MEMORIES & TRADITION
The Crockett Collection

Volume 1
1977-1980

JEFF RUDD

Copyright © 2013 Jeff Rudd
All rights reserved.

ISBN-13:
978-1491023587

ISBN-10:
1491023589

Mid Atlantic Legends Rich Landrum, Sandy Scott, Johnny Weaver, Rocky Kernodle, Don Kernodle & Jim Nelson appearing for CWF Mid-Atlantic. Photo courtesy of Randy Hedrick.

Dedicated to all the fans that were luckly enough to grow up watching Jim Crockett Promotions and had the opportunity to watch this great wrestling in person. Not only was I lucky to watch it but I also made great friends with many I grew up watching.

This book is especially dedicated to my friends
Don Kernodle, Rocky Kernodle,
and in memory of Johnny Weaver.

Special thanks to Rich Blevins for giving this collection to me many years ago. It's time more people have the opportunity to remember these "golden years" and for those that actually study this profession, it provides a wealth of information to learn from. These are the scans of original print ads and results.

Thanks to Michael Bochicchio for the idea and distribution of this project in addition to everything he does!

Thanks to Wayne Culler & Eddie Cheslock for the great photos.

And thanks to Caroline Rudd for her help too!

CONTENTS

1977	11
1978	59
1979	85
1980	139

1977

Ads & Results from

Park Center
Charlotte Coliseum
Hickory Motor Speedway
Chark Griffith Park
Jim Crockett Sr. Park
Greensboro Coliseum
Asheville Civic Center

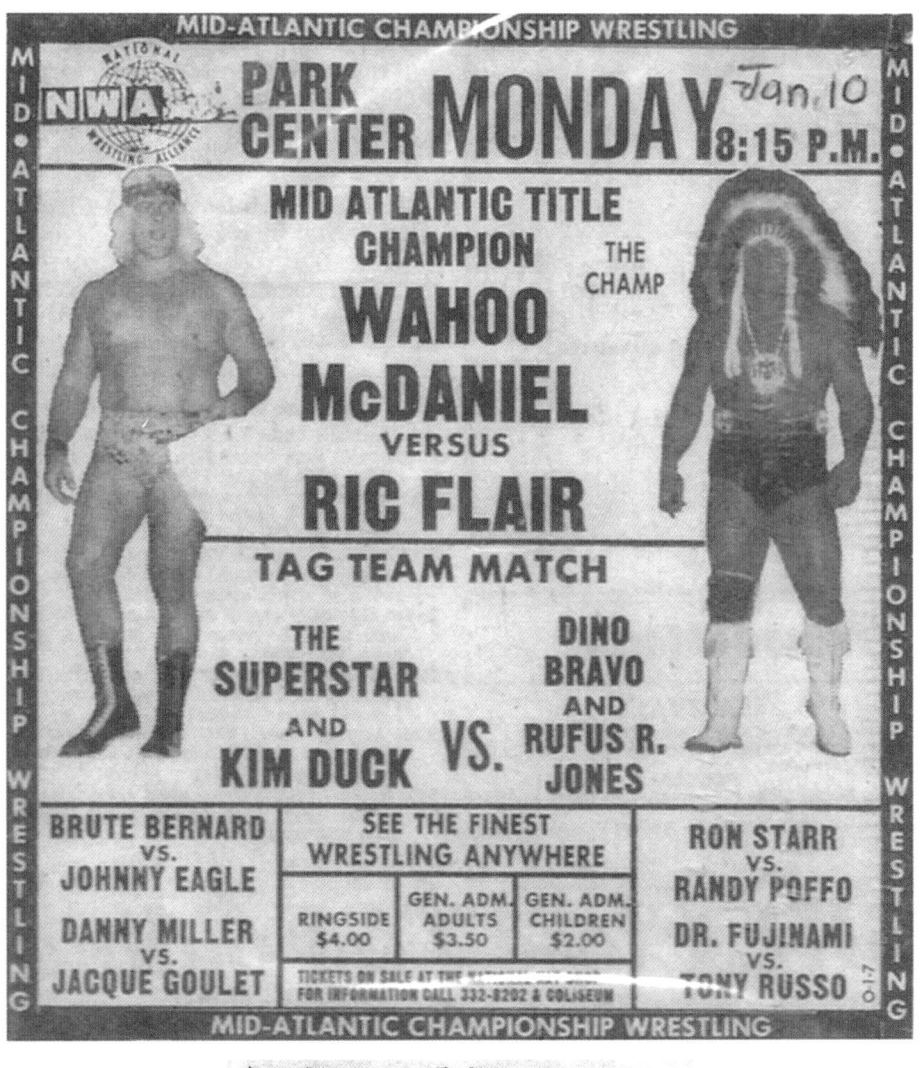

McDaniel Defeats Flair In Feature

Wahoo McDaniel whipped Ric Flair in the main event of the weekly wrestling card at Park Center Monday night.

Kim Duck and Superstar stopped Dino Bravo and Rufus Jones in a tag-team match. Brute Bernard beat Johnny Eagle, Ron Starr defeated Randy Poffo, and Tony Russo topped Dr. Fujinami. Danny Miller and Jacque Goulet fought to a draw.

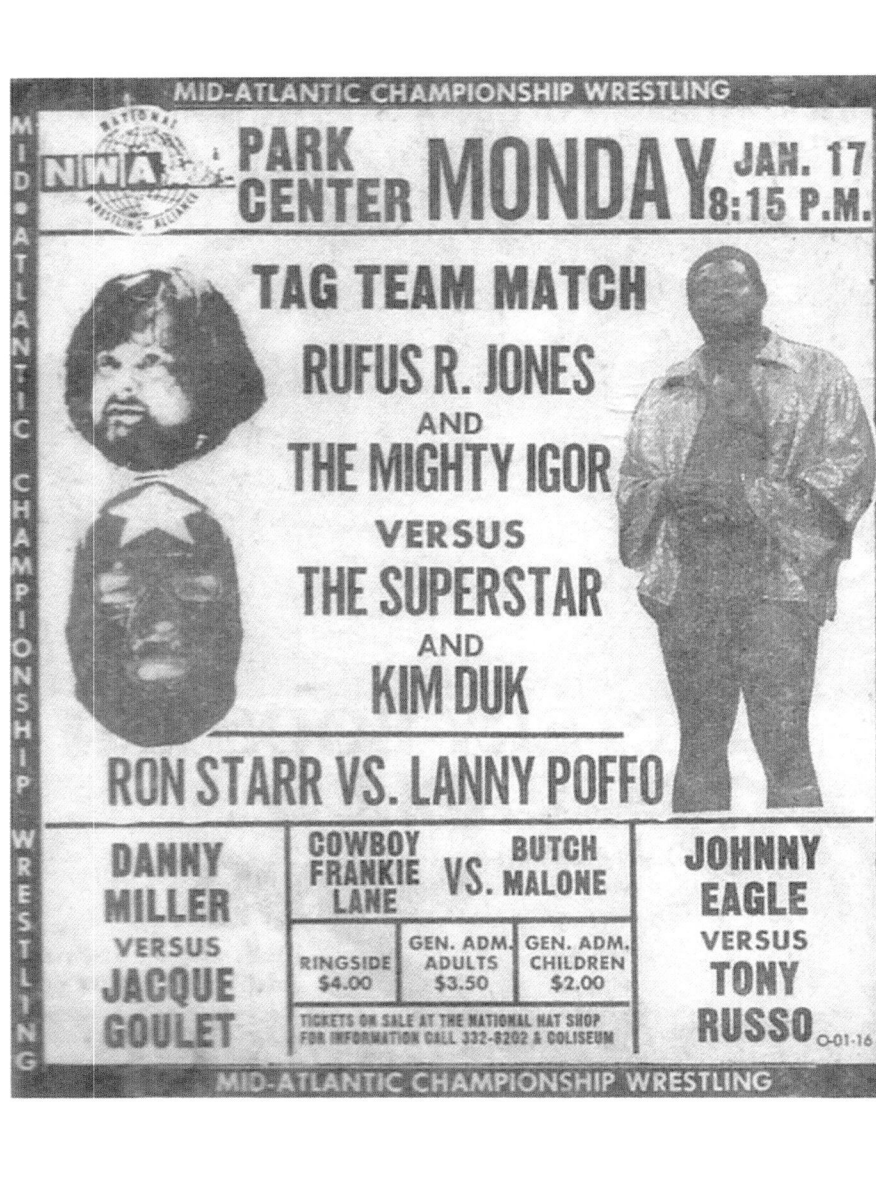

McDaniel Wins Feature Bout

Wahoo McDaniel and Rufus R. Jones won their main event wrestling matches at the Charlotte Coliseum Sunday night while the third featured bout between Blackjack Mulligan and Thunderbolt Patterson ended with a no-contest ruling.

McDaniel won by disqualification over Harley Race and Jones beat Greg Valentine.

In other matches, Tiger Conway and Dino Bravo combined to whip the Hollywood Blonds, Danny Miller beat Tony Russo, former North Mecklenburg High School athlete Rick McGraw bested Bill White and Jacques Goulet topped Herb Gallant.

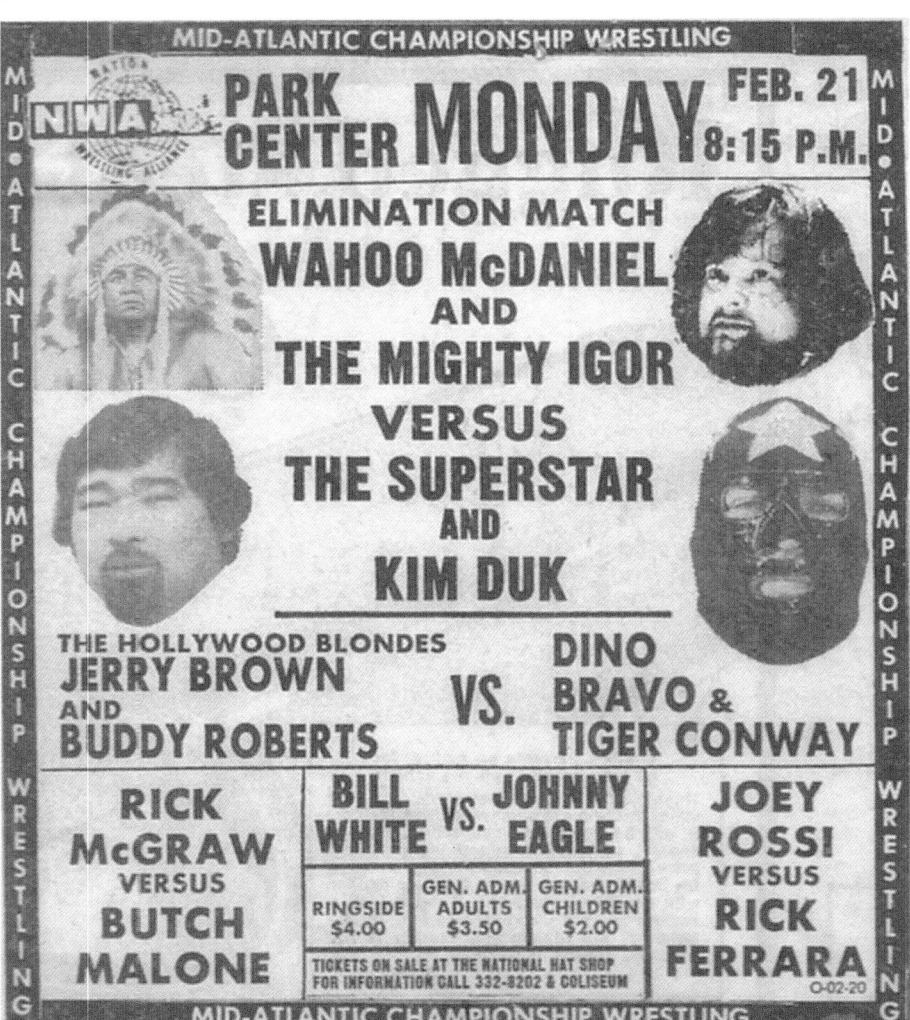

Duk, Superstar Win In Match

Associated Press

Kim Duk and The Superstar defeated Wahoo McDaniel and The Mighty Igor in Monday night's main wrestling event at Charlotte's Park Center.

In other action the Hollywood Blondes defeated Tiger Conway and Dino Bravo, Rick McGraw beat Butch Malone, Johnny Eagle and Bill White fought to a 20-minute draw, and Rick Ferrara outwrestled Joey Rossi.

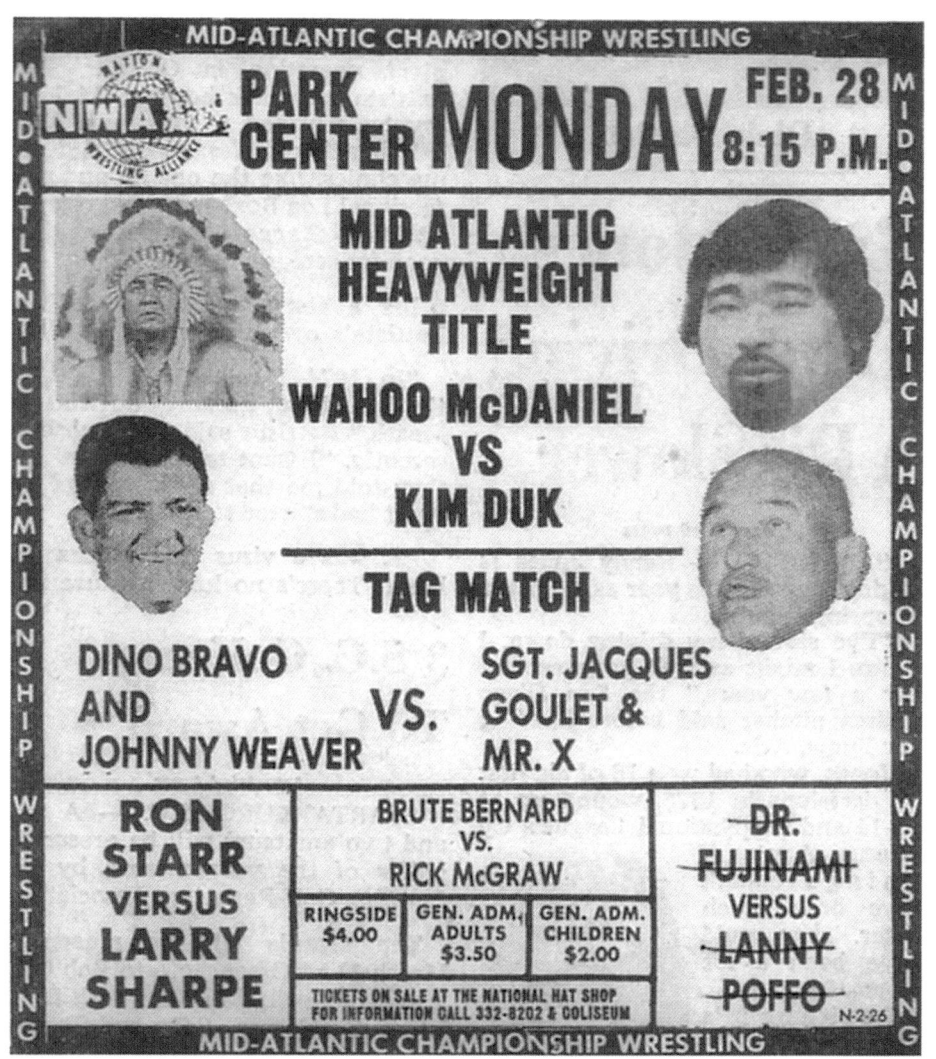

McDaniel Whips Duk

The main wrestling match at Park Center last night had **Wahoo McDaniel** whipping **Kim Duk**. In other matches, **Rick McGraw** beat **Brute Bernard**, **Ron Starr** topped **Larry Sharpe** and **Dino Bravo** teamed with **Johnny Weaver** to whip **Jacques Goulet** and **Mr. X**.

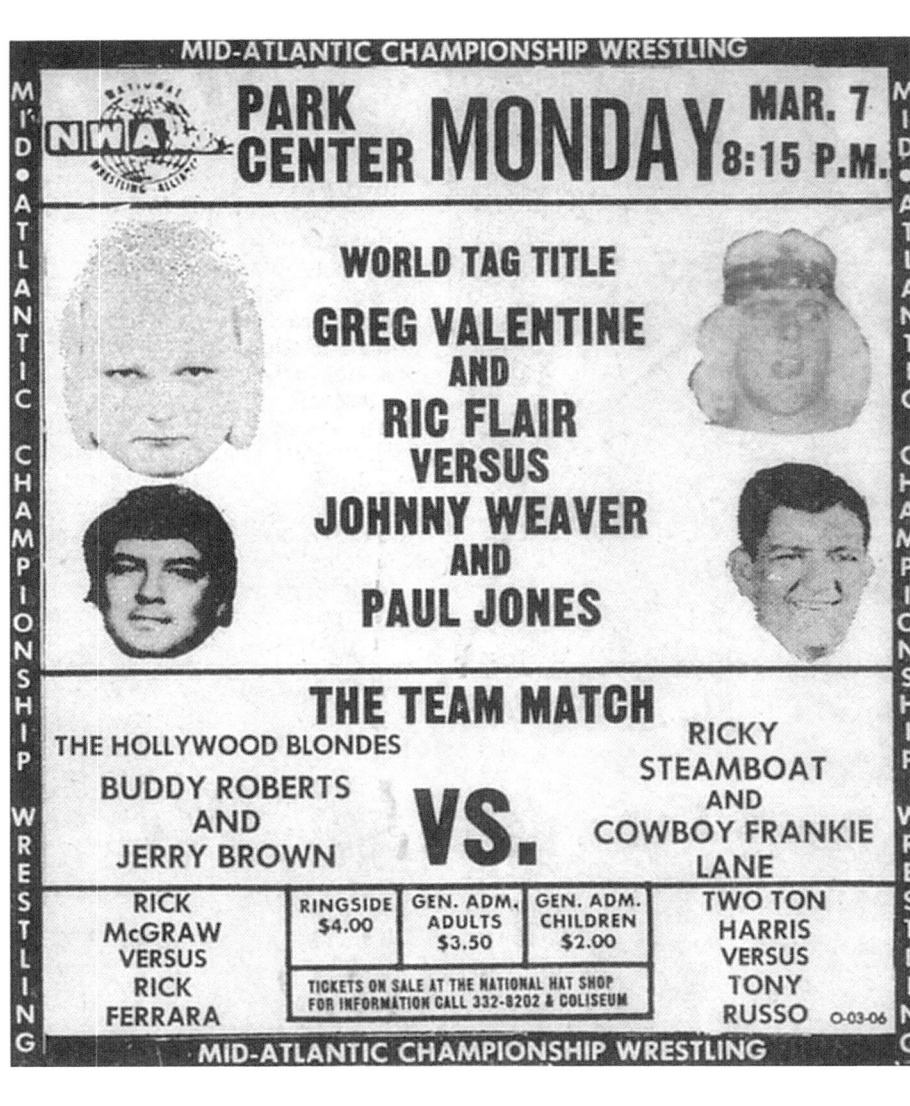

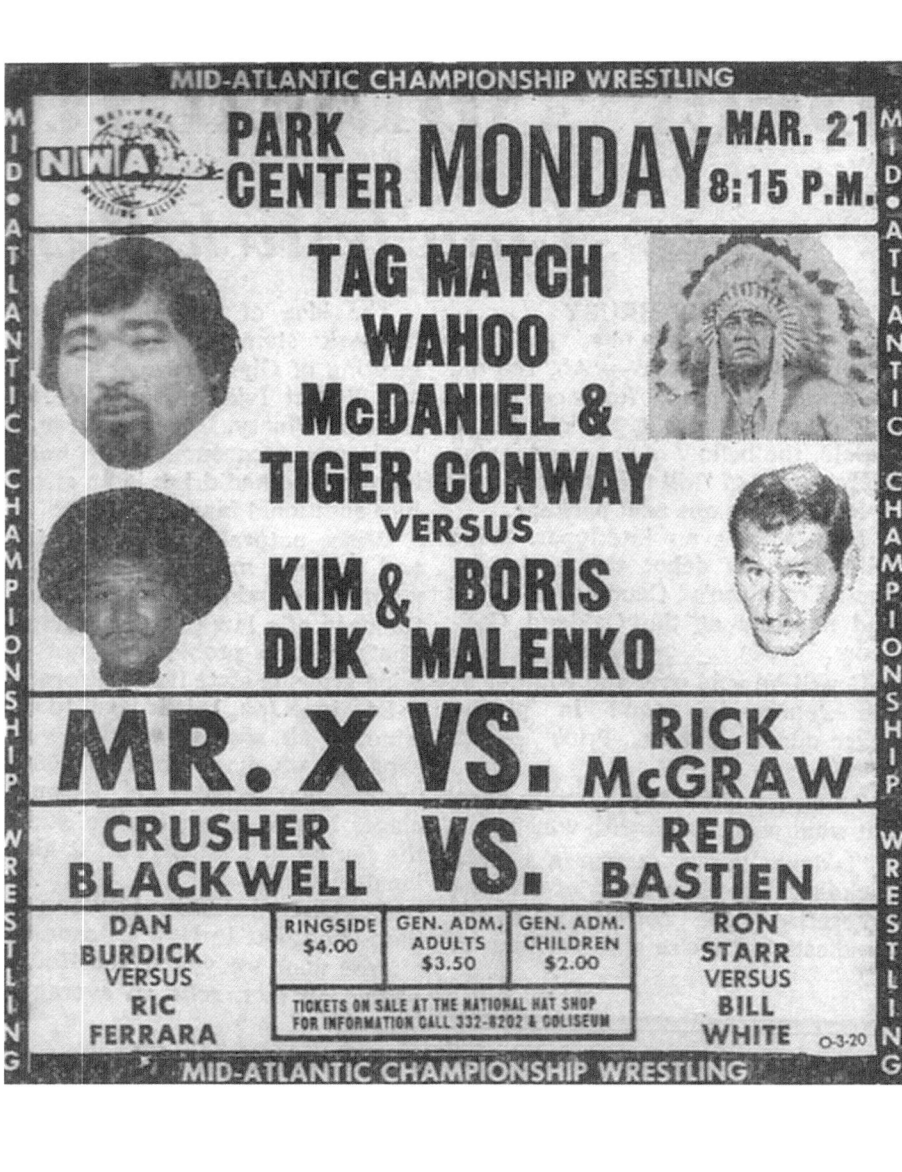

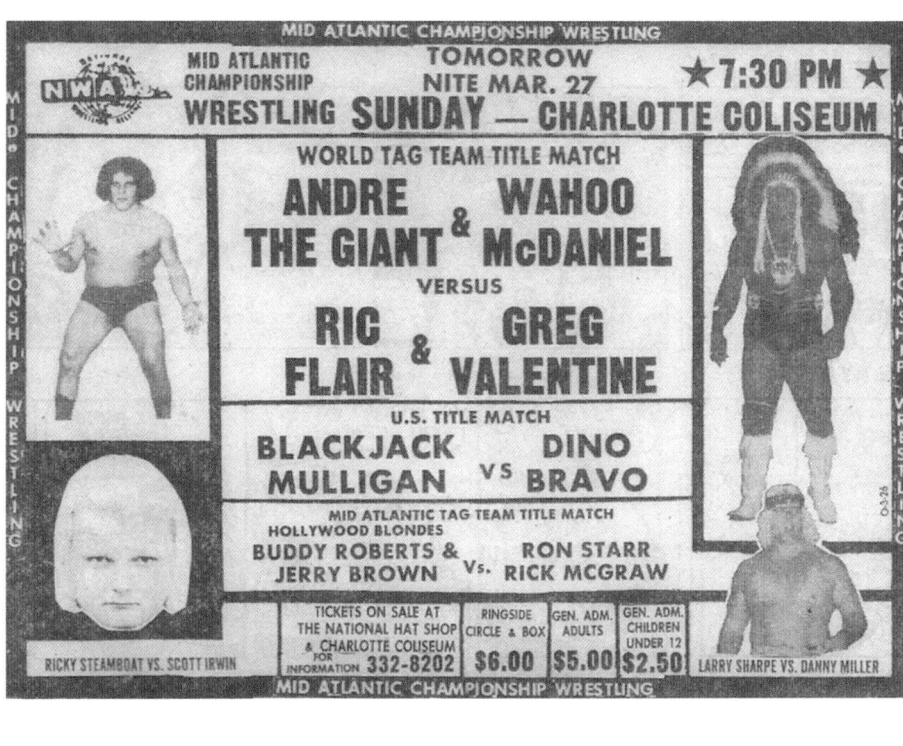

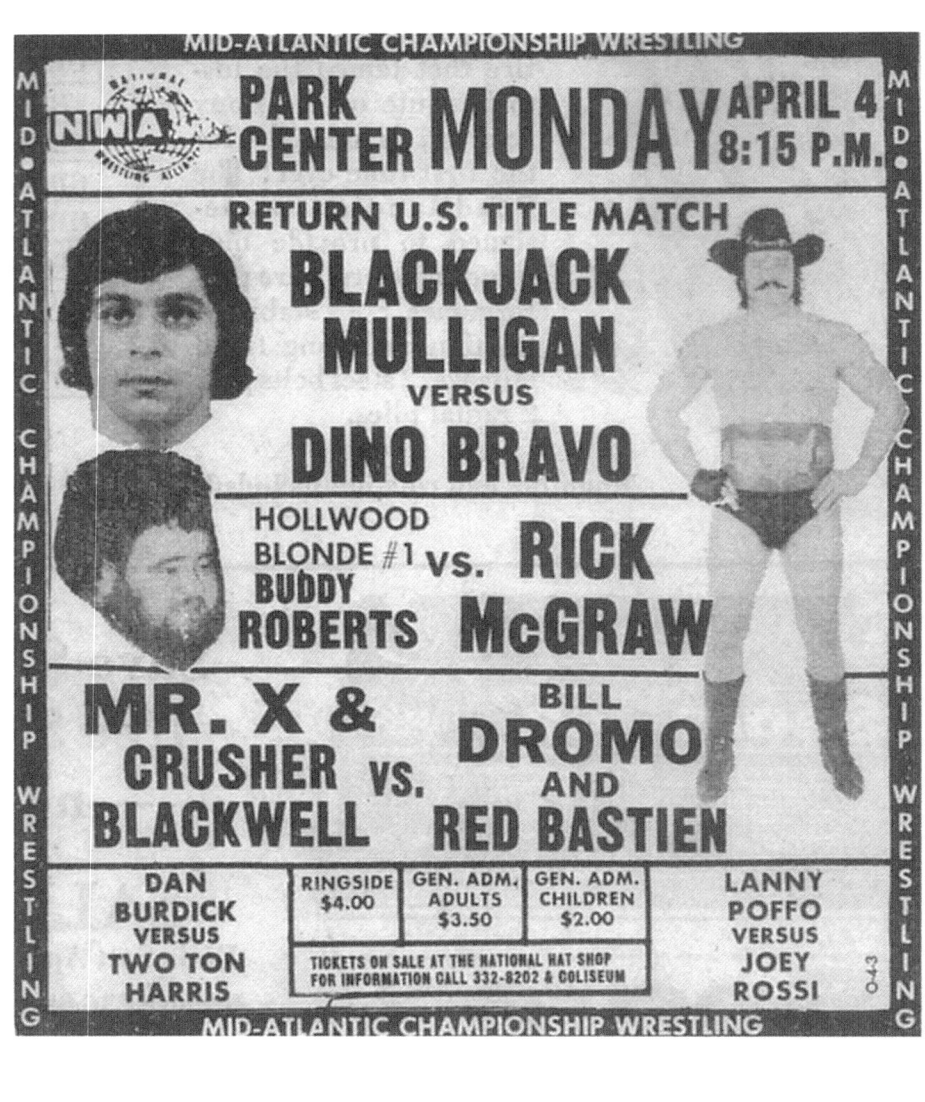

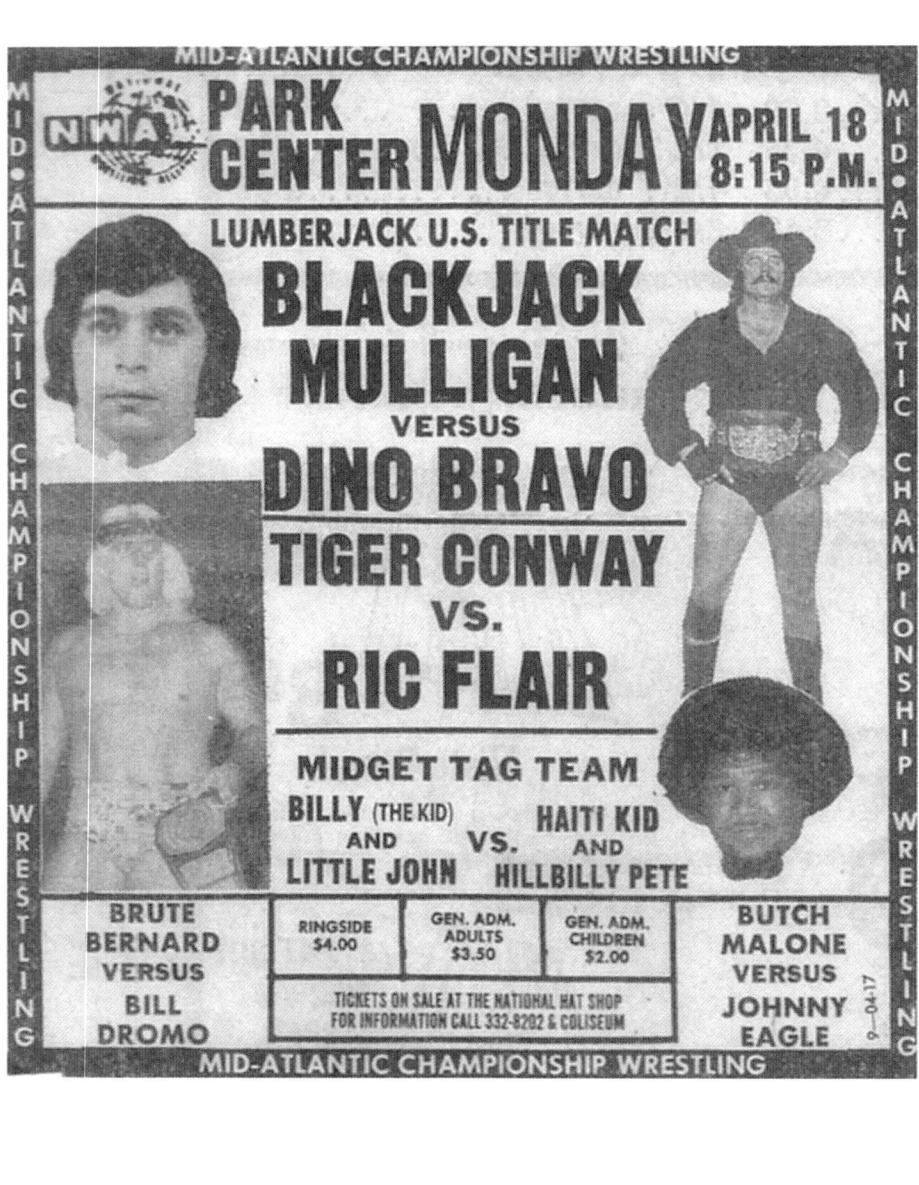

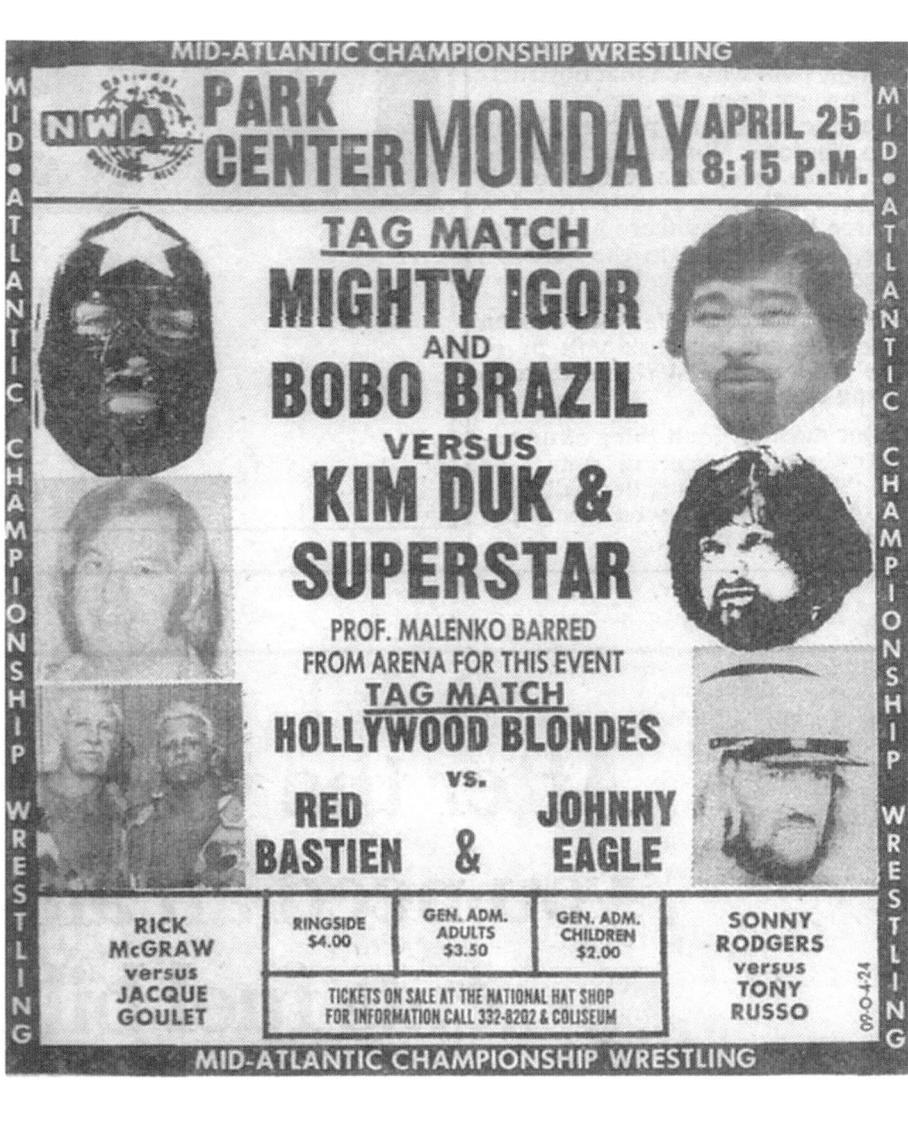

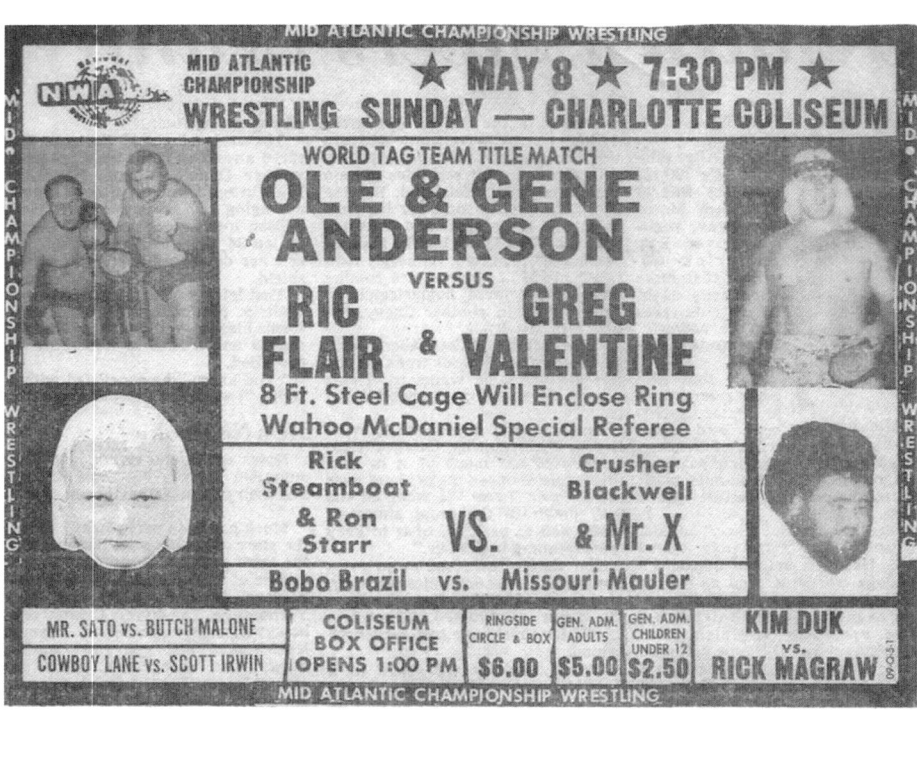

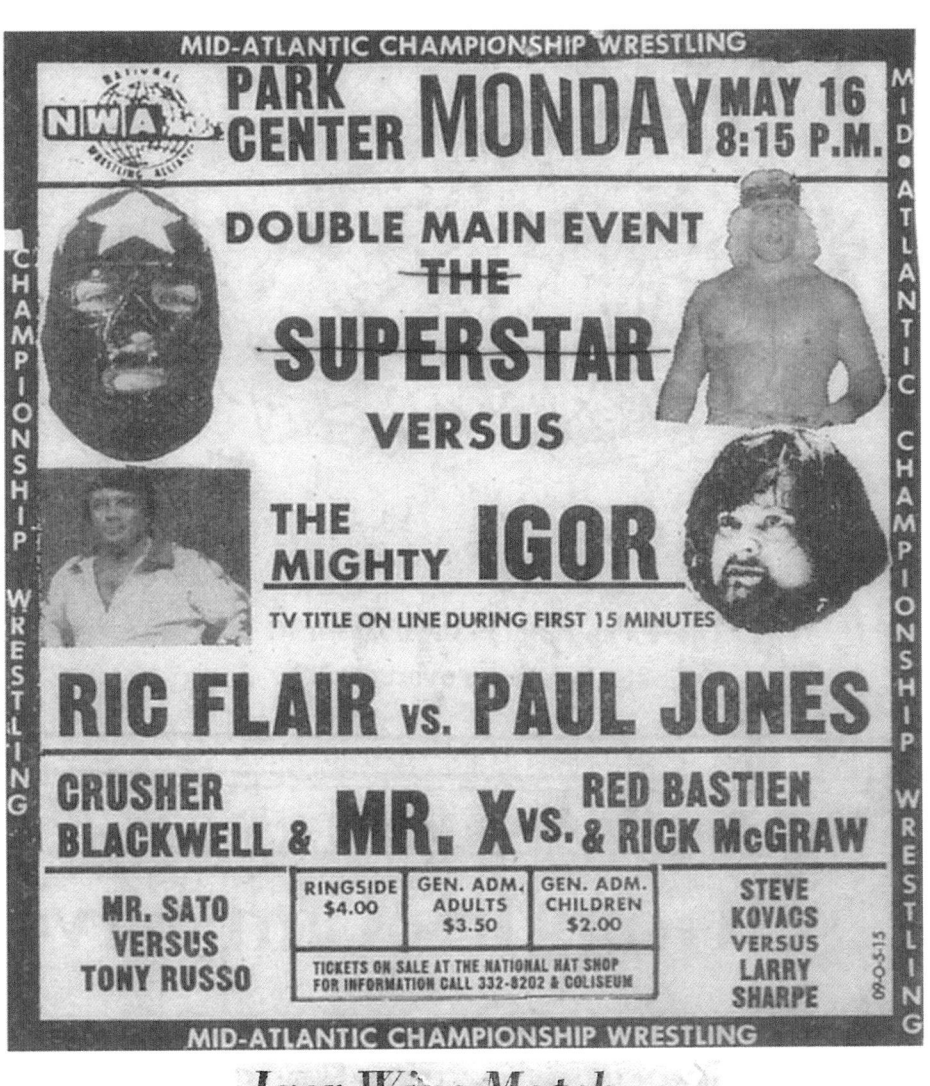

Igor Wins Match Over The Mauler

Paul Jones and the Mighty Igor won the feature events on the Monday night wrestling card at Park Ceter. Jones defeated Ric Flair while Igor turned back the Missouri Mauler.

In tag team action, Red Bastien and Rick McGraw teamed to down Crusher Blackwell and Mr. X. Mr. Sato beat Tony Russo and Steve Kovacs pinned Larry Sharpe.

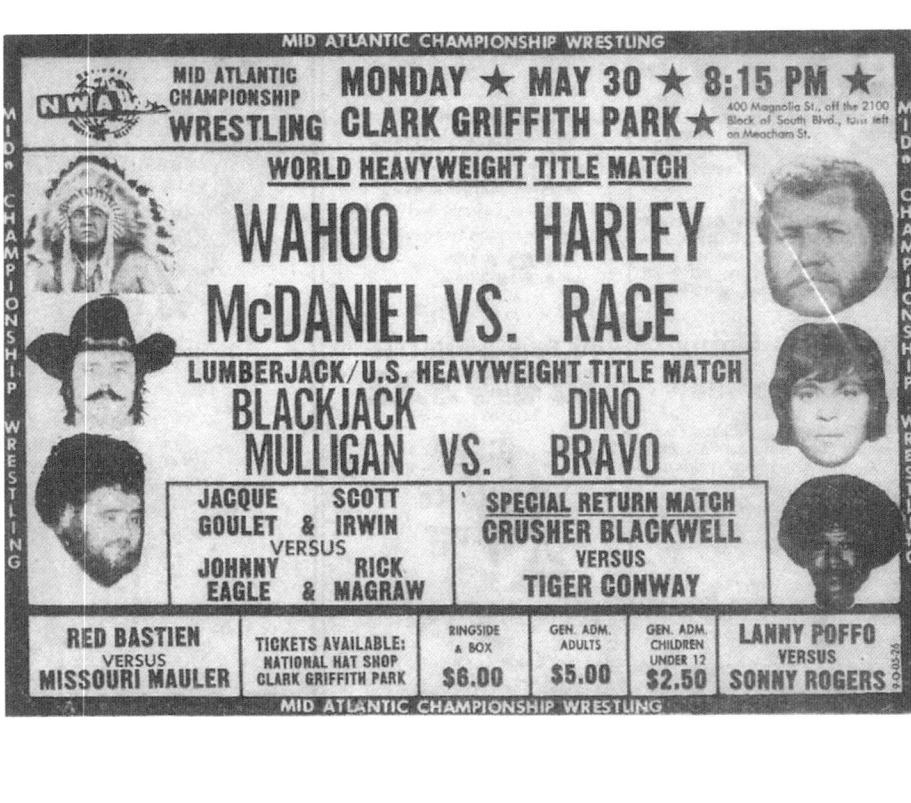

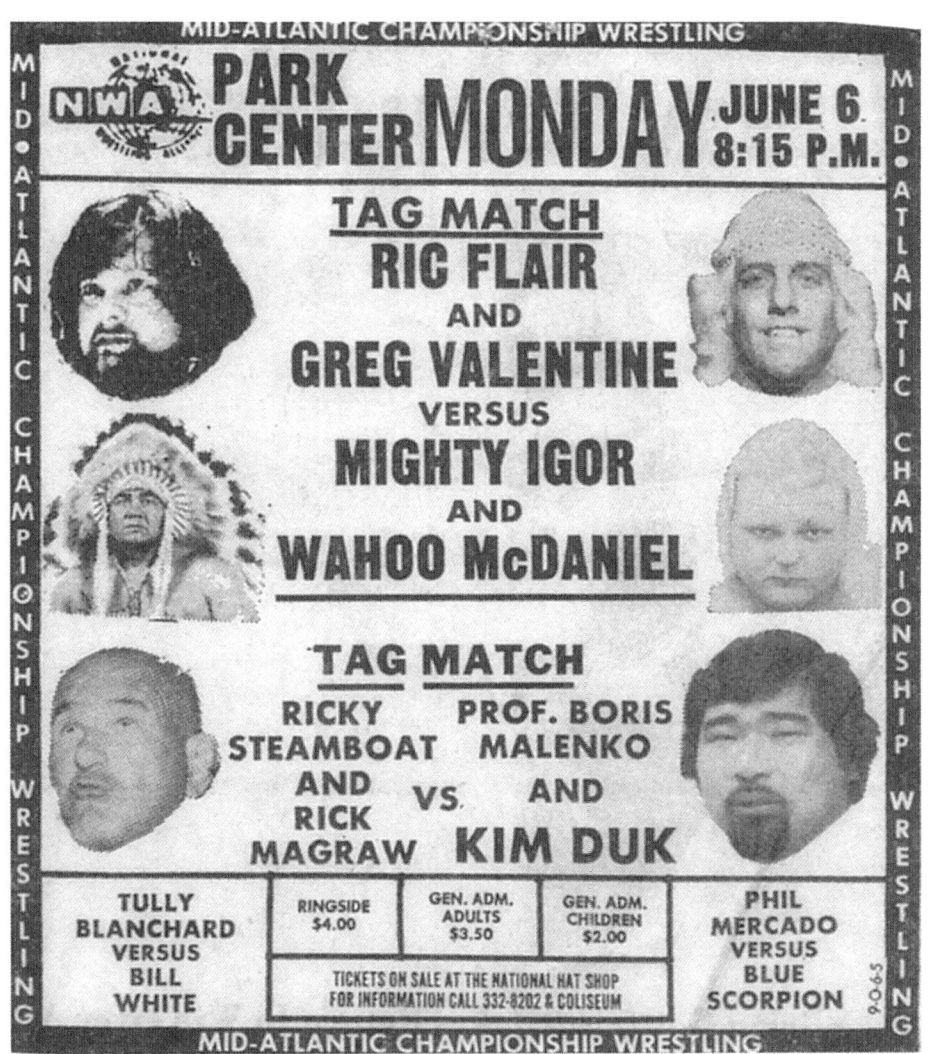

Tag Teams Disqualified

Fighting outside the ring by the tag teams of **Ric Flair-Greg Valentine** and **Wahoo McDaniel-Might Igor** triggered the disqualification off both in the featured pro wrestling match last night at Park Center. In other bouts, **Ricky Steamboat** and **Rick McGraw** beat **Professor Boris Malenko** and **Kim Duk**, **Tully Blanchard** topped **Bill White** and **Phil Mercado** and **The Blue Scorpion** wrestled to a draw.

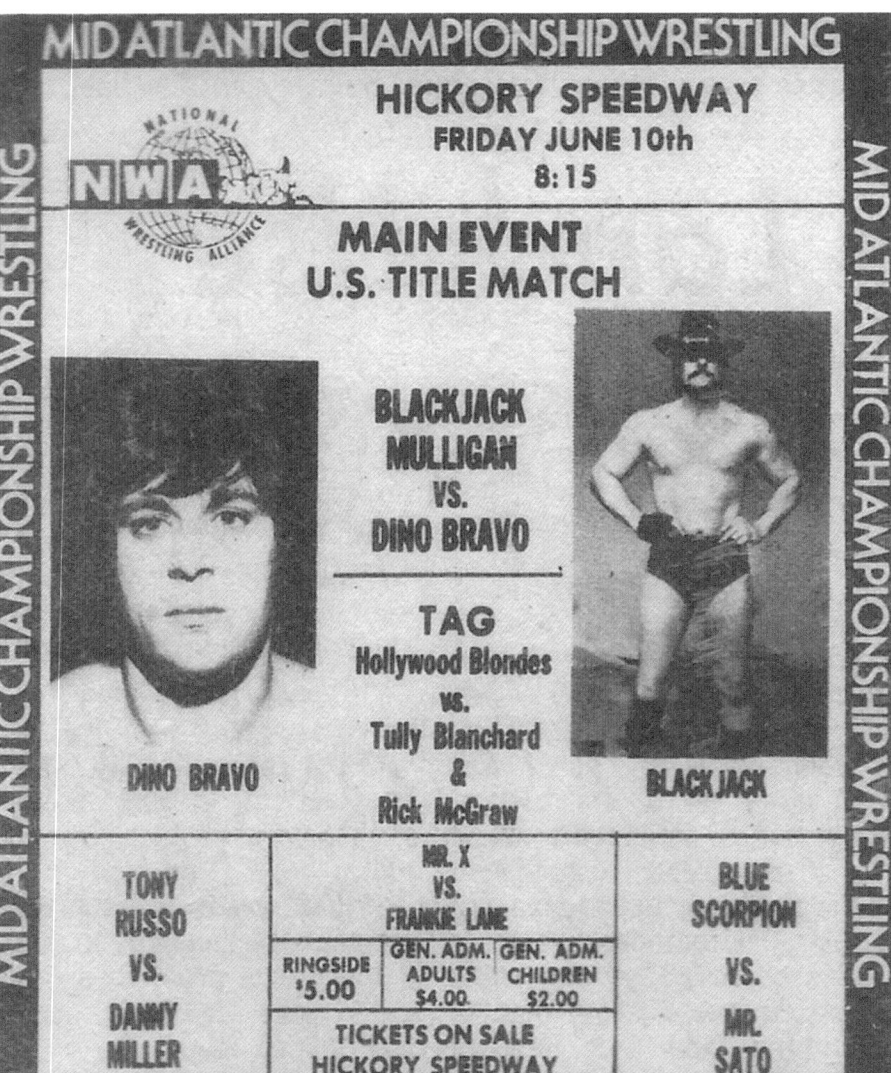

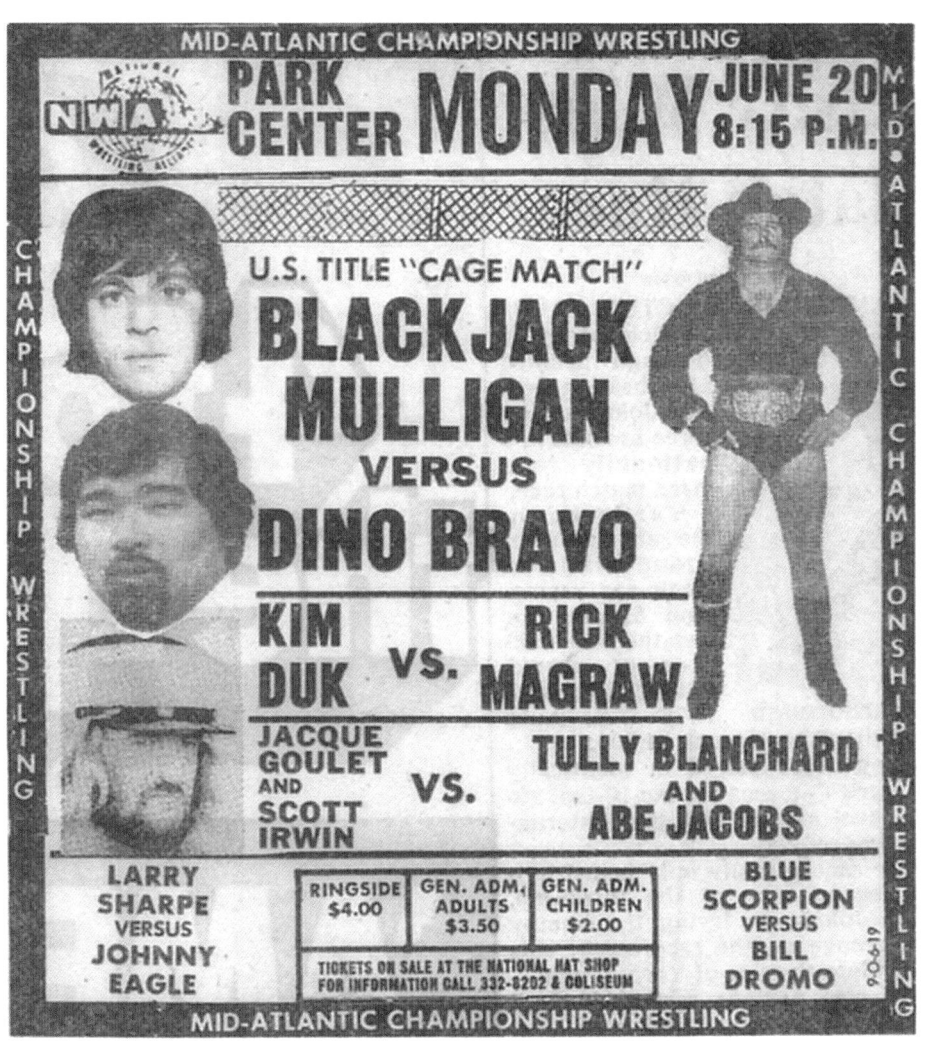

Blackjack Beats Bravo In Feature

Blackjack Mulligan won the featured wrestling event at Park Center Monday night by whipping Dino Bravo. In other matches, Charlotte's Rick McGraw beat Kim Duk, Tully Blanchard and Abe Jacobs combined to outlast Scott Irwin and Jacques Goulet and Johnny Eagle downed Larry Sharpe. Bill Dromo and the Blue Scorpion battled to a draw.

Next week's featured match will send The Mighty Igor and Ricky Steamboat against Ric Flair and The Superstar.

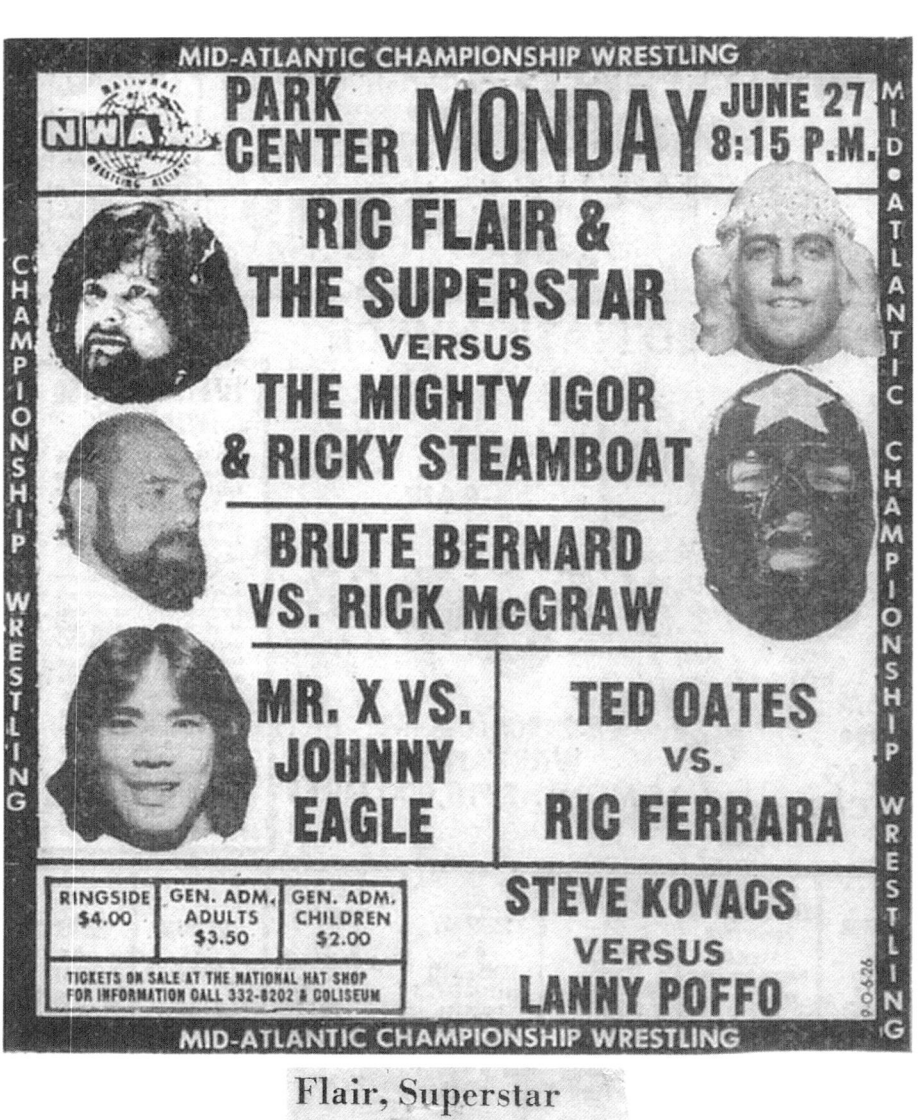

Flair, Superstar Take Tag Bout

Ric Flair and The Superstar won the featured wrestling event at Park Center Monday night, beating Ricky Steamboat and The Mighty Igor in a tag bout.

In other matches, Brute Bernard and Ric McGraw battled to a no contest, Mr. X defeated Johnny Eagle, Ed Oates topped Rick Ferrer and Steve Kovacs turned back Lanny Poffo.

Wrestling moves to Jim Crockett Park Saturday night with a double main event, Wahoo McDaniel vs. Harley Race and Andre The Giant and Bobo Brazil against Greg Valentine and Blackjack Mulligan.

MID ATLANTIC CHAMPIONSHIP WRESTLING

SATURDAY TOMORROW ★ JULY 2 ★ 8:30 P.M.
JIM CROCKETT SR. PARK

400 Magnolia St., off the 2100 Block of South Blvd., turn left on Meacham St.

WORLD TITLE MATCH
HARLEY RACE vs. WAHOO McDANIEL

BLACKJACK MULLIGAN AND GREG VALENTINE vs. BOBO BRAZIL AND ANDRE THE GIANT

WATCH WBTV SATURDAY 3-4 PM

BRUTE BERNARD AND MR. X vs. JOHNNY WEAVER AND RICK McGRAW

TWO TON HARRIS VERSUS STEVE KOVACS

JACQUE GOULET VERSUS TED OATES

TICKETS AVAILABLE:
NATIONAL HAT SHOP
JIM CROCKETT SENIOR PARK
PHONE 332-8202

RINGSIDE & BOX	GEN. ADM. ADULTS	GEN. ADM. CHILDREN UNDER 12
$6.00	$5.00	$2.50

MID ATLANTIC CHAMPIONSHIP WRESTLING

MID-ATLANTIC CHAMPIONSHIP WRESTLING

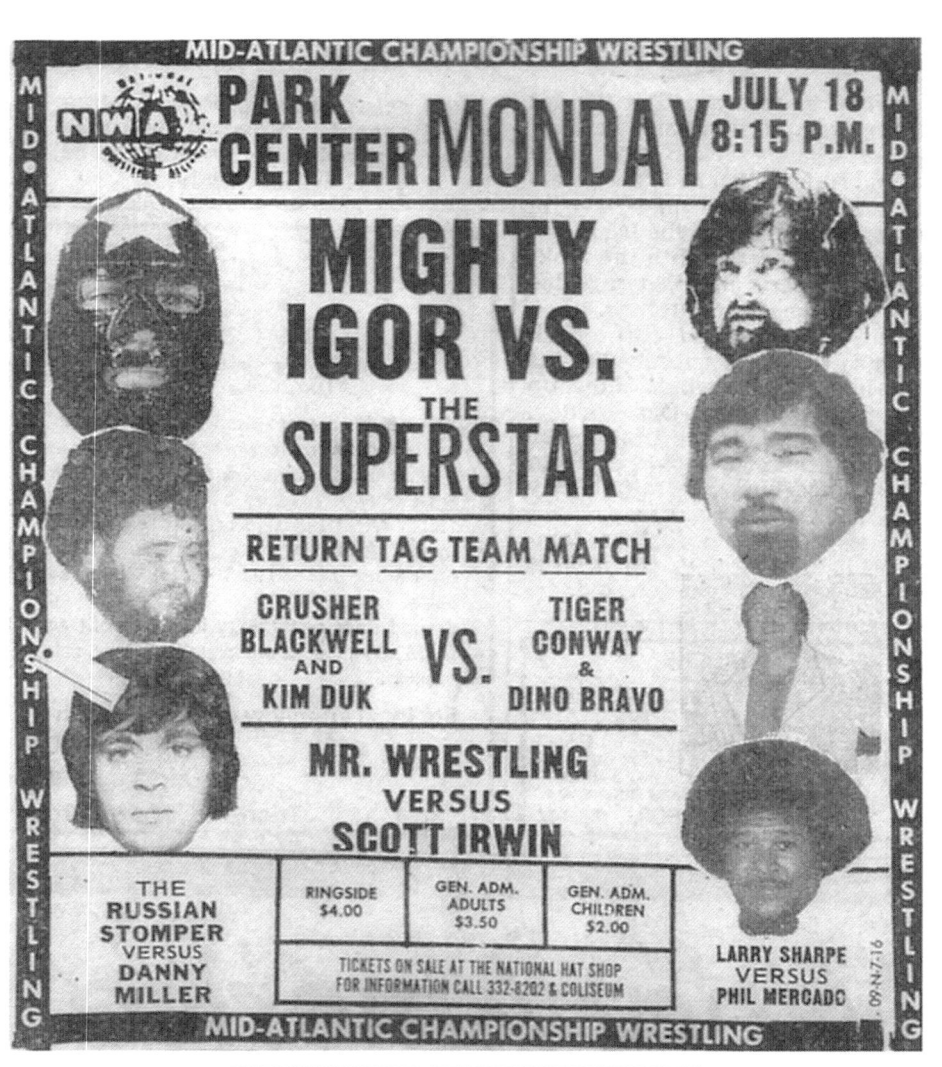

NWA • PARK CENTER • MONDAY
JULY 18 • 8:15 P.M.

MIGHTY IGOR VS. THE SUPERSTAR

RETURN TAG TEAM MATCH
CRUSHER BLACKWELL AND KIM DUK VS. **TIGER CONWAY & DINO BRAVO**

MR. WRESTLING VERSUS SCOTT IRWIN

THE RUSSIAN STOMPER VERSUS DANNY MILLER

LARRY SHARPE VERSUS PHIL MERCADO

RINGSIDE	GEN. ADM. ADULTS	GEN. ADM. CHILDREN
$4.00	$3.50	$2.00

TICKETS ON SALE AT THE NATIONAL HAT SHOP
FOR INFORMATION CALL 332-8202 & COLISEUM

Mighty Igor Wins On Disqualification

Mighty Igor defeated Superstar on a disqualification in the main event at Park Center Monday night.

Larry Sharpe, forced to wrestle twice when the Russian Stomper didn't appear, beat Phil Macado, then lost to Danny Miller.

In other matches, Crusher Blackwell and Kim Duk beat Dino Bravo and Tiger Conway Jr., and Mr. Wrestling whipped Scott Irwin.

MID ATLANTIC CHAMPIONSHIP WRESTLING

HICKORY SPEEDWAY
FRIDAY, JULY 22
TICKETS ON SALE HICKORY SPEEDWAY

NWA — National Wrestling Alliance

MAIN EVENT
"Mid Atlantic Title"

MIGHTY IGOR
vs.
CHAMPION GREG VALENTINE

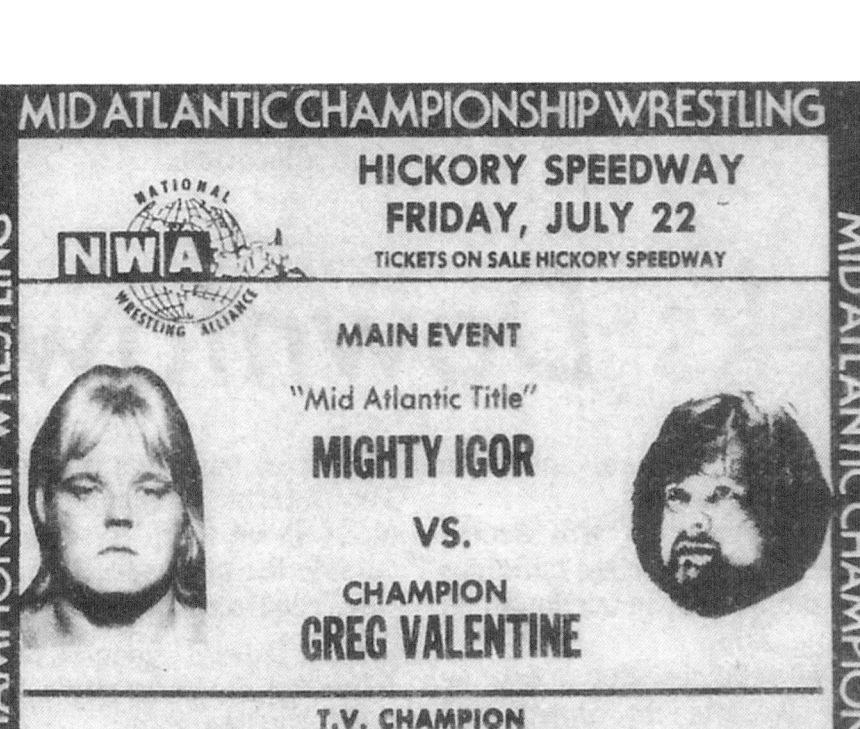

T.V. CHAMPION
RICK STEAMBOAT
vs.
SCOTT ERWIN

LITTLE TOKYO vs. **COWBOY LANG**

TAG TEAM MATCH
TONY RUSSO & CHARLIE FULTON
vs.
STEVE KOVACKS & RICK McGRAW

PHIL MERCADO vs. **LARRY SHARP**

RINGSIDE	GEN. ADM. ADULTS	GEN. ADM. CHILDREN
$5.00	$4.00	$2.00

MID ATLANTIC CHAMPIONSHIP WRESTLING

MID-ATLANTIC CHAMPIONSHIP WRESTLING

NWA PARK CENTER — MONDAY JULY 25, 8:15 P.M.

MID-ATLANTIC TAG TEAM CHAMPIONSHIP

THE CHAMPIONS
GREG VALENTINE / RICK FLARE
VS.
WAHOO McDANIEL / RICKY STEAMBOAT

CRUSHER BLACKWELL vs. **RICK McGRAW**

TED OATS VERSUS **SCOTT IRWIN**

JOHNNY WEAVER VERSUS **MR. X**

ABE JACOBS VERSUS **LARRY SHARPE**

RINGSIDE $4.00 | GEN. ADM. ADULTS $3.50 | GEN. ADM. CHILDREN $2.00

TICKETS ON SALE AT THE NATIONAL HAT SHOP
FOR INFORMATION CALL 332-8202 & COLISEUM

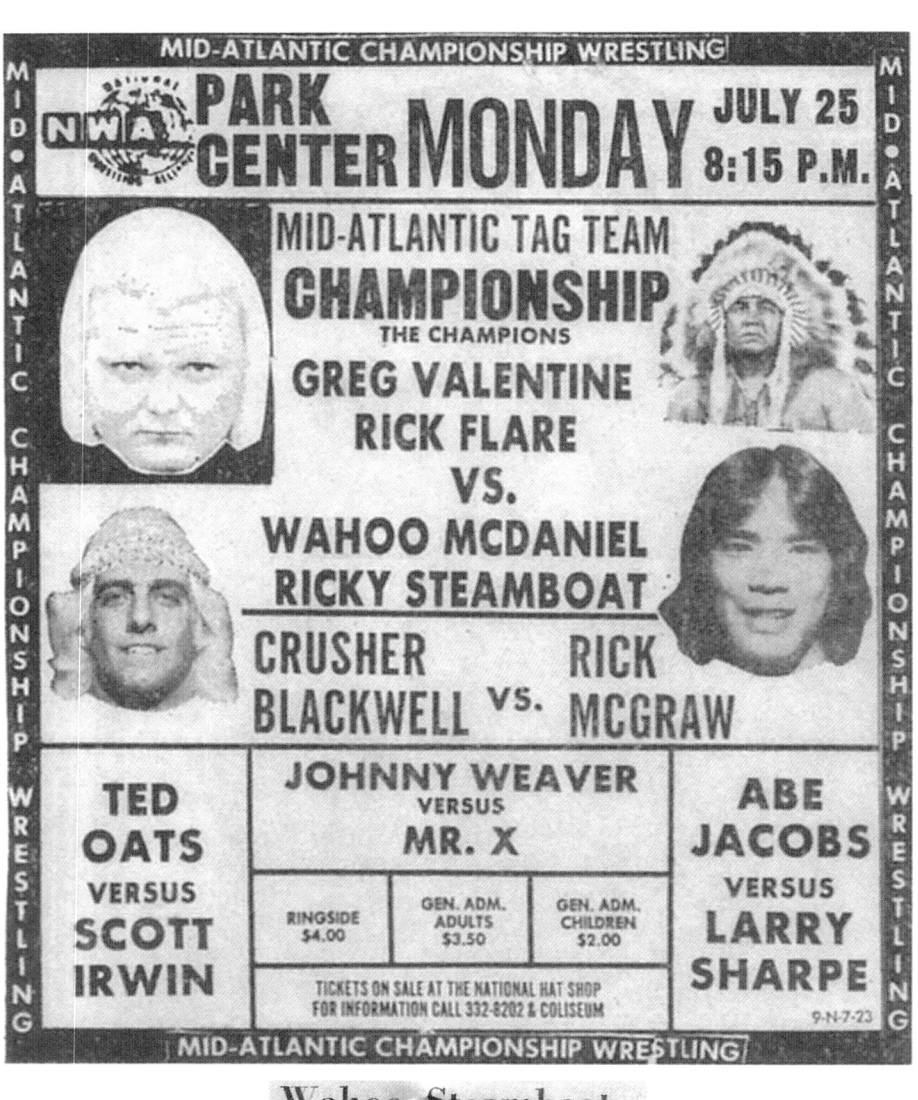

Wahoo-Steamboat Win Mat Feature

Wahoo McDaniel and Ricky Steamboat won the main event of wrestling at Park Center Monday night as Ric Flair and Greg Valentine were disqualified.

In other matches Johnny Weaver defeated Mr. X; Scott Irwin and Ted Oates fought to a draw; Abe Jacobs beat Larry Sharpe and Rick McGraw wo over Crusher Blackwell, who was disqualified when he failed to break an illegal hold on a five count.

Next Monday night features Blackjack Mulligan meeting No. 1 Paul Jones.

MID-ATLANTIC CHAMPIONSHIP WRESTLING

NWA PARK CENTER — MONDAY AUG. 1 8:15 P.M.

MIDATLANTIC HEAVYWEIGHT CHAMPIONSHIP

WAHOO McDANIEL
VERSUS
GREG VALENTINE

PAUL JONES
VERSUS
BLACKJACK MULLIGAN

| CHARLIE FULTON & SCOTT IRWIN | VS. | ABE JACOBS & TULLY BLANCHARD |

RUSSIAN STOMPER VS. DANNY MILLER

MR. SATO VS. TWO TON HARRIS

| RINGSIDE $4.00 | GEN. ADM. ADULTS $3.50 | GEN. ADM. CHILDREN $2.00 |

TICKETS ON SALE AT THE NATIONAL HAT SHOP
FOR INFORMATION CALL 332-8202 & COLISEUM

9-0-8-1

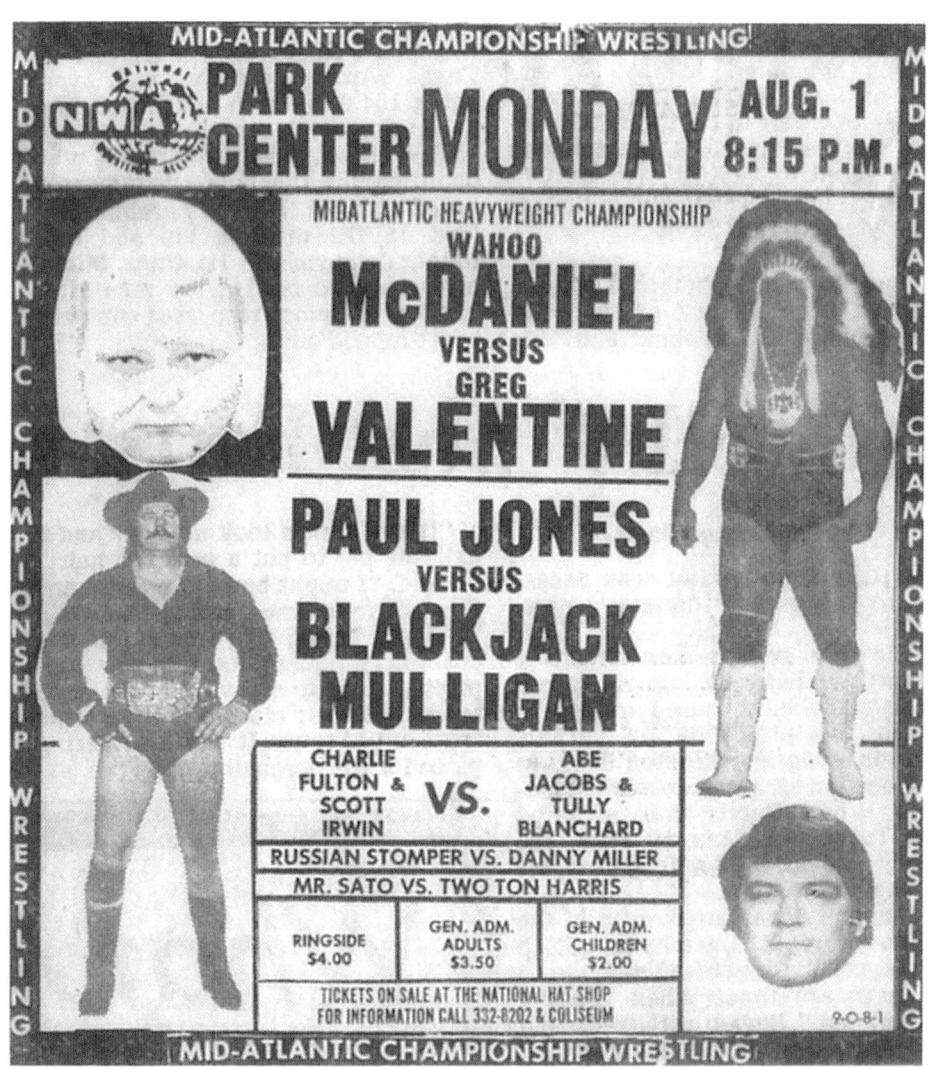

McDaniel Wins On Disqualification

Wahoo McDaniel defeated Greg Valentine on a disqualification Monday in the main event of the wrestling card at Park Center. In other matches, Paul Jones won on a reversed decision over Blackjack Mulligan; The Russian Stomper walked over Danny Miller; Abe Jacobs and Tully Blanchard defeated Charlie Fulton and Scott Irwin in the tag team match, and Mr. Sato defeated Two-Ton Harris.

The next wrestling card will be next Monday at The Coliseum including a match between Crusher Blackwell and Charlotte's Rick McGraw.

Tickets On Sale—Greensboro Coliseum Box Office

GREENSBORO COLISEUM
WRESTLING

TONITE at August 7 — 7:30 PM

FOR THE WORLD'S HEAVYWEIGHT CHAMPIONSHIP!
WAHOO McDANIEL
—versus—
HARLEY RACE

FOR THE U.S. HEAVYWEIGHT CHAMPIONSHIP!
RIC FLAIR —versus— RICKY STEAMBOAT

—HANDICAP MATCH—
BLACK JACK MULLIGAN
—versus—
DUSTY RHODES and GEORGE SCOTT

—TAG TEAM MATCH—
PAUL JONES and MR. WRESTLING
—versus—
KIM DUC and THE SUPERSTAR

*THE STOMPER vs. DANNY MILLER

*TED OATES vs. JOHNNY WEAVER

*TULLY BLANCHARD vs. SCOTT IRWIN

MR. X versus ABE JACOBS

TICKET PRICES $5 - $6 - $7

Children—under age 10 — ½ PRICE — in $5 and $6 Sections

MID ATLANTIC CHAMPIONSHIP WRESTLING

★ AUGUST 8 ★ 8:15 PM ★
MONDAY — CHARLOTTE COLISEUM

3 BIG MAIN EVENTS

INDIAN STRAP MATCH
WAHOO McDANIEL VS. GREG VALENTINE

HANDICAP MATCH
GEORGE SCOTT AND RICKY STEAMBOAT VERSUS BLACKJACK MULLIGAN

U.S. TITLE MATCH
BOBO BRAZIL VS. RIC FLAIR

TICKETS ON SALE AT THE NATIONAL HAT SHOP & CHARLOTTE COLISEUM
FOR INFORMATION CALL 332-8202

RINGSIDE & BOX $6.00
GEN. ADM. ADULTS $5.00
GEN. ADM. CHILDREN UNDER 12 $2.50

RETURN MATCH — NO DISQUALIFICATIONS
RICK McGRAW VS. JERRY BLACKWELL
TIGER CONWAY & STEVE KOVACS VS. MR. X & RUSSIAN STOMPER
RICK FERRARA VS. TED OATES   DANNY MILLER VS. SCOTT IRWIN

McDaniel Straps Valentine In Ring

Wahoo McDaniel defeated Greg Valentine in an Indian strap match in the feature bout of Sunday's professional wrestling show at the Charlotte Coliseum.

In two other main events Baron Von Raschke defended his television title by beating Mr. Wrestling and Paul Jones was declared the winner over Superstar when Superstar left the ring and was counted out.

Cyclone Negro and Crusher Blackwell defeated Tiger Conway, Jr. and Johnny Weaver, Mighty Igor beat the Missouri Mauler, Jerry Stubbs and Danny Miller wrestled to a draw and Brian St. John and Richard Blood defeated Frank Monte and Hartford Love.

The next show at the Coliseum will be at 7:30 p.m., Sunday, Feb. 12.

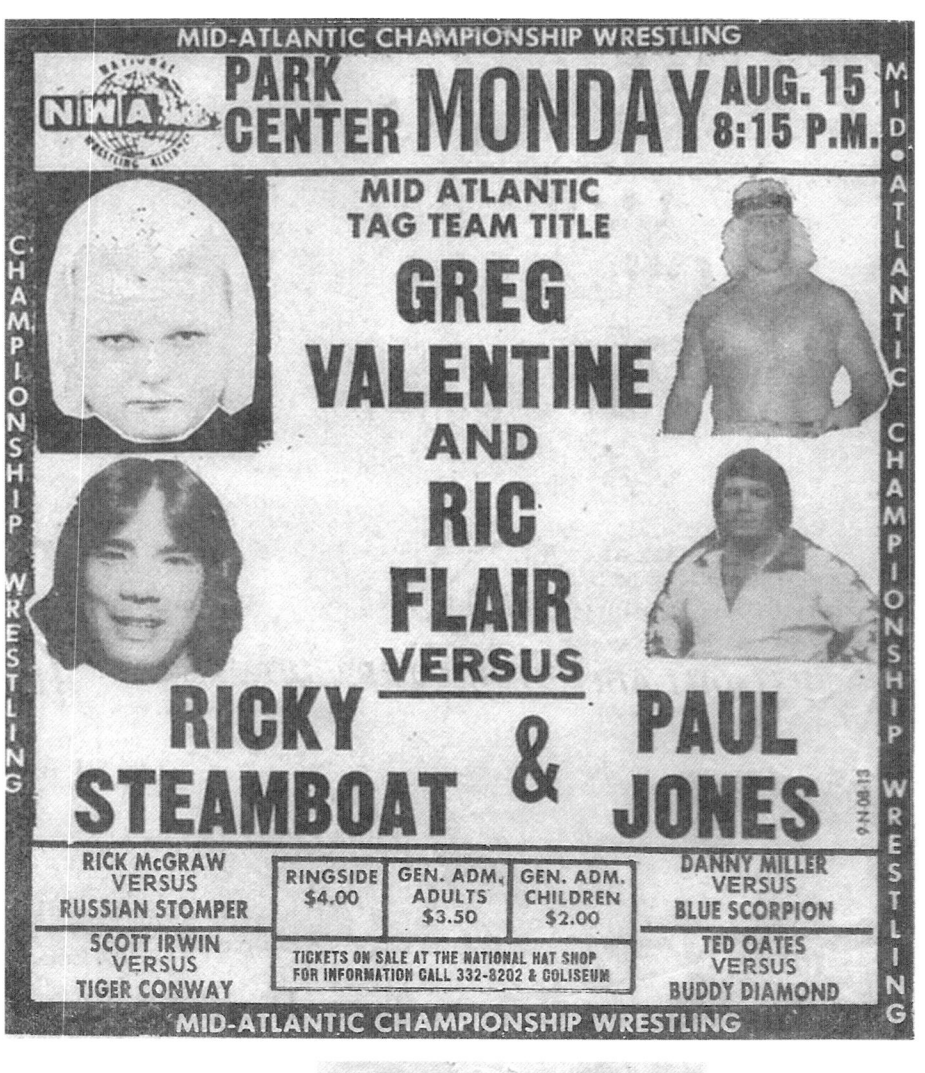

MID-ATLANTIC CHAMPIONSHIP WRESTLING

PARK CENTER — MONDAY AUG. 15, 8:15 P.M.

NWA

MID ATLANTIC TAG TEAM TITLE

GREG VALENTINE AND RIC FLAIR
VERSUS
RICKY STEAMBOAT & PAUL JONES

RICK McGRAW VERSUS RUSSIAN STOMPER

SCOTT IRWIN VERSUS TIGER CONWAY

DANNY MILLER VERSUS BLUE SCORPION

TED OATES VERSUS BUDDY DIAMOND

RINGSIDE $4.00 | GEN. ADM. ADULTS $3.50 | GEN. ADM. CHILDREN $2.00

TICKETS ON SALE AT THE NATIONAL HAT SHOP
FOR INFORMATION CALL 332-8202 & COLISEUM

MID-ATLANTIC CHAMPIONSHIP WRESTLING

Valentine, Flair Retain Crown

Greg Valentine and Ric Flair defeated Ricky Steamboat and Paul Jones to retain their Mid-Atlantic tag-team wrestling title Monday.

In singles matches, Rick McGraw beat The Russian Stomper, Tiger Conway Jr. whipped Scott Irwin, Danny Miller won over The Blue Scorpion, and Ted Oates defeated Buddy Diamond.

Next Monday at Park Center, Bobo Brazil face Blackjack Mulligan, and other matches feature Mr. Wrestling, Mr. Sato, Mr. X and others.

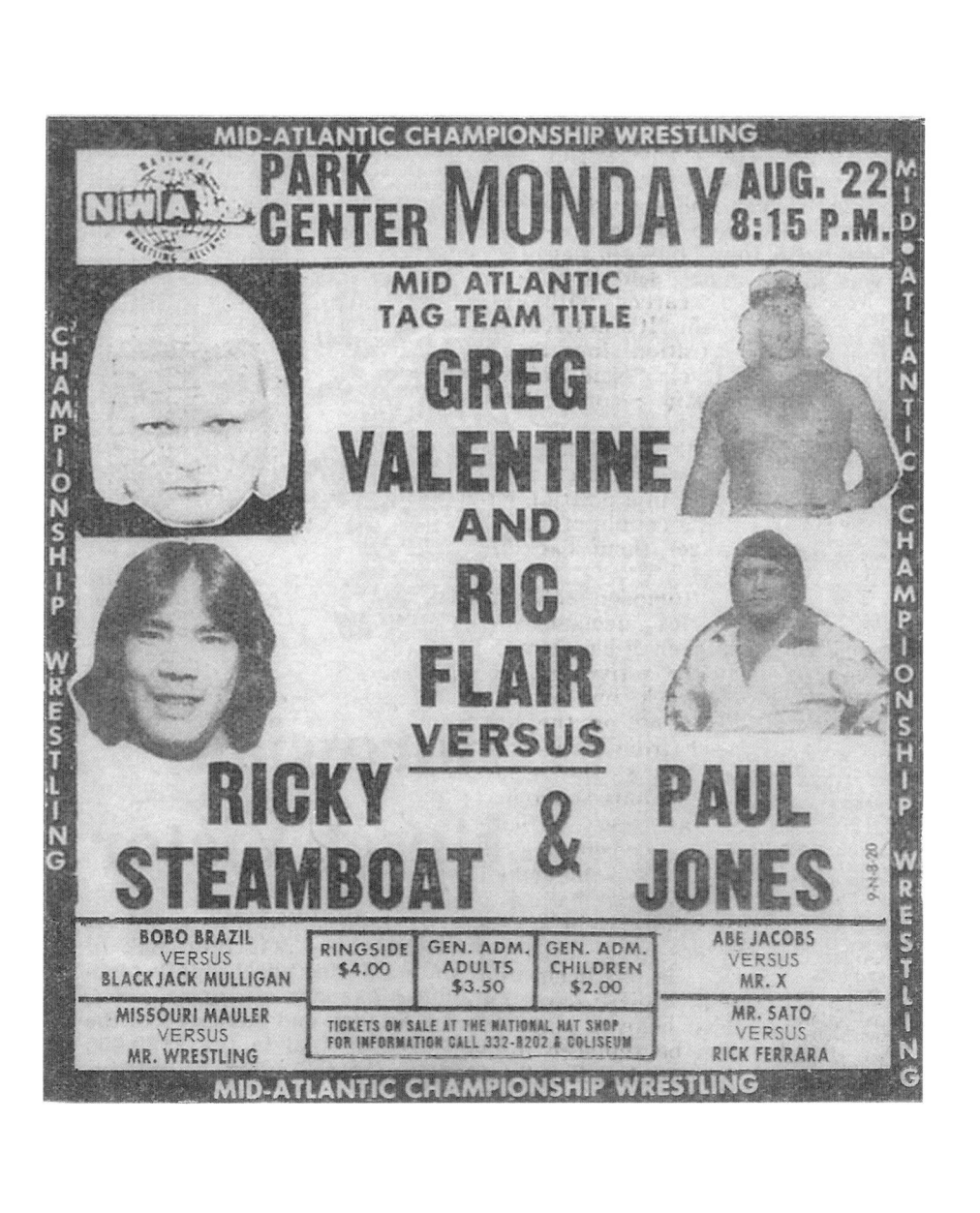

MID-ATLANTIC CHAMPIONSHIP WRESTLING

NWA PARK CENTER
MONDAY AUG. 22 8:15 P.M.

MID ATLANTIC TAG TEAM TITLE

GREG VALENTINE AND RIC FLAIR
VERSUS
RICKY STEAMBOAT & PAUL JONES

BOBO BRAZIL VERSUS BLACKJACK MULLIGAN	RINGSIDE $4.00	GEN. ADM. ADULTS $3.50	GEN. ADM. CHILDREN $2.00	ABE JACOBS VERSUS MR. X
MISSOURI MAULER VERSUS MR. WRESTLING		TICKETS ON SALE AT THE NATIONAL HAT SHOP FOR INFORMATION CALL 332-R202 & COLISEUM		MR. SATO VERSUS RICK FERRARA

MID-ATLANTIC CHAMPIONSHIP WRESTLING

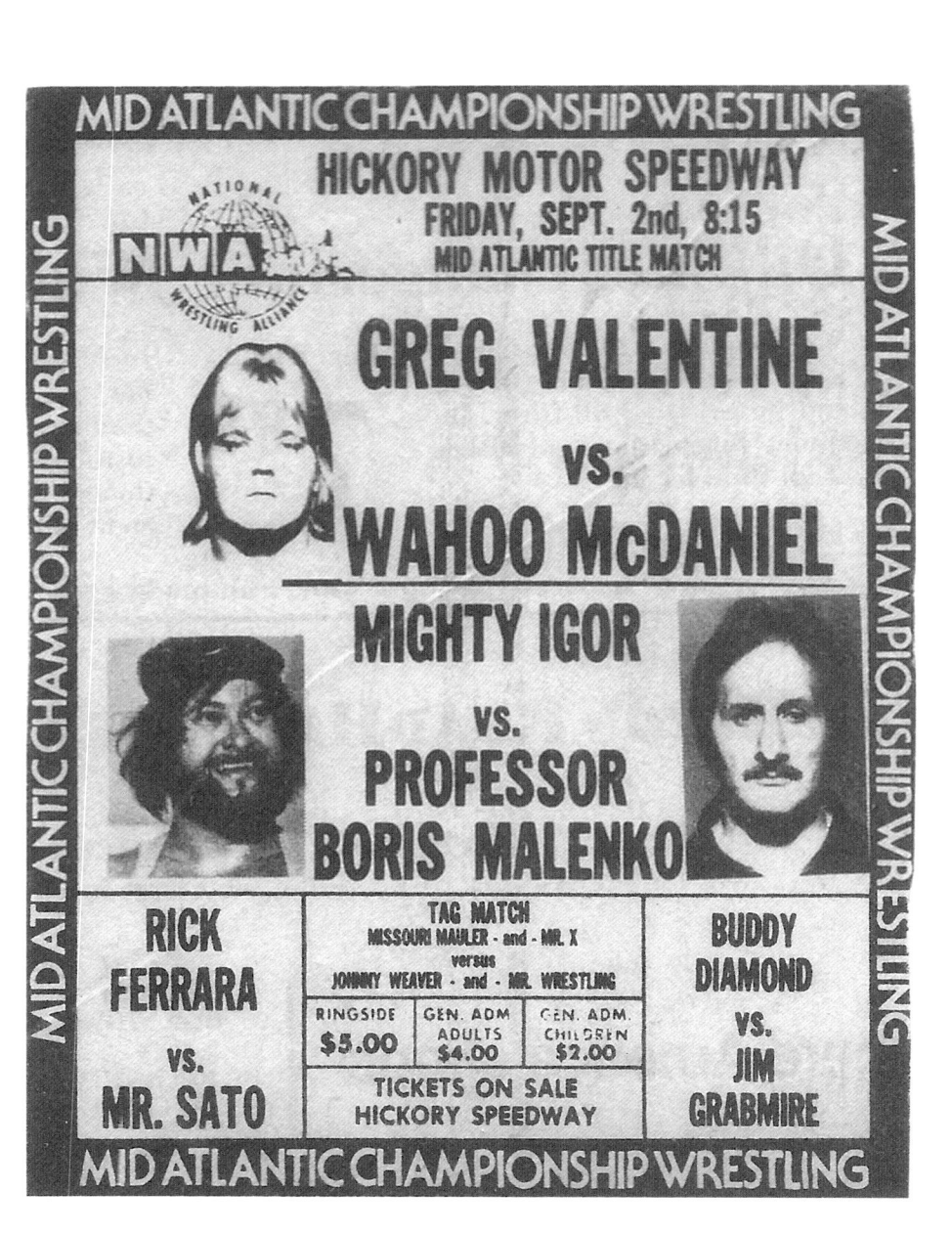

MID ATLANTIC CHAMPIONSHIP WRESTLING

HICKORY MOTOR SPEEDWAY
FRIDAY, SEPT. 2nd, 8:15
MID ATLANTIC TITLE MATCH

NWA — National Wrestling Alliance

GREG VALENTINE
vs.
WAHOO McDANIEL

MIGHTY IGOR
vs.
PROFESSOR BORIS MALENKO

RICK FERRARA
vs.
MR. SATO

TAG MATCH
MISSOURI MAULER - and - MR. X
versus
JOHNNY WEAVER - and - MR. WRESTLING

RINGSIDE	GEN. ADM ADULTS	GEN. ADM CHILDREN
$5.00	$4.00	$2.00

TICKETS ON SALE HICKORY SPEEDWAY

BUDDY DIAMOND
vs.
JIM GRABMIRE

MID ATLANTIC CHAMPIONSHIP WRESTLING

MID ATLANTIC CHAMPIONSHIP WRESTLING

NWA MID ATLANTIC CHAMPIONSHIP WRESTLING TONIGHT—CHARLOTTE COLSEUM
★ SEPT. 3 ★ 8:15 PM ★

3 BIG MAIN EVENTS

U.S. TITLE MATCH
WAHOO McDANIEL VS. RIC FLAIR

T.V. TITLE MATCH
RICKY STEAMBOAT VS. GREG VALENTINE

LUMBERJACK MATCH
MIGHTY IGOR VS. SUPER STAR

TIGER CONWAY & MR. WRESTLING VERSUS JERRY BLACKWELL & PROF. BORIS MALENKO

TULLY BLANCHARD VS. SCOTT IRWIN
RICK McGRAW VS. MR. X
BURRHEAD JONES VS. RICK FERRARA
LARRY SHARP VS. MR. SATO

TICKETS ON SALE AT THE NATIONAL HAT SHOP & CHARLOTTE COLISEUM
FOR INFORMATION CALL 332-8202

RINGSIDE & BOX	GEN. ADM. ADULTS	GEN. ADM. CHILDREN UNDER 12
$6.00	$5.00	$2.50

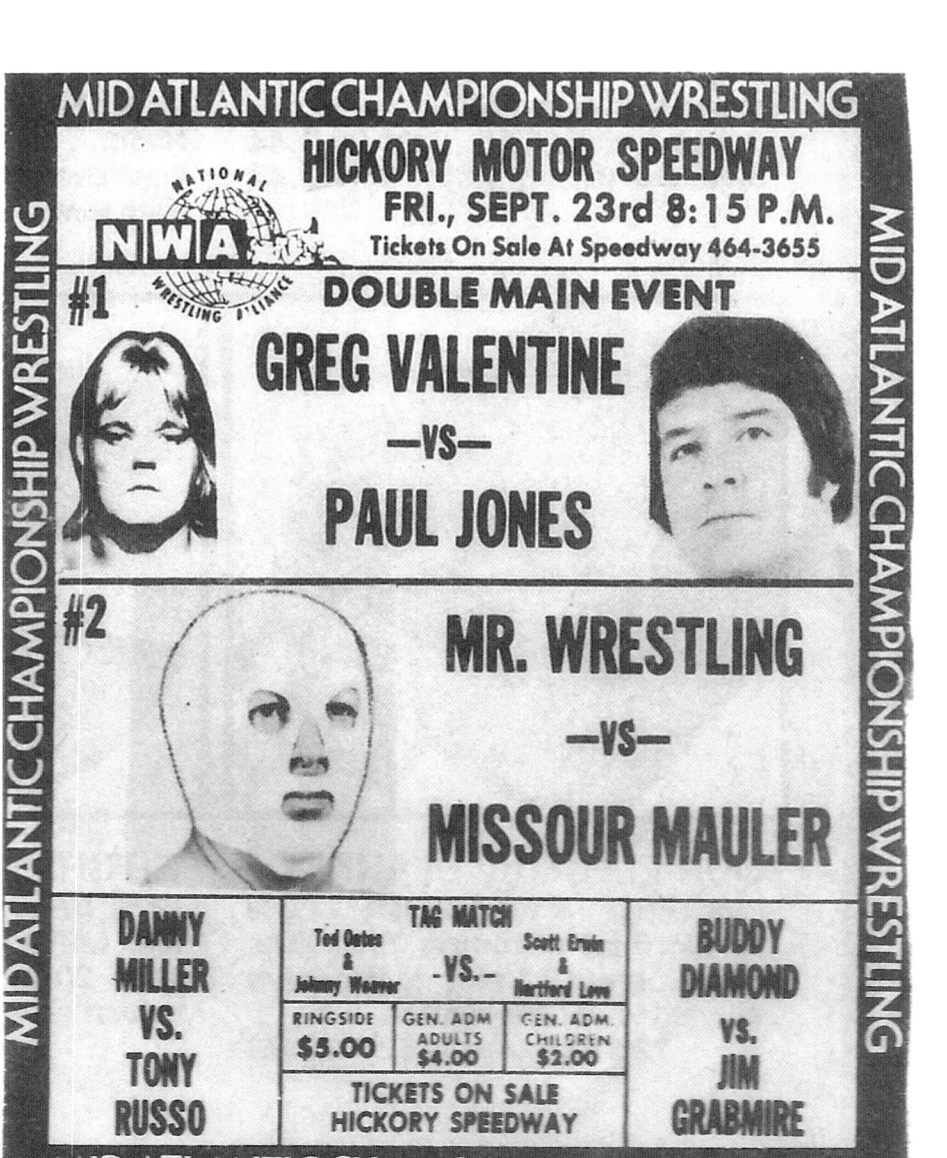

MID ATLANTIC CHAMPIONSHIP WRESTLING

HICKORY MOTOR SPEEDWAY
FRI., SEPT. 23rd 8:15 P.M.
Tickets On Sale At Speedway 464-3655

NWA — NATIONAL WRESTLING ALLIANCE

DOUBLE MAIN EVENT

#1 GREG VALENTINE -vs- PAUL JONES

#2 MR. WRESTLING -vs- MISSOUR MAULER

DANNY MILLER VS. TONY RUSSO

TAG MATCH
Ted Oates & Johnny Weaver -VS- Scott Erwin & Hartford Love

RINGSIDE	GEN. ADM. ADULTS	GEN. ADM. CHILDREN
$5.00	$4.00	$2.00

TICKETS ON SALE HICKORY SPEEDWAY

BUDDY DIAMOND VS. JIM GRABMIRE

MID ATLANTIC CHAMPIONSHIP WRESTLING

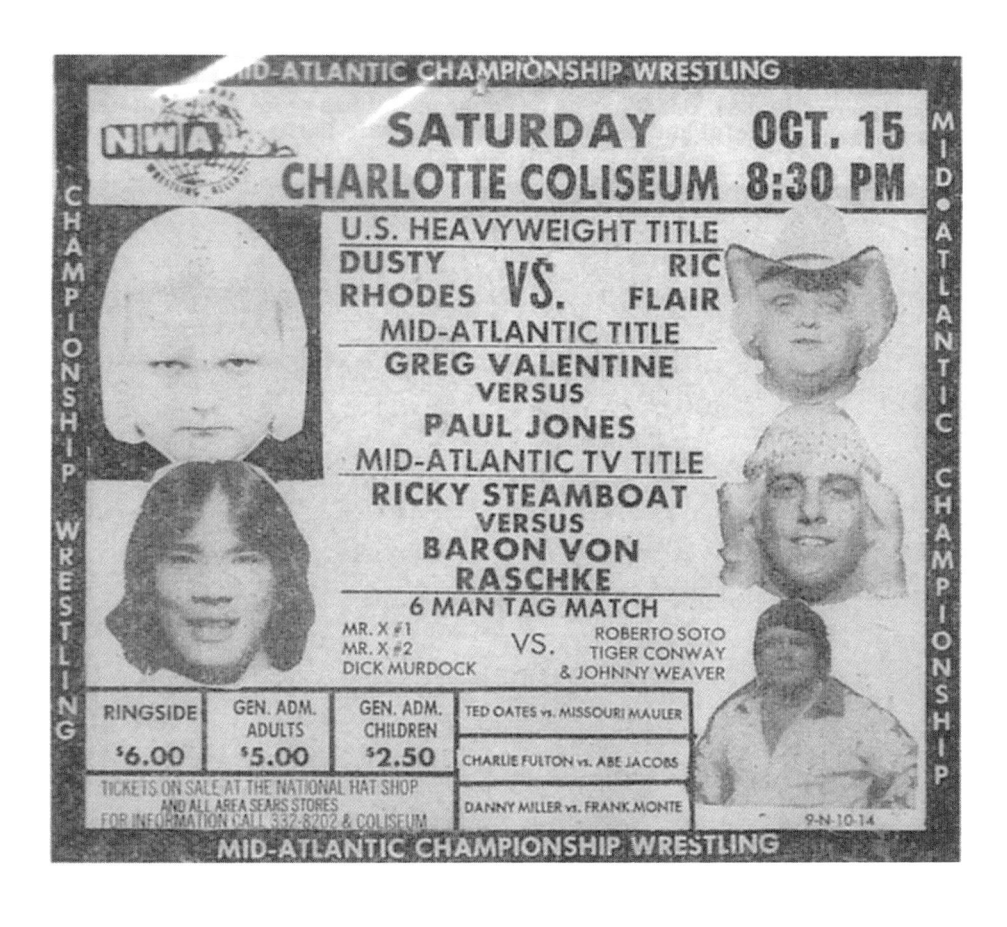

MID-ATLANTIC CHAMPIONSHIP WRESTLING

NWA

SATURDAY OCT. 15
CHARLOTTE COLISEUM 8:30 PM

U.S. HEAVYWEIGHT TITLE
DUSTY RHODES vs. RIC FLAIR

MID-ATLANTIC TITLE
GREG VALENTINE VERSUS PAUL JONES

MID-ATLANTIC TV TITLE
RICKY STEAMBOAT VERSUS BARON VON RASCHKE

6 MAN TAG MATCH
MR. X #1, MR. X #2, DICK MURDOCK vs. ROBERTO SOTO, TIGER CONWAY & JOHNNY WEAVER

RINGSIDE	GEN. ADM. ADULTS	GEN. ADM. CHILDREN
$6.00	$5.00	$2.50

TED OATES vs. MISSOURI MAULER
CHARLIE FULTON vs. ABE JACOBS
DANNY MILLER vs. FRANK MONTE

TICKETS ON SALE AT THE NATIONAL HAT SHOP AND ALL AREA SEARS STORES
FOR INFORMATION CALL 332-8202 & COLISEUM

Wrestlers Retain Assorted Titles

Ric Flair, Greg Valentine and Baron Von Raschke all retained their various NWA professional wrestling titles Saturday night at the Charlotte Coliseum.

Dusty Rhodes got the win over Flair in a U.S. heavyweight championship match, but it was via a disqualification, and a title cannot change hands in such a manner. Valentine and challenger Paul Jones were both counted out of the ring, so the former kept his Mid-Atlantic title. And in the third main event, Von Raschke, who just recently had taken the Mid-Atlantic TV belt from Ricky Steamboat, retained it. Steamboat beat Von Raschke in 22 minutes Saturday, but the title is up for grabs only in the first 15 minutes of a match.

The crowd of 7,272 also saw Roberto Soto, Tiger Conway and Johnny Weaver team to defeat Mr. X Nos. 1 and 2 and Dick Murdock; Missouri Mauler defeat Ted Oates; Abe Jacobs top Charlie Fulton and Danny Miller and Frank Monte fight to a draw.

MID ATLANTIC CHAMPIONSHIP WRESTLING

★ MONDAY ★ OCT. 31, ★ 8:15 PM ★
—Charlotte Coliseum

U.S. HEAVYWEIGHT TITLE
RIC FLAIR vs. RICKY STEAMBOAT

BARON VON RASCHKE & THE SUPERSTAR vs. MR. WRESTLING AND PAUL JONES

MIGHTY IGOR vs. PROF. BORIS MALENKO

BLACKJACK MULLIGAN VERSUS RICKY McGRAW

RIC FERRARA vs. JIM GARVIN

CHARLEY FULTON vs. TULLI BLANCHARD

MR. X #1 AND MR. X #2 vs. TIGER CONWAY AND JOHNNY WEAVER

TICKETS ON SALE AT THE NATIONAL HAT SHOP & CHARLOTTE COLISEUM THE ALAMO, 4447 SOUTH BLVD.
FOR INFORMATION CALL 332-8202

RINGSIDE & BOX	GEN. ADM. ADULTS	GEN. ADM. CHILDREN UNDER 12
$6.00	$5.00	$2.50

WIDE WORLD WRESTLING

SUNDAY
November 6
3:00 P.M.

BIG DOUBLE MAIN EVENT

GRUDGE MATCH

Paul Jones
(½ Holder Mid-Atlantic Tag Team Belt)

VS

The Masked Superstar

Paul — Superstar

U.S. HEAVYWEIGHT TITLE MATCH

Ricky Steamboat
(U.S. Heavyweight Champ)

VS

Blackjack Mulligan

Ricky — Blackjack

TAG MATCH

Mighty Igor & Johnny Weaver

VS

MRX-1 & MRX-2

Danny Miller VS Mr. Sato

Box Office-255-5771. Ringside-$5.00, Center Balcony-$4.00
Other Balcony: Adults-$4.00, Children under 12-$2.00
Box Office Open Mon.-Fri. 10:00-5:30, Sat. 11:00-4:00, Day of
Match 1:00 P.M. NO CHECKS OR CREDIT CARDS DAY OF MATCH.

SEE NWA WIDE WORLD WRESTLING SATURDAY
ON WLOS-TV CHANNEL 13 11:30 PM-12:30 AM

Asheville Civic Center

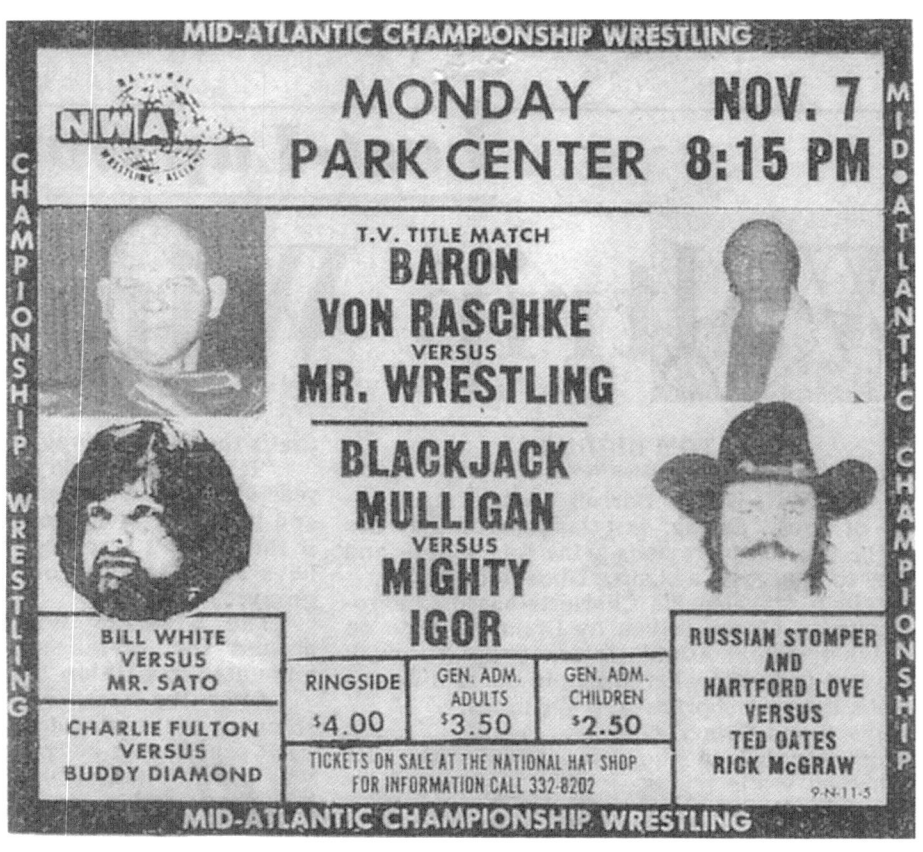

MID-ATLANTIC CHAMPIONSHIP WRESTLING

MONDAY PARK CENTER — NOV. 7 — 8:15 PM

T.V. TITLE MATCH
BARON VON RASCHKE
versus
MR. WRESTLING

BLACKJACK MULLIGAN
versus
MIGHTY IGOR

BILL WHITE VERSUS MR. SATO

CHARLIE FULTON VERSUS BUDDY DIAMOND

RUSSIAN STOMPER AND HARTFORD LOVE
VERSUS
TED OATES RICK McGRAW

RINGSIDE $4.00 | GEN. ADM. ADULTS $3.50 | GEN. ADM. CHILDREN $2.50

TICKETS ON SALE AT THE NATIONAL HAT SHOP
FOR INFORMATION CALL 332-8202

Von Raschke Keeps TV Championship

Baron von Raschke retained his Mid-Atlantic TV title by defeating Mr. Wrestling in Monday night professional wrestling at Park Center.

In other matches: the Mighty Igor defeated Black Jack Mulligan by disqualification; the Russian Stomper and Hartford Love teamed to whip Ted Oates and Ric McGraw; Bill White and Mr. Sato fought to a draw, and Charlie Fulton defeated Buddy Diamond.

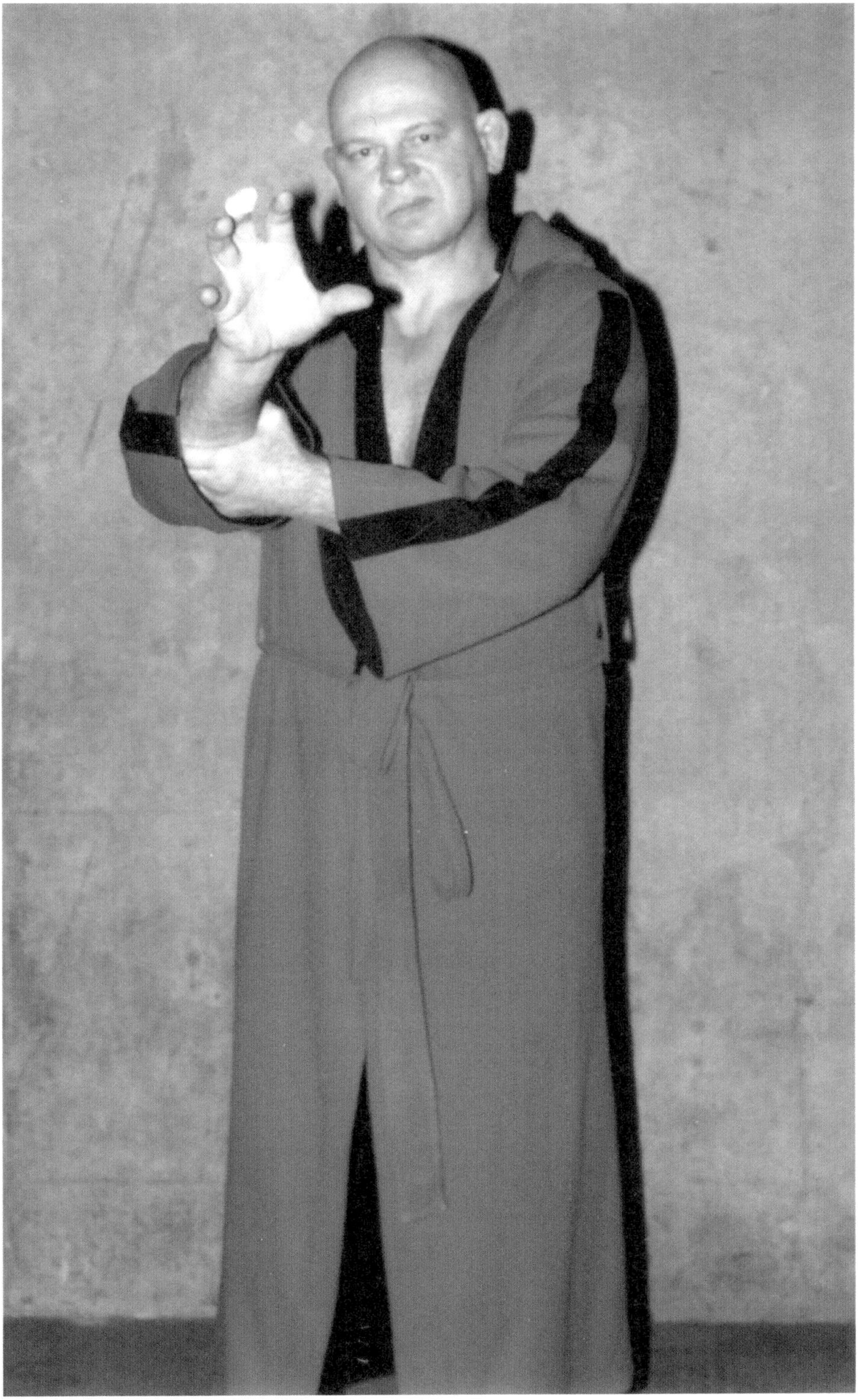

MID ATLANTIC CHAMPIONSHIP WRESTLING

NWA

★ SUNDAY ★ NOV. 27 ★ 7:30 PM ★
— CHARLOTTE COLISEUM

WORLD TAG TEAM TITLE MATCH

CHAMPIONS
RIC FLAIR
AND
GREG VALENTINE

VS.

CHALLENGERS
DUSTY "THE AMERICAN DREAM" RHODES
AND
WAHOO McDANIEL

U.S. TITLE MATCH

CHAMPION
RICKY STEAMBOAT

VERSUS

CHALLENGER
BLACKJACK MULLIGAN

ROBERTO SOTO vs. HARTFORD LOVE | ABE JACOBS vs. FRANK MONTE

TICKETS ON SALE AT THE NATIONAL HAT SHOP & CHARLOTTE COLISEUM THE ALAMO, 4447 SOUTH BLVD. FOR INFORMATION CALL 332-8202

RINGSIDE & BOX $6.00 | GEN. ADM. ADULTS $5.00 | GEN. ADM. CHILDREN UNDER 12 $2.50

TONY BLANCHARD vs. RIC FERRARA

JOHNNY WEAVER & RICK McGRAW VS. DICK MURDOCK & MISSOURI MAULER

MID ATLANTIC CHAMPIONSHIP WRESTLING

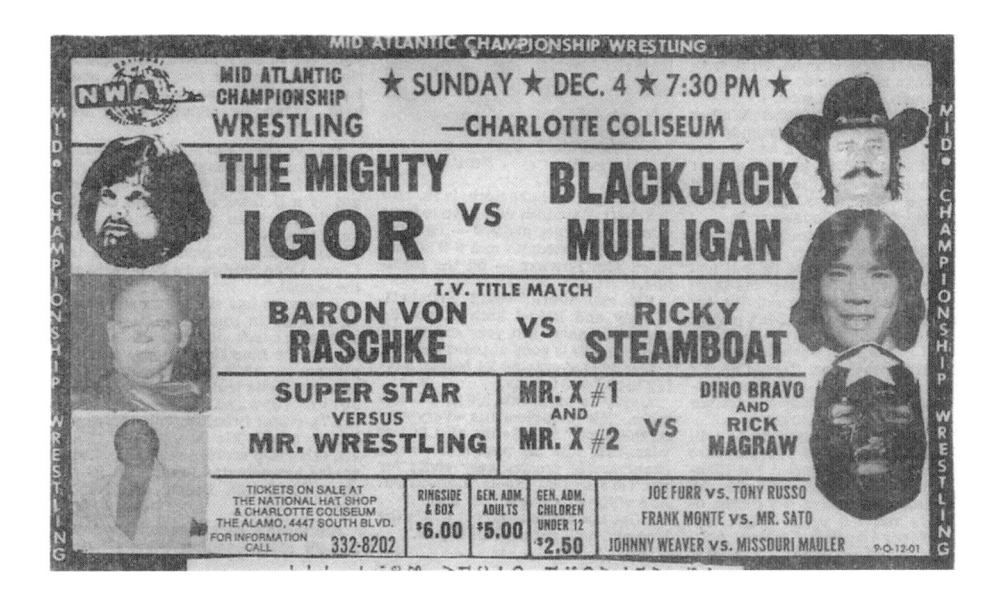

MID ATLANTIC CHAMPIONSHIP WRESTLING

NWA — MID ATLANTIC CHAMPIONSHIP WRESTLING

★ SUNDAY ★ DEC. 4 ★ 7:30 PM ★
—CHARLOTTE COLISEUM

THE MIGHTY IGOR vs **BLACKJACK MULLIGAN**

T.V. TITLE MATCH
BARON VON RASCHKE vs **RICKY STEAMBOAT**

SUPER STAR VERSUS **MR. WRESTLING**

MR. X #1 AND MR. X #2 VS **DINO BRAVO AND RICK MAGRAW**

TICKETS ON SALE AT THE NATIONAL HAT SHOP & CHARLOTTE COLISEUM, THE ALAMO, 4447 SOUTH BLVD.
FOR INFORMATION CALL 332-8202

RINGSIDE & BOX $6.00 | GEN. ADM. ADULTS $5.00 | GEN. ADM. CHILDREN UNDER 12 $2.50

JOE FURR vs. TONY RUSSO
FRANK MONTE vs. MR. SATO
JOHNNY WEAVER vs. MISSOURI MAULER

Igor Big Winner In Pro Wrestling

The Mighty Igor was the big winner in Sunday night's National Wrestling Alliance activity at the Coliseum.

Igor first defeated Blackjack Mulligan in an arm-wrestling event, which earned him the right to face Mulligan in a $5,000-purse wrestling bout. Igor won that, too.

In the other main event, Ricky Steamboat retained his U.S. title and Baron Von Raschke his Mid-Atlantic TV title when the former was disqualified for using a karate thrust to the Baron's throat.

In other matches: Superstar and Tim Woods were both disqualified; Mr. X Nos. 1 and 2 defeated Dino Bravo and Rick McGraw; Johnny Weaver topped Missouri Mauler; Mr. Sato and Frank Monte fought to a draw and Joe Furr defeated Tony Russo.

Next pro wrestling in Charlotte is Christmas night, with Wahoo McDaniel vs. Greg Valentine a main event.

MID ATLALANTIC CHAMPIONSHIP WRESTLING

NWA — MID ATLANTIC CHAMPIONSHIP WRESTLING

★ SUNDAY ★ DEC. 25 ★ 7:30 PM ★
—CHARLOTTE COLISEUM

MID-ATLANTIC HEAVYWEIGHT TITLE

GREG VALENTINE vs. **WAHOO McDANIEL**

MIGHTY IGOR AND KEN PATERA vs. **BLACK JACK MULLIGAN AND THE SUPERSTAR**

TIGER CONWAY, JR. AND TIGER CONWAY, SR. vs. **HARTFORD LOVE AND THE RUSSIAN STOMPER**

EMPTY STOCKING FUND MATCHES

TICKETS ON SALE AT THE NATIONAL HAT SHOP & CHARLOTTE COLISEUM THE ALAMO, 4447 SOUTH BLVD. FOR INFORMATION CALL 332-8202

RINGSIDE & BOX	GEN. ADM. ADULTS	GEN. ADM. CHILDREN UNDER 12
$6.00	$5.00	$2.50

TONY RUSSO VS. SWEDE HANSON
MR. SATO VS. RICK McGRAW
CHARLEY FULTON VS. ABE JACOBS

McDaniel Wins, But Doesn't Get Belt

Wahoo McDaniel was awarded a disqualification victory over Greg Valentine in the main event of professional werestling Sunday night at the Coliseum. But Valentine retained his Mid-Atlantic championship, because titles cannot change hands on a disqualification.

The main tag-team event had a different twist, as Mighty Igor and Ken Patera defeated Blackjack Mulligan and The Superstar. Superstar and manager Boris Malenko abandoned Mulligan and Igor pinned him.

Also, Tiger Conway Jr.-Tiger Conway Sr. defeated Russian Stomper and Hartford Love; Swede Hanson pinned Tony Russo; Rick McGraw of Charlotte and Mr. Sato fought to a 20-minute draw, and Abe Jacobs defeated Charlie Fulton.

Next wrestling in Charlotte is Sunday, Jan. 15.

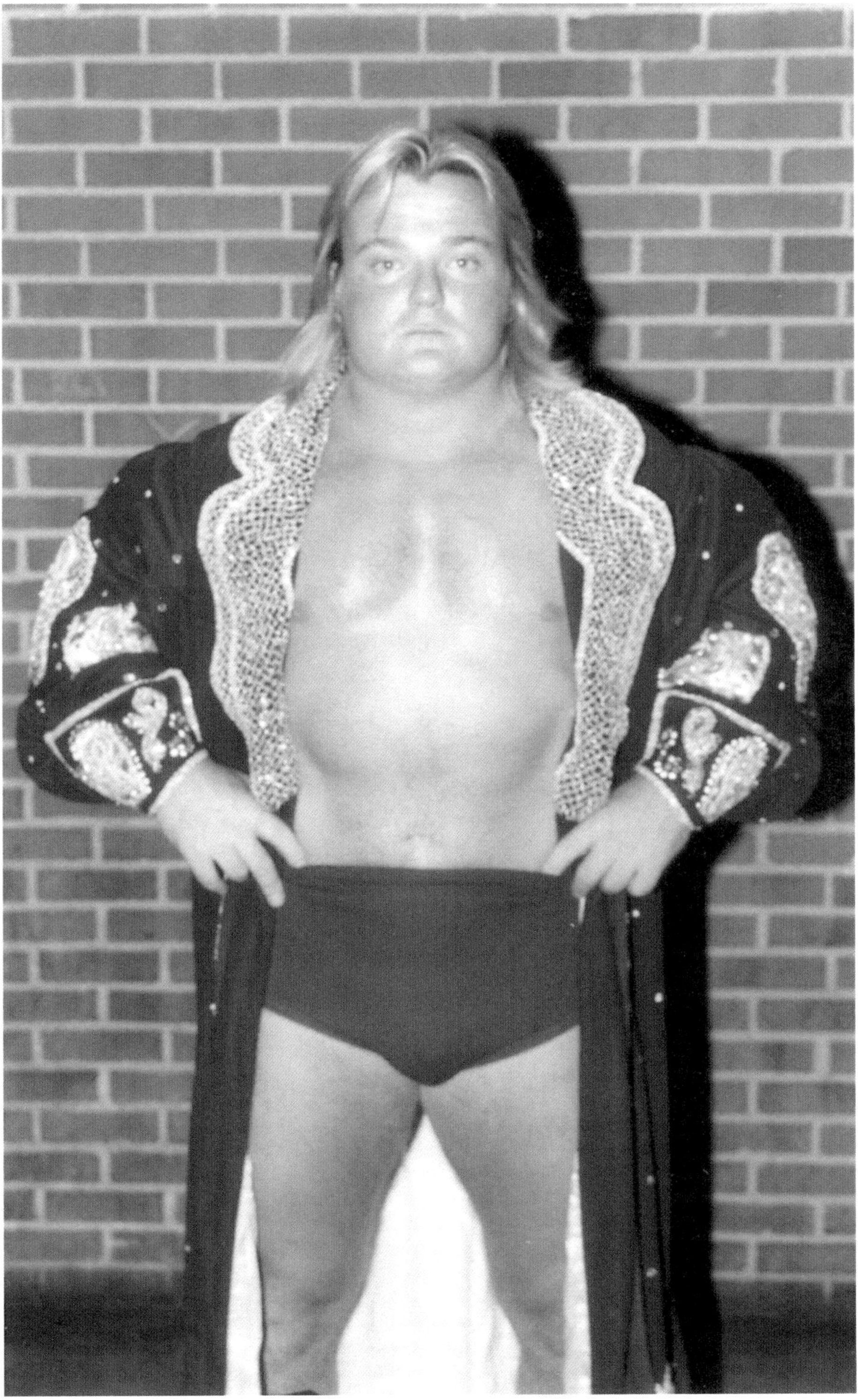

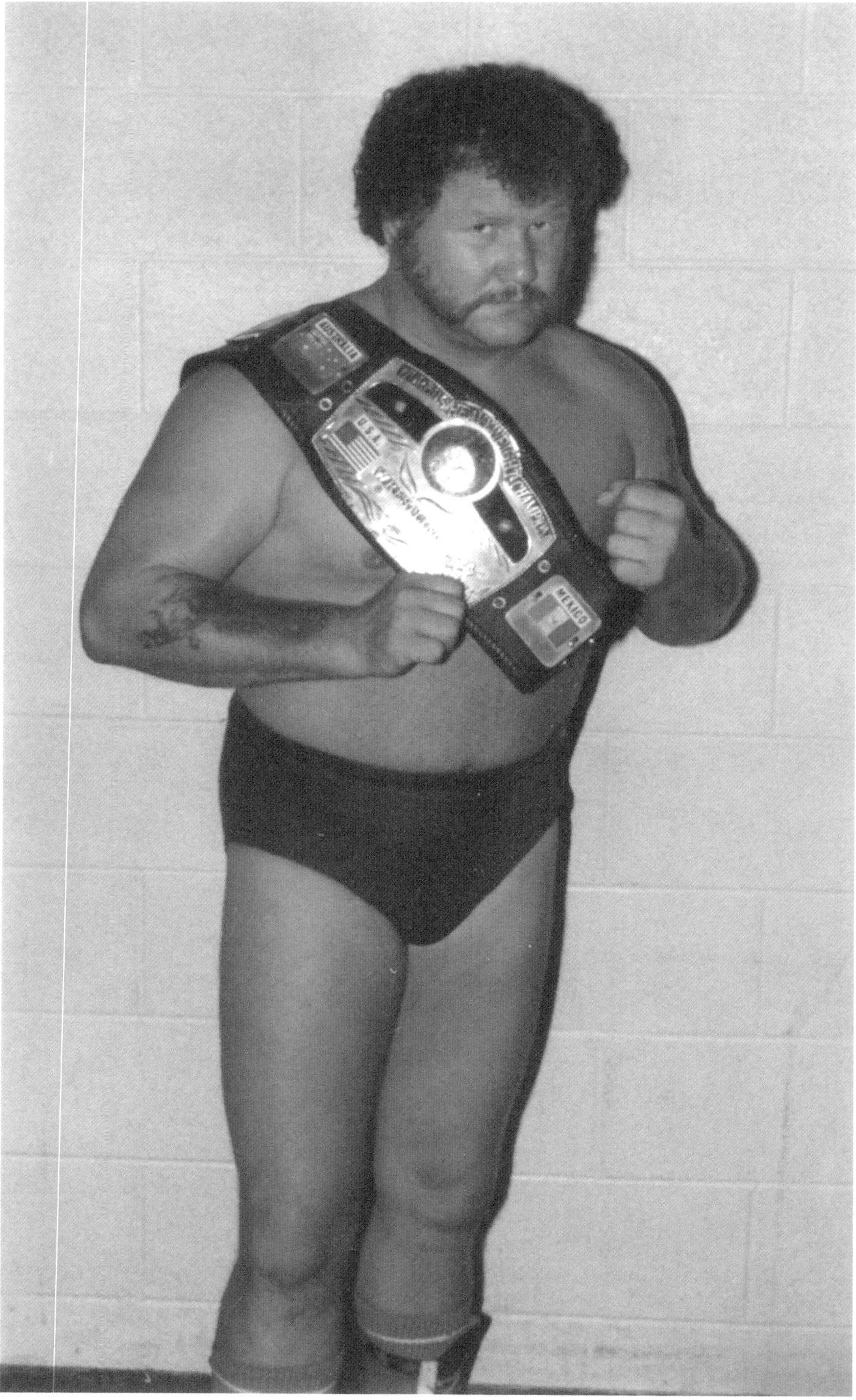
AUSTRALIA
U.S.A.
MEXICO

1978

Ads & Results from

Charlotte Coliseum
Cumberland County Memorial Arena
Dorton Arena
Lineburger Stadium

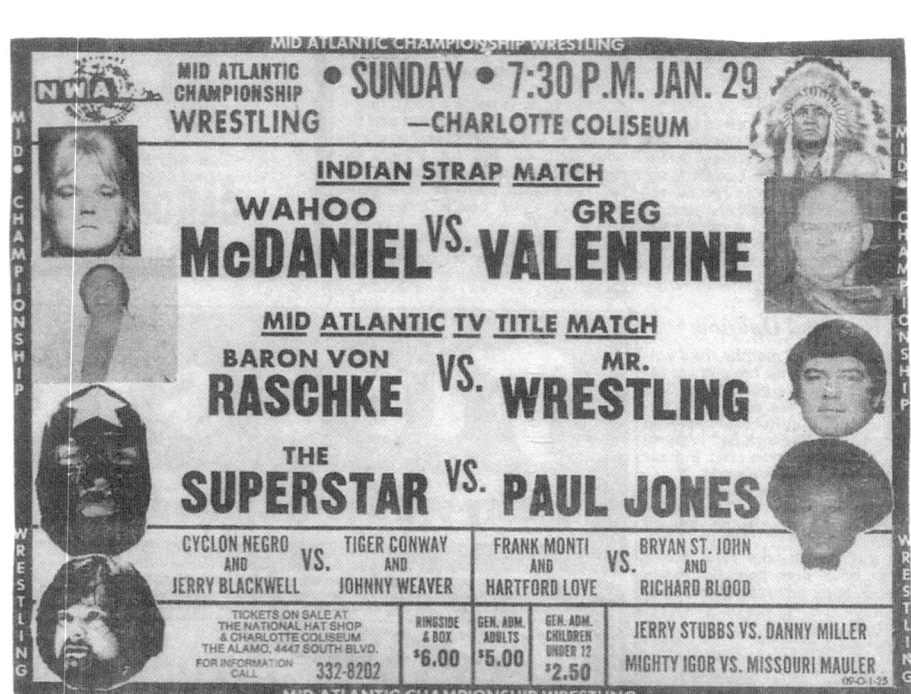

MID ATLANTIC CHAMPIONSHIP WRESTLING
TODAY · 2:00 P.M. · JAN. 15TH
—CHARLOTTE COLISEUM

WORLD TAG TEAM CHAMPIONSHIP

RIC FLAIR & GREG VALENTINE

VERSUS

OLE ANDERSON & WAHOO McDANIEL

U.S. TITLE MATCH

BLACKJACK MULLIGAN vs THE SUPERSTAR

BOBO BRAZIL & TIGER CONWAY JR. vs BARON VON RASCHKE & MISSOURI MAULER

RUSSIAN STOMPER VS BRYAN ST. JOHN

SCOTT IRWIN VS RICHARD BLOOD

MR. X #2 VS. TIM WOODS

MR. X #1 VS TED OATES

TICKETS ON SALE AT THE NATIONAL HAT SHOP & CHARLOTTE COLISEUM THE ALAMO, 4447 SOUTH BLVD.
FOR INFORMATION CALL 332-8202

RINGSIDE & BOX $6.00 — GEN. ADM. ADULTS $5.00 — GEN. ADM. CHILDREN UNDER 12 $2.50

MID ATLANTIC CHAMPIONSHIP WRESTLING
SUNDAY · 7:30 P.M. JAN. 29
—CHARLOTTE COLISEUM

INDIAN STRAP MATCH

WAHOO McDANIEL vs. GREG VALENTINE

MID ATLANTIC TV TITLE MATCH

BARON VON RASCHKE vs. MR. WRESTLING

THE SUPERSTAR vs. PAUL JONES

CYCLON NEGRO AND JERRY BLACKWELL vs. TIGER CONWAY AND JOHNNY WEAVER

FRANK MONTI AND HARTFORD LOVE vs. BRYAN ST. JOHN AND RICHARD BLOOD

JERRY STUBBS VS. DANNY MILLER

MIGHTY IGOR VS. MISSOURI MAULER

TICKETS ON SALE AT THE NATIONAL HAT SHOP & CHARLOTTE COLISEUM THE ALAMO, 4447 SOUTH BLVD.
FOR INFORMATION CALL 332-8202

RINGSIDE & BOX $6.00 — GEN. ADM. ADULTS $5.00 — GEN. ADM. CHILDREN UNDER 12 $2.50

MID-ATLANTIC CHAMPIONSHIP WRESTLING

2 BIG MAIN EVENTS
Charlotte Coliseum
Sunday Feb. 12, 7:30 p.m.

For the World Tag Team Championship — 2 refs.

Ole Anderson & Wahoo McDaniel
vs.
Ric Flair & Greg Valentine

Baron Von Raschke
vs.
Mr. Wrestling

Cyclone Negro vs. Tiger Conway
Mr. X #1 & Mr. X #2 vs. Johnny Weaver & Roberto Soto
Dick Murdock vs. Bill White
Bryan St. John vs. Abe Jacobs
Richard Blood vs. Tony Russo

★ See Wrestling Sat. Feb. 11 on WBTV Channel 3 — 4:00 to 5:00 p.m. ★

TICKETS AVAILABLE AT COLISEUM BOX OFFICE, NATIONAL HAT SHOP, THE ALAMO - 4447 S. BLVD.

Flair, Valentine Run With Belts

Greg Valentine and Ric Flair had enough of challengers Wahoo McDaniel and Ole Anderson, so the reigning U.S. Tag Team champions took their belts and ran from the ring during the professional wrestling main event Sunday night at the Coliseum.

The maneuver resulted in a countout, but Valentine and Flair retained their titles since they cannot change hands on a disqualification.

In an amateur-rules match for the TV title, Tim Woods (Mr. Wrestling) pinned Baron Von Raschke after 23 minutes but Von Raschke retained his championship because it is at stake only during the first 15 minutes of a match.

In other bouts: Cyclone Negro pinned Tiger Conway Jr.; Mr. X Nos. 1 and 2 beat Johnny Wezver and Roberto Soto; Dick Murdock defeated Bill White; Bryan St. John and Abe Jacobs fought to a draw; and Richard Blood defeated Tony Russo.

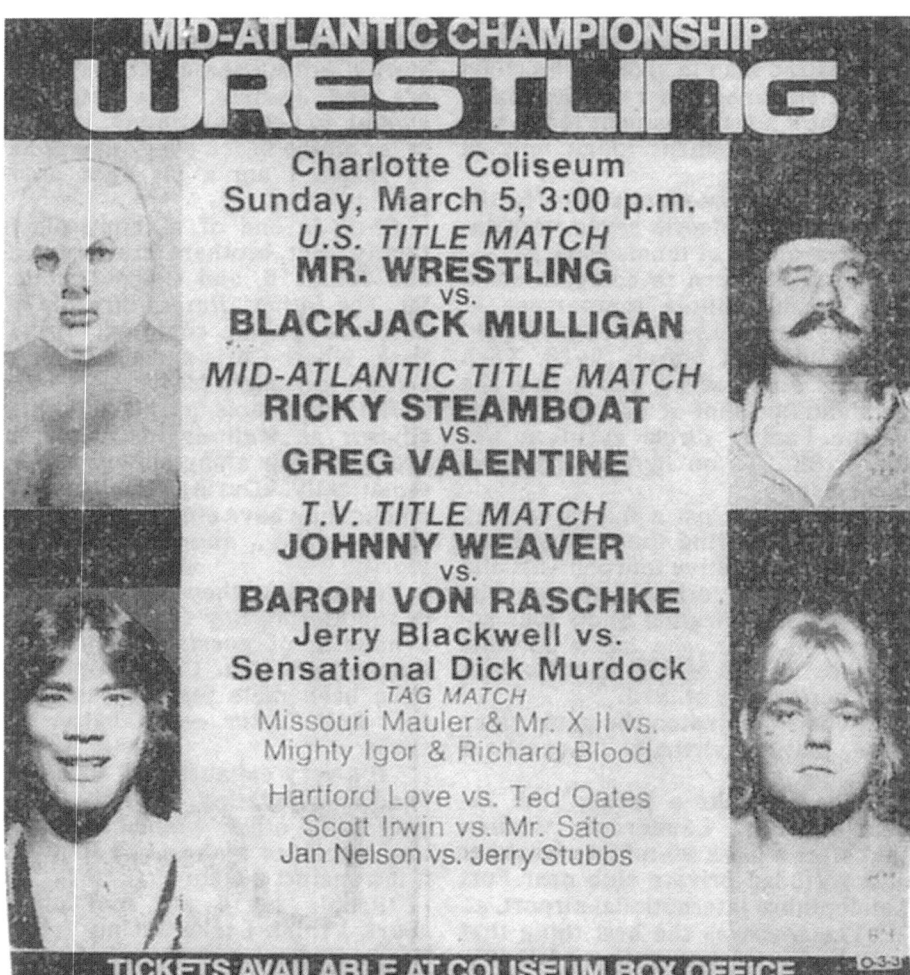

MID-ATLANTIC CHAMPIONSHIP WRESTLING

Charlotte Coliseum
Sunday, March 5, 3:00 p.m.

U.S. TITLE MATCH
MR. WRESTLING
vs.
BLACKJACK MULLIGAN

MID-ATLANTIC TITLE MATCH
RICKY STEAMBOAT
vs.
GREG VALENTINE

T.V. TITLE MATCH
JOHNNY WEAVER
vs.
BARON VON RASCHKE

Jerry Blackwell vs.
Sensational Dick Murdock

TAG MATCH
Missouri Mauler & Mr. X II vs.
Mighty Igor & Richard Blood

Hartford Love vs. Ted Oates
Scott Irwin vs. Mr. Sato
Jan Nelson vs. Jerry Stubbs

TICKETS AVAILABLE AT COLISEUM BOX OFFICE, NATIONAL HAT SHOP, THE ALAMO - 4447 S. BLVD.

Weaver Beats Baron

Johnny Weaver pinned Baron Von Raschke after 12 minutes of wrestling Sunday to take Von Raschke's TV title, the highlight of pro wrestling event at the Coliseum.

In two other title bouts, U.S. champ Blackjack Mulligan and Mid-Atlantic champ Greg Valentine each retained their titles. Mulligan and foe Mr. Wrestling both were disqualified and Valentine was counted out of the ring in his match, giving the victory but not the belt to Ricky Steamboat.

In other matches: Dick Murdock defeated Crusher Blackwell; Mighty Igor and Richard Blood teamed to top Missouri Mauler and Mr. X No. 2; Ted Oates defeated Hartford Love; Scott Irwin pinned Mr. Sato and Jan Nelson and Jerry Stubbs fought to a 15-minute draw.

MID-ATLANTIC CHAMPIONSHIP WRESTLING

Charlotte Coliseum
Sunday, March 26, 7:30 p.m.

WORLD TAG TEAM TITLE MATCH
PAUL JONES
and
RICKY STEAMBOAT
versus
RIC FLAIR
and
GREG VALENTINE

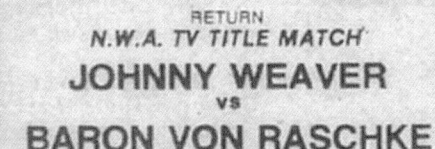

RETURN N.W.A. TV TITLE MATCH
JOHNNY WEAVER
vs
BARON VON RASCHKE

Dick Murdock vs Jan Nelson

Mr. X1 and Mr. X2 vs Denny Miller and Abe Jacobs

Jerry Stubbs vs Bill White

Mr. Sato vs Frank Monte

See Wrestling Sat., March 18 on WBTV Channel 3 - 3:30 to 4:30 p.m.

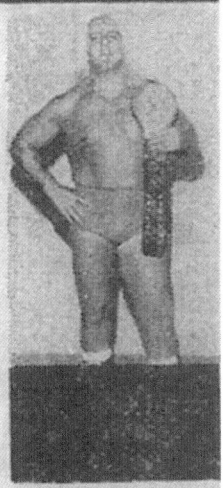

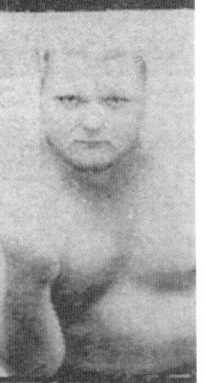

TICKETS AVAILABLE AT COLISEUM BOX OFFICE, NATIONAL HAT SHOP, THE ALAMO - 4447 S. BLVD.

Flair, Valentine Retain Tag Belts

Ric Flair and Greg Valentine successfully defended their World Tag-Team titles to highlight Sunday's professional wrestling show at the Coliseum. They defeated challengers Paul Jones and Ricky Steamboat when Flair pinned Jones.

In a second main event, Johnny Weaver retained his television title by turning back Baron Von Raschke.

In other results: Dick Murdock pinned Jan Nelson; Mr. X Nos. 1 and 2 teamed to defeat Danny Miller and Abe Jacobs; Jerry Stubbs defeated Bill White and Mr. Sato earned a 20-minute decision over Frank Monte.

MID-ATLANTIC CHAMPIONSHIP WRESTLING

Charlotte Coliseum
April 9th 7:30 P.M.

U.S. TITLE MATCH

MR. WRESTLING
VERSUS
RIC FLAIR
(TITLE VERSUS HAIR)

WAHOO McDANIEL
VERSUS
KEN PATERA

BLACKJACK MULLIGAN
VERSUS
BOBO BRAZIL

TAG ACTION
Mr. X 1 & 2 versus
Richard Blood & Ted Oates

Crusher Blackwell vs. Bryan St. John

Charlie Fulton vs. Frank Monte

Mr. Sato vs. Bill Howard

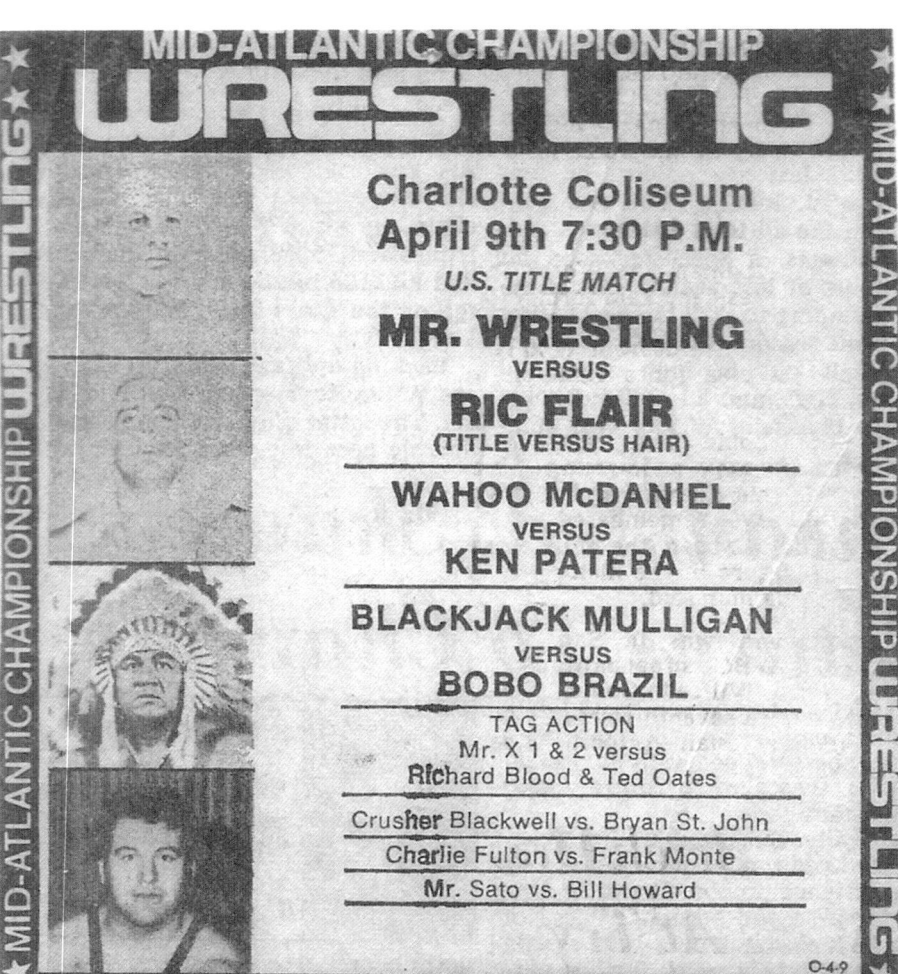

TICKETS AVAILABLE AT COLISEUM BOX OFFICE, NATIONAL HAT SHOP, THE ALAMO - 4447 S. BLVD.

Flair, Patera Top Woods, McDaniel

Two championship belts changed hands during Sunday night's professional wrestling card at the Charlotte Coliseum, as Ric Flair pinned Mr. Wrestling, Tim Woods, for the National Wrestling Alliance U.S. championship and Ken Patera pinned Wahoo McDaniel for the Mid-Atlantic belt.

In other singles matches: Blackjack Mulligan d. Bobo Brazil; Crusher Blackwell d. Bryan St. John, Frank Monte d. Charlie Fulton and Mr. Sato d. Bill Howard.

In the night's lone tag-team bout, Mr. X Nos. 1 and 2 defeated Richard Blood and Ted Oates.

MID-ATLANTIC CHAMPIONSHIP WRESTLING

Charlotte Coliseum
Sunday, April 30, 7:30 P.M.

TWO OF THE WORLDS STRONGEST MEN
ANDRE' THE GIANT
VERSUS
KEN PATERA

BLACKJACK MULLIGAN
VERSUS
THE SUPERSTAR

NWA T.V. TITLE
BARON VON RASCHKE
VERSUS
JOHNNY WEAVER

TAG ACTION
Mr. Wrestling and Tony Atlas VS. Cyclone Negro and Jerry Blackwell

Mr. X #1 VS. Roberto Soto

Richard Blood VS. Hartford Love

Bill Howard VS. Joe Furr

See Wrestling Sat. April 29
WBTV Channel 3 - 3:30 to 4:30 p.m.

TICKETS AVAILABLE AT COLISEUM BOX OFFICE, NATIONAL HAT SHOP, THE ALAMO - 4447 S. BLVD.

Disqualifications Reign

Disqualifications were the order of the day in Sunday's professional wrestling show at the Charlotte Coliseum.

Ken Patera was disqualified for throwing Andre the Giant over the top rope and in another match both Blackjack Mulligan and the Superstar were disqualified.

Baron Von Raschke defeated Johnny Weaver to retain his television title belt.

In other matches Mr. Wrestling and Tony Atlas defeated Cyclone Negro and Crusher Blackwell, Mr. X No. 1 was disqualified against Roberto Soto, Richard Blood defeated Hartford Love, Mr. Sato beat Scott Irvin and Bill Howard defeated Joe Furr.

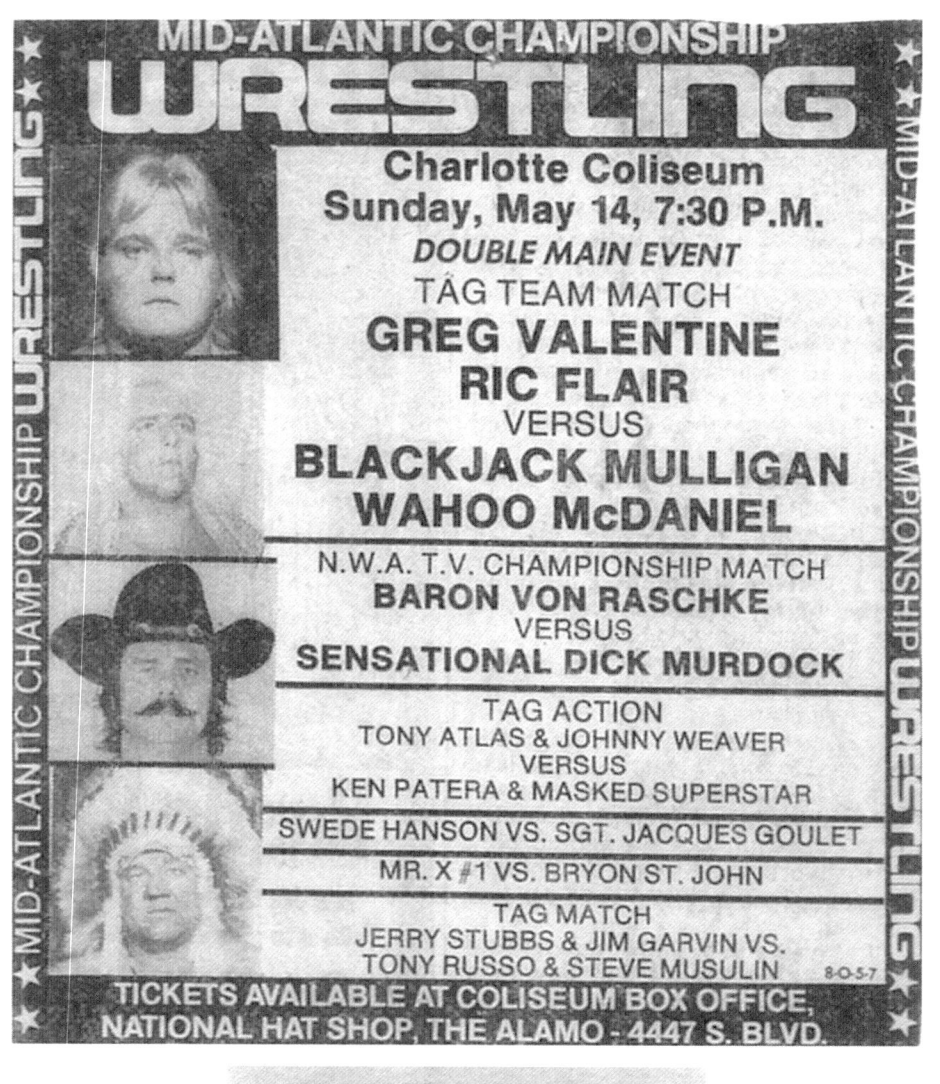

MID-ATLANTIC CHAMPIONSHIP WRESTLING

Charlotte Coliseum
Sunday, May 14, 7:30 P.M.

DOUBLE MAIN EVENT

TAG TEAM MATCH
GREG VALENTINE
RIC FLAIR
VERSUS
BLACKJACK MULLIGAN
WAHOO McDANIEL

N.W.A. T.V. CHAMPIONSHIP MATCH
BARON VON RASCHKE
VERSUS
SENSATIONAL DICK MURDOCK

TAG ACTION
TONY ATLAS & JOHNNY WEAVER
VERSUS
KEN PATERA & MASKED SUPERSTAR

SWEDE HANSON VS. SGT. JACQUES GOULET

MR. X #1 VS. BRYON ST. JOHN

TAG MATCH
JERRY STUBBS & JIM GARVIN VS.
TONY RUSSO & STEVE MUSULIN

TICKETS AVAILABLE AT COLISEUM BOX OFFICE, NATIONAL HAT SHOP, THE ALAMO - 4447 S. BLVD.

Pro Wrestling

At Charlotte Coliseum

Blackjack Mulligan-Wahoo McDaniel d. Ric Flair-Greg Valentine, disqualification.
Dick Murdock d. Baron Von Raschke, 15:20, 20 seconds too late for Von Raschke to lose TV title.
Ken Patera-The Superstar d. Tony Atlas-Johnny Weaver.
Jacques Goulet d. Swede Hansen.
Bryan St. John d. Mr. X. No. 1
Jerry Stubbs-Jim Garvin d. Steve Musilin-Tony Russo.

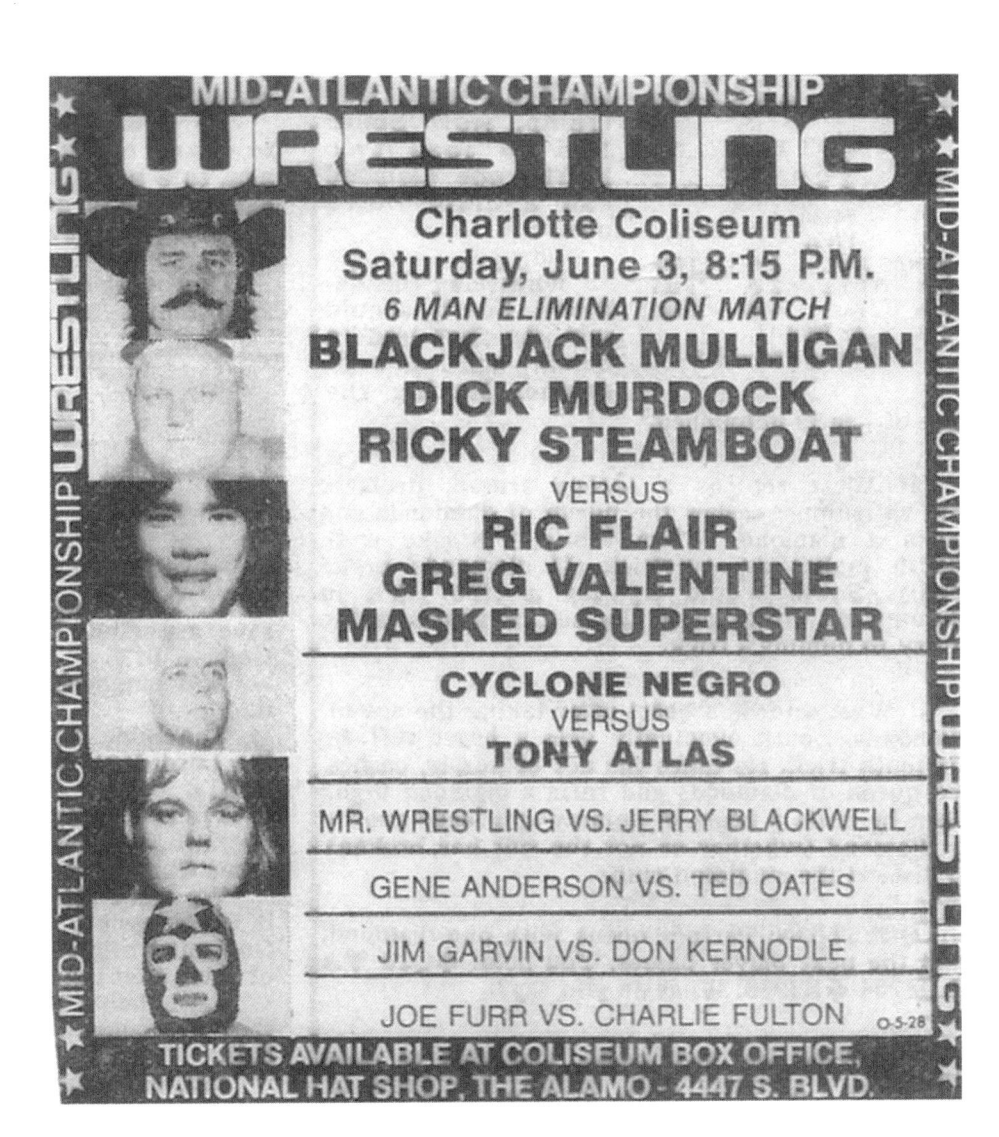

MID-ATLANTIC CHAMPIONSHIP WRESTLING

Charlotte Coliseum
Saturday, June 3, 8:15 P.M.

6 MAN ELIMINATION MATCH

BLACKJACK MULLIGAN
DICK MURDOCK
RICKY STEAMBOAT

VERSUS

RIC FLAIR
GREG VALENTINE
MASKED SUPERSTAR

CYCLONE NEGRO
VERSUS
TONY ATLAS

MR. WRESTLING VS. JERRY BLACKWELL

GENE ANDERSON VS. TED OATES

JIM GARVIN VS. DON KERNODLE

JOE FURR VS. CHARLIE FULTON

TICKETS AVAILABLE AT COLISEUM BOX OFFICE, NATIONAL HAT SHOP, THE ALAMO - 4447 S. BLVD.

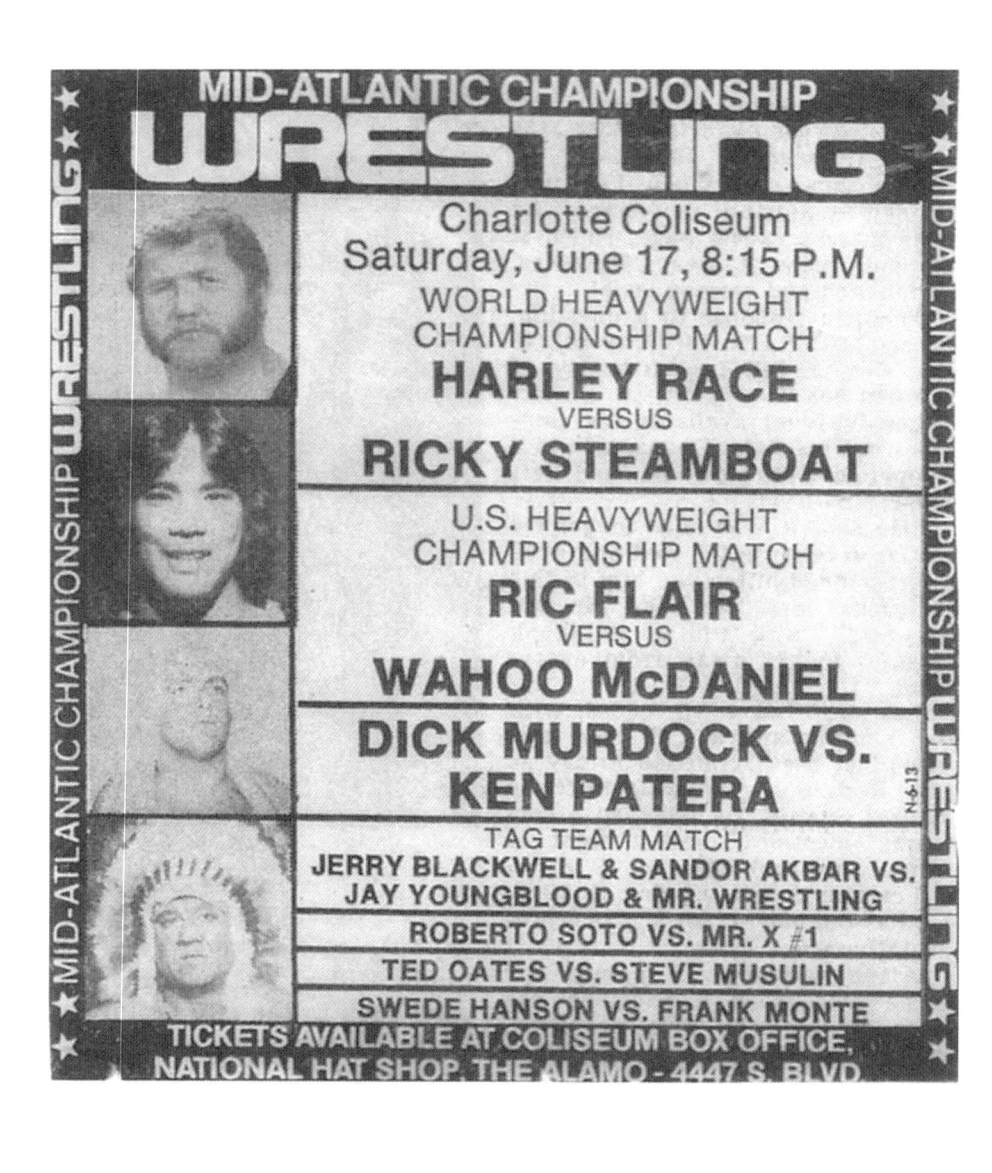

MID-ATLANTIC CHAMPIONSHIP WRESTLING

Charlotte Coliseum
Saturday, June 17, 8:15 P.M.

WORLD HEAVYWEIGHT CHAMPIONSHIP MATCH
HARLEY RACE
VERSUS
RICKY STEAMBOAT

U.S. HEAVYWEIGHT CHAMPIONSHIP MATCH
RIC FLAIR
VERSUS
WAHOO McDANIEL

DICK MURDOCK VS. KEN PATERA

TAG TEAM MATCH
JERRY BLACKWELL & SANDOR AKBAR VS.
JAY YOUNGBLOOD & MR. WRESTLING

ROBERTO SOTO VS. MR. X #1

TED OATES VS. STEVE MUSULIN

SWEDE HANSON VS. FRANK MONTE

TICKETS AVAILABLE AT COLISEUM BOX OFFICE,
NATIONAL HAT SHOP, THE ALAMO - 4447 S. BLVD.

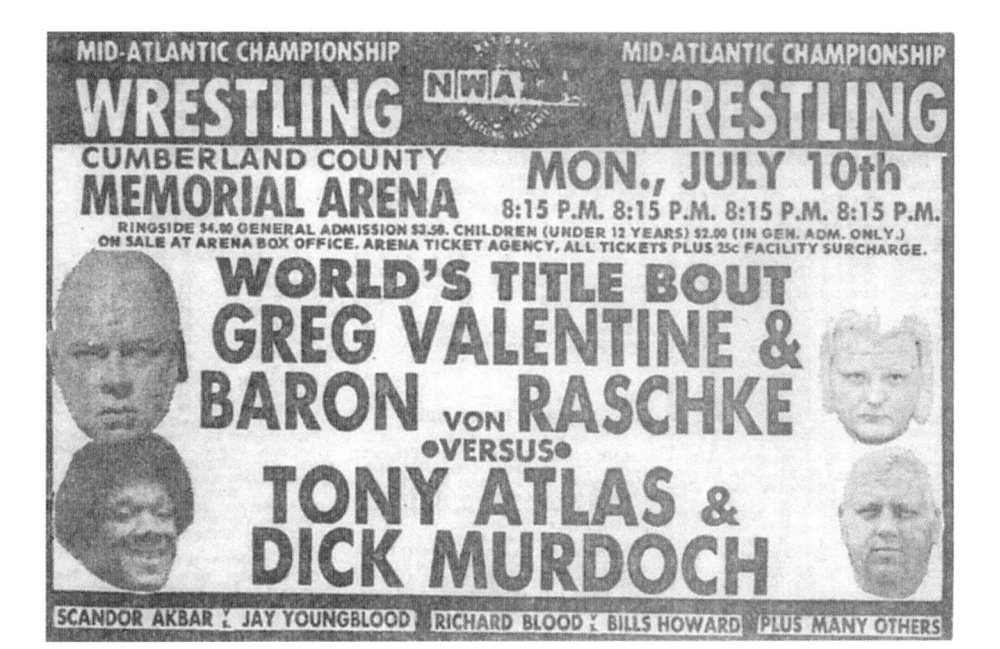

MID-ATLANTIC CHAMPIONSHIP WRESTLING — NWA

CUMBERLAND COUNTY MEMORIAL ARENA — MON., JULY 10th 8:15 P.M.

RINGSIDE $4.00 GENERAL ADMISSION $3.50. CHILDREN (UNDER 12 YEARS) $2.00 (IN GEN. ADM. ONLY). ON SALE AT ARENA BOX OFFICE. ARENA TICKET AGENCY, ALL TICKETS PLUS 25c FACILITY SURCHARGE.

WORLD'S TITLE BOUT
GREG VALENTINE & BARON von RASCHKE
• VERSUS •
TONY ATLAS & DICK MURDOCH

SCANDOR AKBAR v. JAY YOUNGBLOOD | RICHARD BLOOD v. BILLS HOWARD | PLUS MANY OTHERS

MID-ATLANTIC CHAMPIONSHIP WRESTLING — NWA

DORTON ARENA • TUES., JULY 11th, 8:15 P.M.

RINGSIDE $5.00, GEN. ADM. $4.00. CHILDREN (UNDER 12) $2.00 ADM.

FOR UNITED STATES TITLE
RIC FLAIR
• VERSUS •
BLACKJACK MULLIGAN

TONY ATLAS
• VERSUS •
THE SUPERSTAR

MR. X No. 1 & MR. X No. 2 vs. TED OATES & JERRY OATES | ROBERTO SOTO vs FRANK MONTE | MR. SATO vs STEVE MUSULIN

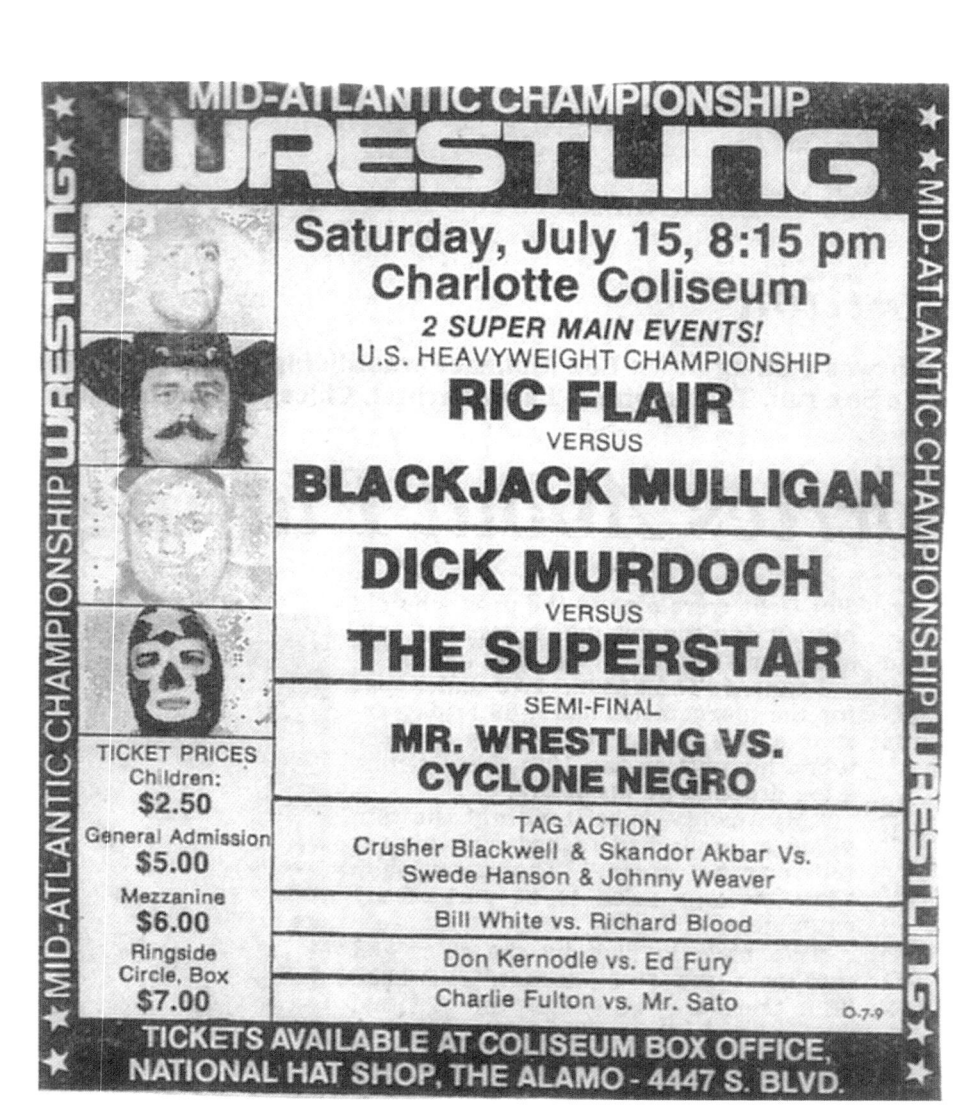

MID-ATLANTIC CHAMPIONSHIP WRESTLING

Saturday, July 15, 8:15 pm
Charlotte Coliseum

2 SUPER MAIN EVENTS!

U.S. HEAVYWEIGHT CHAMPIONSHIP

RIC FLAIR
VERSUS
BLACKJACK MULLIGAN

DICK MURDOCH
VERSUS
THE SUPERSTAR

SEMI-FINAL
MR. WRESTLING VS. CYCLONE NEGRO

TAG ACTION
Crusher Blackwell & Skandor Akbar Vs. Swede Hanson & Johnny Weaver

Bill White vs. Richard Blood

Don Kernodle vs. Ed Fury

Charlie Fulton vs. Mr. Sato

TICKET PRICES
Children: $2.50
General Admission: $5.00
Mezzanine: $6.00
Ringside Circle, Box: $7.00

TICKETS AVAILABLE AT COLISEUM BOX OFFICE, NATIONAL HAT SHOP, THE ALAMO - 4447 S. BLVD.

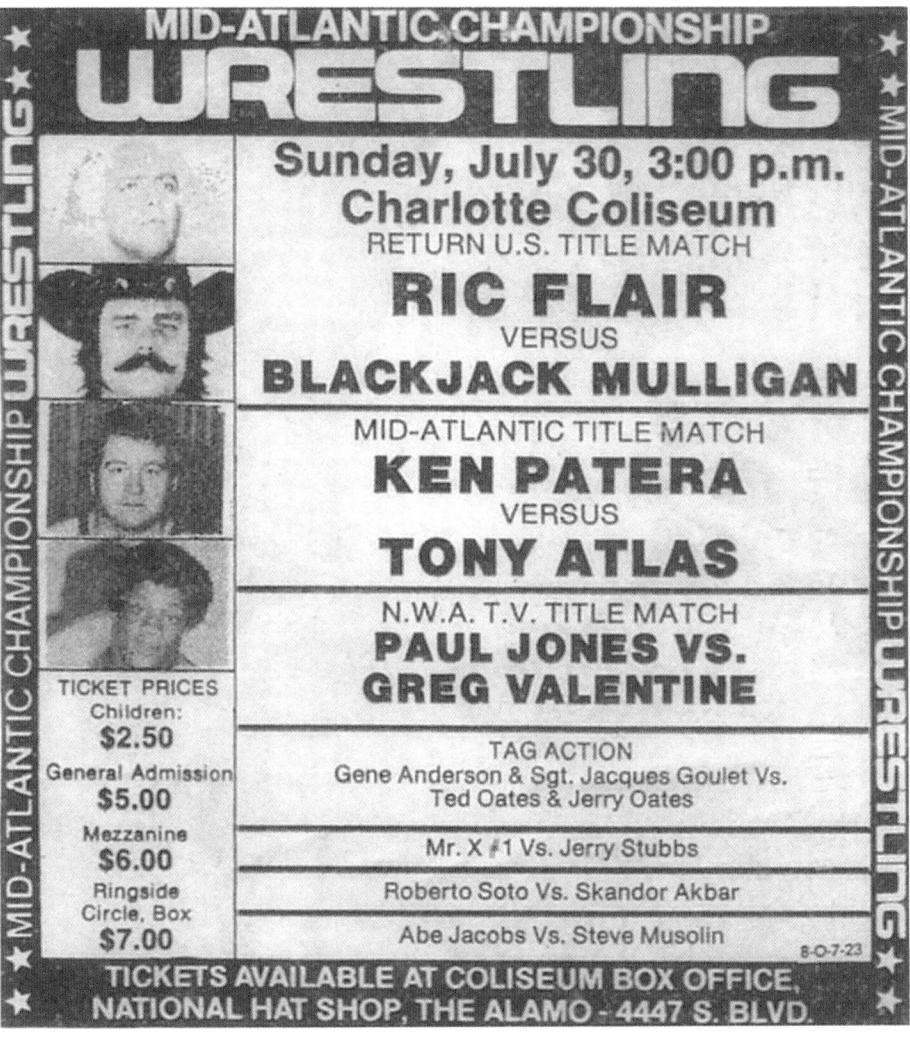

MID-ATLANTIC CHAMPIONSHIP WRESTLING

Sunday, July 30, 3:00 p.m.
Charlotte Coliseum

RETURN U.S. TITLE MATCH
RIC FLAIR
VERSUS
BLACKJACK MULLIGAN

MID-ATLANTIC TITLE MATCH
KEN PATERA
VERSUS
TONY ATLAS

N.W.A. T.V. TITLE MATCH
PAUL JONES VS. GREG VALENTINE

TAG ACTION
Gene Anderson & Sgt. Jacques Goulet Vs. Ted Oates & Jerry Oates
Mr. X #1 Vs. Jerry Stubbs
Roberto Soto Vs. Skandor Akbar
Abe Jacobs Vs. Steve Musolin

TICKET PRICES
Children: $2.50
General Admission: $5.00
Mezzanine: $6.00
Ringside, Circle, Box: $7.00

TICKETS AVAILABLE AT COLISEUM BOX OFFICE, NATIONAL HAT SHOP, THE ALAMO - 4447 S. BLVD.

Mulligan, Flair Both Disqualified

Ric Flair and Blackjack Mulligan both were disqualified from their National Wrestling Alliance U.S. title wrestling bout Sunday at the Charlotte Coliseum Sunday for disregarding and then roughing up the referee.

In other action, Ken Patera was disqualified from his Mid-Atlantic championship bout but retained the title when he threw Tony Atlas over the top rope; Paul Jones defeated Greg Valentine; Gene Anderson and Jaques Goulet topped Ted and Jerry Oates in a tag-team match; Mr. X No. 1 defeated Jerry Stubbs; Roberto Soto was decisioned by Skandar Akbar and Abe Jacobs beat Steve Musolin.

MID-ATLANTIC CHAMPIONSHIP WRESTLING

TRIPLE MAIN EVENT
Charlotte Coliseum
Saturday, August 12, 1978 8:15 p.m.

U.S. TITLE MATCH
RIC FLAIR VS DICK MURDOCH

No Disqualification
Blackjack Mulligan VS Superstar

Ricky Steamboat VS Gene Anderson

TAG TEAM MATCH

Crusher Blackwell AND Sgt. Jacques Goulet VS Mr. X #1	Ted Oates AND Jerry Oates VS Skip Young	Doug Gilbert VS Bryan St. John Charlie Fulton VS Richard Blood Steve Musulin VS Swede Hanson

Ringside $7.00 Reserved $6.00 Adult General Admission $5.00 Children 11 yrs and under $2.50

TICKETS AVAILABLE AT COLISEUM BOX OFFICE, NATIONAL HAT SHOP, THE ALAMO - 4447 S. BLVD.

MID ATLANTIC CHAMPIONSHIP WRESTLING
Sponsored by BELMONT JAYCEES
MONDAY, AUGUST 21-8 P.M.
LINEBURGER STADIUM at South Point High in Belmont

12 WRESTLERS-DOUBLE MAIN EVENT
Gene Anderson vs. Ricky Steamboat
Mr. Wrestling vs. Cyclone Negro

Cyclone Negro vs. Mr. Wrestling

Ricky Steamboat vs. Gene Anderson

TICKETS ON SALE AT:
Dixon Ford, B & K Auto Parts, Security Bank, & Textile Bowling Lanes
CALL 825-9635

MID-ATLANTIC CHAMPIONSHIP WRESTLING

Charlotte Coliseum
September 3, 1978 3:00 P.M.

LUMBERJACK MATCH
BLACKJACK MULLIGAN vs. SUPERSTAR

U.S. TITLE MATCH
RIC FLAIR vs RICKY STEAMBOAT

MID-ATLANTIC TITLE MATCH
Prior to Match: ARM WRESTLING
TONY ATLAS VS KEN PATERA (Champion)

TAG-TEAM MATCH
DICK MURDOCH and JAY YOUNGBLOOD
VS
CYCLONE NEGRO and SGT. JACQUES GOULET

TAG-TEAM MATCH
TED OATES and JERRY OATES
VS
SKANDOR AKBAR and BILL WHITE

FRANK MONTE VS ABE JACOBS

SWEDE HANSON VS DAVID PATTERSON

Ringside $7.00, Reserved $6.00, Adult General Admission $5.00, Children 11 yrs and under $2.50   O-8-27

TICKETS AVAILABLE AT COLISEUM BOX OFFICE,
NATIONAL HAT SHOP, THE ALAMO - 4447 S. BLVD.

Mulligan Unmasks Loser Superstar

Blackjack Mulligan defeated The Superstar in the lumberjack main event wrestling match Sunday at the Charlotte Coliseum. Mulligan took the Superstar's mask off, but the loser escaped without being identified.

In two title bouts, Ric Flair was disqualified but retained his U.S. crown against Ricky Steamboat and Ken Patera, Mid-Atlantic titleholder, defeated Tony Atlas.

In tag-team matches, Dick Murdock-Jay Youngblood pinned Cyclone Negro-Jacques Goulet and Ted and Jerry Oates topped Skandar Akbar-Bill White. In other singles bouts, Abe Jacobs pinned Frank Monte and Swede Hanson defeated Steve Patterson.

Attendance was 7,119.

MID ATLANTIC CHAMPIONSHIP WRESTLING

MATCHES: MON., SEPT. 11, 8:15

HICKORY SPEEDWAY
HWY. 64-70   HICKORY, N.C.

NWA - NATIONAL WRESTLING ALLIANCE

DOUBLE MAIN EVENTS

N.W.A. TV TITLE MATCH
CHAMPION PAUL JONES
VS.
BARON VON RASCHKE

SENSATIONAL DICK MURDOCK
VS.
CYCLONE NEGRO

TAG MATCH	BILL WHITE VS. ABE JACOBS	BILL HOWARD VS. BRYON ST. JOHN
TED BATES & JERRY OATES VS. SWEDE HANSON & MR. X #2	RINGSIDE $5.00 GEN. ADM. ADULTS $4.00 CHILDREN UNDER 11 $2.50	

TICKETS ON SALE HICKORY SPEEDWAY

MID ATLANTIC CHAMPIONSHIP WRESTLING

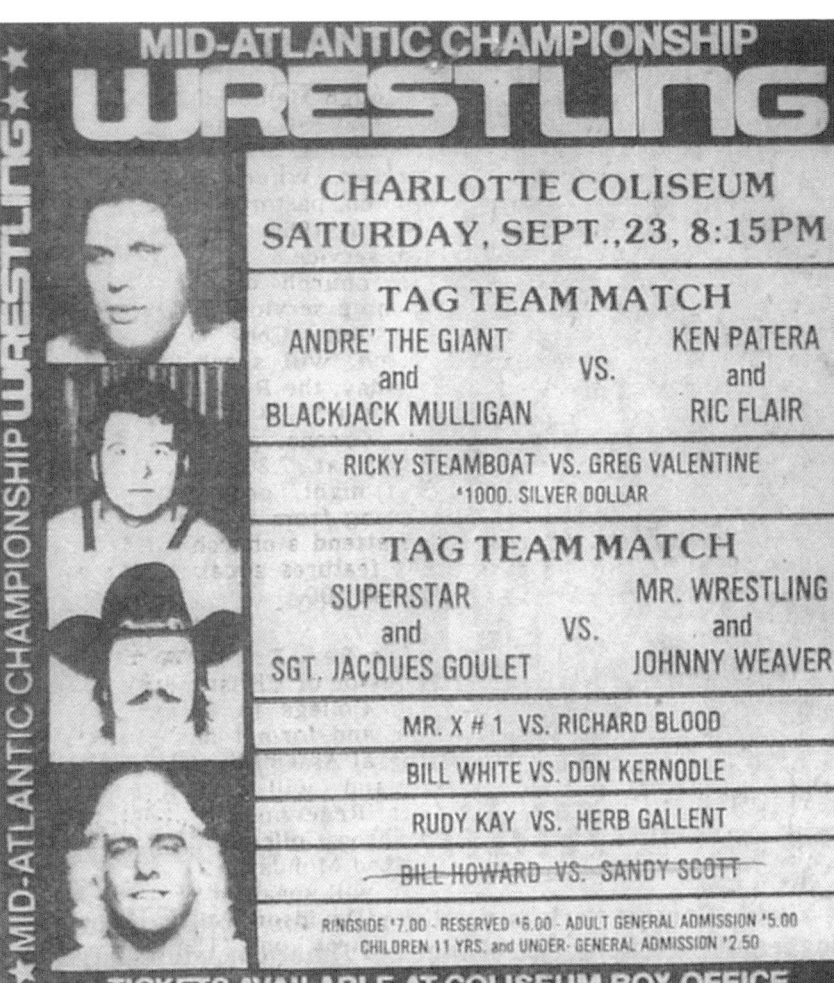

MID-ATLANTIC CHAMPIONSHIP WRESTLING

CHARLOTTE COLISEUM
SATURDAY, SEPT. 23, 8:15 PM

TAG TEAM MATCH

ANDRE' THE GIANT and BLACKJACK MULLIGAN vs. KEN PATERA and RIC FLAIR

RICKY STEAMBOAT vs. GREG VALENTINE
$1000. SILVER DOLLAR

TAG TEAM MATCH

SUPERSTAR and SGT. JACQUES GOULET vs. MR. WRESTLING and JOHNNY WEAVER

MR. X #1 vs. RICHARD BLOOD

BILL WHITE vs. DON KERNODLE

RUDY KAY vs. HERB GALLENT

~~BILL HOWARD vs. SANDY SCOTT~~

RINGSIDE $7.00 - RESERVED $6.00 - ADULT GENERAL ADMISSION $5.00
CHILDREN 11 YRS. and UNDER- GENERAL ADMISSION $2.50

TICKETS AVAILABLE AT COLISEUM BOX OFFICE, NATIONAL HAT SHOP, THE ALAMO - 4447 S. BLVD.

Andre, Blackjack Win Mat Feature

Andre the Giant and Blackjack Mulligan defeated Ken Patera and Rick Flair Saturday night in the feature tag team event on Saturday night's pro wrestling program at Charlotte Coliseum.

In the top singles match, Ricky Steamboat defeated Greg Valentine, while Mr. Wrestling and Johnny Weaver won their tag-team match when Superstar and Jacques Goulet were disqualified for making a two saves (tag teams are permitted only one save).

In other matches, Mr. X No.1 defeated Richard Blood, Don Kernodle pinned Bill White, and Herb Gallent and Rudy Kay wrestled to a 20-minute draw.

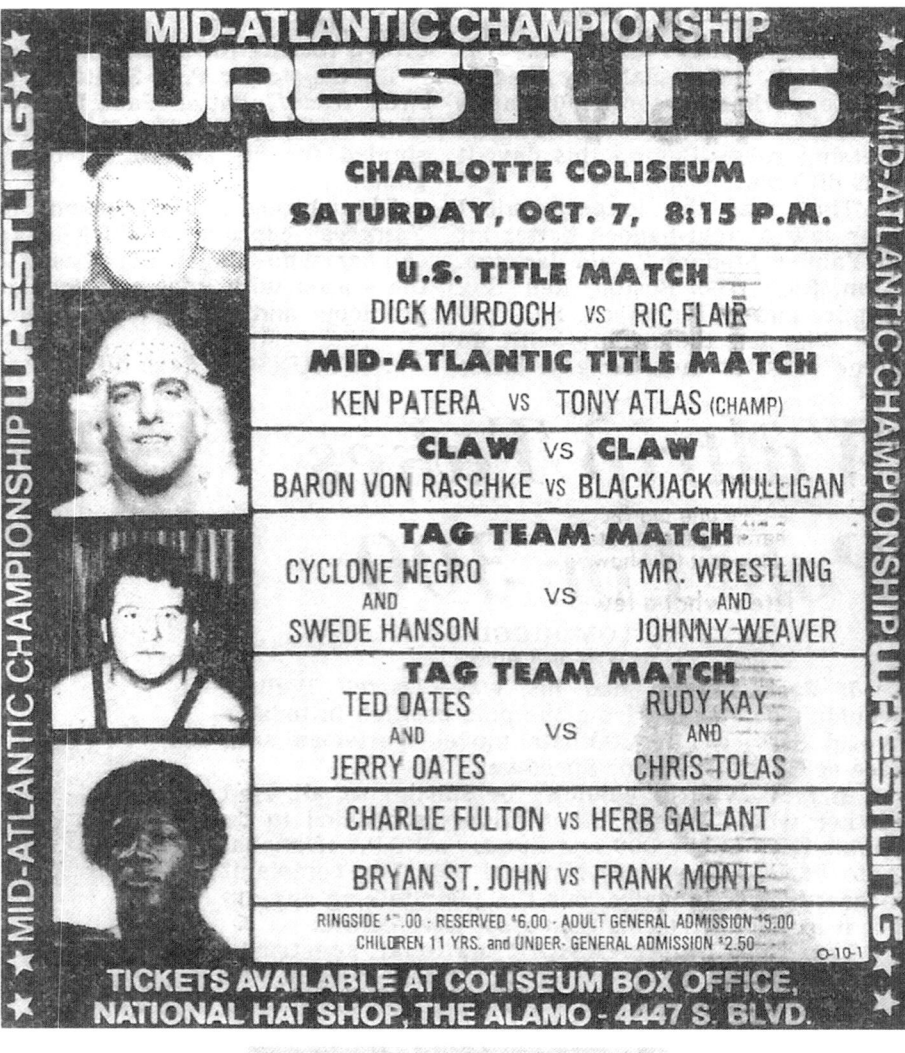

MID-ATLANTIC CHAMPIONSHIP WRESTLING

CHARLOTTE COLISEUM
SATURDAY, OCT. 7, 8:15 P.M.

U.S. TITLE MATCH
DICK MURDOCH vs RIC FLAIR

MID-ATLANTIC TITLE MATCH
KEN PATERA vs TONY ATLAS (CHAMP)

CLAW vs CLAW
BARON VON RASCHKE vs BLACKJACK MULLIGAN

TAG TEAM MATCH
CYCLONE NEGRO AND SWEDE HANSON vs MR. WRESTLING AND JOHNNY WEAVER

TAG TEAM MATCH
TED OATES AND JERRY OATES vs RUDY KAY AND CHRIS TOLAS

CHARLIE FULTON vs HERB GALLANT

BRYAN ST. JOHN vs FRANK MONTE

RINGSIDE $7.00 - RESERVED $6.00 - ADULT GENERAL ADMISSION $5.00
CHILDREN 11 YRS. and UNDER- GENERAL ADMISSION $2.50

TICKETS AVAILABLE AT COLISEUM BOX OFFICE, NATIONAL HAT SHOP, THE ALAMO - 4447 S. BLVD.

Mulligan, Flair, Atlas Win Matches

In pro wrestling action at the Charlotte Coliseum Saturday, Blackjack Mulligan defeated Baron Von Raschke; Tony Atlas defeated Ken Patera, and Ric Flair beat Dick Murdock.

Bryan St. John won a 15-minute decision over Frank Monte; Ted and Jerry Oates defeated Rudy Kay and Chris Tolas, and Johnny Weaver teamed up with Mr. Wrestling to defeat Cyclone Negro and Swede Hanson.

MID-ATLANTIC CHAMPIONSHIP WRESTLING

CHARLOTTE COLISEUM
SUNDAY, OCT. 22, 3:00 P.M.

WORLD TITLE MATCH
$10,000 Bounty
HARLEY RACE vs. BLACKJACK MULLIGAN

WORLD TAG TEAM MATCH
BARON VON RASCHKE and GREG VALENTINE vs. PAUL JONES and DICK MURDOCH

TAG TEAM MATCH
HERB GALLANT and GARY YOUNG vs. RUDY KAY AND CHRIS TOLAS

JERRY OATES vs. SKANDOR AKBAR

SKIP YOUNG vs. CYCLONE NEGRO

JOHN STUDD vs. TED OATES

DON KERNODLE vs. FRANK MONTE

RINGSIDE $7.00 - RESERVED $6.00 - ADULT GENERAL ADMISSION $5.00
CHILDREN 11 YRS. and UNDER - GENERAL ADMISSION $2.50

TICKETS AVAILABLE AT COLISEUM BOX OFFICE, NATIONAL HAT SHOP, THE ALAMO - 4447 S. BLVD.

Champions Retain Wrestling Titles

No titles changed hands during Sunday's professional wrestling show at the Coliseum. In the two main events, world champion Harley Race retained his crown when challenger Blackjack Mulligan was disqualified for throwing Race over top rope, and Greg Valentine and Baron Von Raschke kept their world tag-team belts by defeating challengers Paul Jones and Dick Murdock.

In other matches, Skip Young defeated Swede Hansen; John Studd bested Ted Oates; Jerry Oates pinned Skandar Akbar; Herb Gallant and Gary Young teamed to top Rudy Kaye and Chris Tolos on a disqualification, and Don Kernodle defeated Frank Monte.

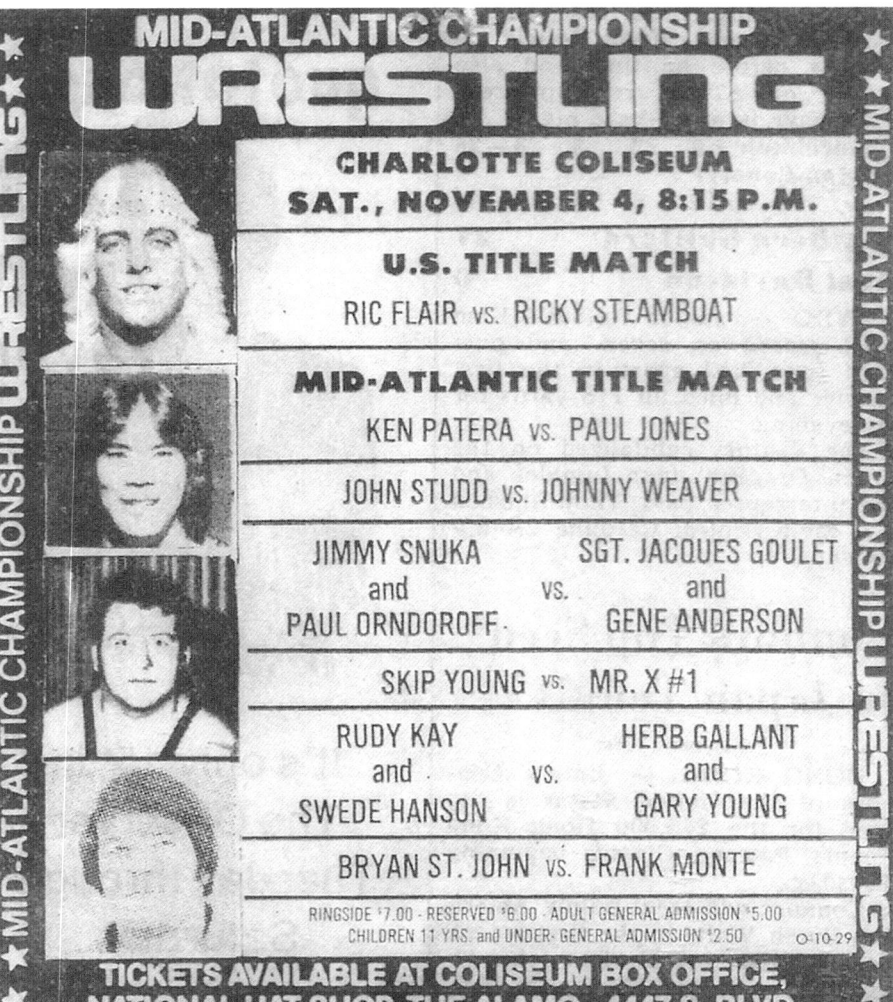

MID-ATLANTIC CHAMPIONSHIP WRESTLING

CHARLOTTE COLISEUM
SAT., NOVEMBER 4, 8:15 P.M.

U.S. TITLE MATCH
RIC FLAIR vs. RICKY STEAMBOAT

MID-ATLANTIC TITLE MATCH
KEN PATERA vs. PAUL JONES

JOHN STUDD vs. JOHNNY WEAVER

JIMMY SNUKA and PAUL ORNDOROFF vs. SGT. JACQUES GOULET and GENE ANDERSON

SKIP YOUNG vs. MR. X #1

RUDY KAY and SWEDE HANSON vs. HERB GALLANT and GARY YOUNG

BRYAN ST. JOHN vs. FRANK MONTE

RINGSIDE $7.00 - RESERVED $6.00 - ADULT GENERAL ADMISSION $5.00
CHILDREN 11 YRS. and UNDER - GENERAL ADMISSION $2.50

TICKETS AVAILABLE AT COLISEUM BOX OFFICE, NATIONAL HAT SHOP, THE ALAMO - 4447 S. BLVD.

Flair, Patera Keep Titles

Ric Flair kept his U.S. heavyweight title and Ken Patera retained his Mid-Atlantic title to highlight Saturday night's professional wrestling card at the Coliseum

Flair ran from the ring with his belt during a match with challenger Ricky Steamboat. Flair was disqualified, but a belt does not change hands on a disqualification. Patera kept his title by defeating Paul Jones.

In other matches: John Studd d. Johnny Weaver; Paul Orndorff-Jimmy Snuka d. Gene Anderson-Jacques Goulet; Skip Young d. Mr. X No. 1; Rudy Kaye-Swede Hanson d. Gary Young-Herb Gallant and Frank Monte d. Brian St. John.

MID-ATLANTIC CHAMPIONSHIP WRESTLING

CHARLOTTE COLISEUM
SUN., NOVEMBER 26 7:30 P.M.
3 MAIN EVENTS

U.S. TITLE MATCH

RIC FLAIR vs. RICKY STEAMBOAT

ANDRE' THE GIANT vs. JOHN STUDD

JIMMY SNUKA vs. GREG VALENTINE

Paul Orndoroff vs. Gene Anderson

TAG TEAM MATCH

Johnny Weaver and Skip Young vs. Mr. X #1 and Mr. X #2

Chris Tolas vs. Abe Jacobs

Charlie Fulton vs. Steve Regal

RINGSIDE $7.00 - RESERVED $6.00 - ADULT GENERAL ADMISSION $5.00
CHILDREN 11 YRS. and UNDER - GENERAL ADMISSION $2.50

O-11-19

TICKETS AVAILABLE AT COLISEUM BOX OFFICE, NATIONAL HAT SHOP, THE ALAMO - 4447 S. BLVD.

Flair Wins By Disqualification

Ricky Steamboat was disqualified for refusing to break an illegal hold, allowing Ric Flair to retain his U.S. title in a professional wrestling match Sunday at the Coliseum.

In other matches:

Jimmy Snuka defeated Greg Valentine; Andre the Giant and John Studd were disqualified for fighting outside the ring; Paul Orndoff defeated Gene Anderson; Abe Jacobs won a 20-minute decision over Chris Tolas; Steve Regal defeated Charlie Fulton; and the tag team of Johnny Weaver and Skip Young defeated Mr. X Nos. 1 and 2.

MID-ATLANTIC CHAMPIONSHIP WRESTLING

CHARLOTTE COLISEUM
SUNDAY, DEC. 3   7:30 P.M.

24 MAN ELIMINATION MATCH

2 Rings Set Up (full Size)
All men in rings at same time
Eliminate down to 2
Last 2 wrestle for a

$10,000 PURSE

FEATURING:

Baron Von Raschke	Blackjack Mulligan
Greg Valentine	Ricky Steamboat
Big John Studd	Paul Orndorff
Ric Flair	Paul Jones
Swede Hanson	Tony Atlas
Chris Tolos	Jay Youngblood
Steve Musulin	Johnny Weaver
Mr. X #1	Skip Young
Charlie Fulton	Gary Young
Sgt. Jacques Goulet	Richard Blood
Rudy Kay	Abe Jacobs
Ken Patera	Steve Regal

RINGSIDE $7.00 - RESERVED $6.00 - ADULT GENERAL ADMISSION $5.00
CHILDREN 11 YRS. and UNDER: GENERAL ADMISSION $2.50

**TICKETS AVAILABLE AT COLISEUM BOX OFFICE,
NATIONAL HAT SHOP, THE ALAMO - 4447 S. BLVD.**

MID-ATLANTIC CHAMPIONSHIP WRESTLING

CHARLOTTE COLISEUM
MON. DECEMBER 25, 8:15 P.M.
3 MAIN EVENTS

U.S. TITLE MATCH-CAGE
BLACKJACK MULLIGAN vs. RIC FLAIR

PAUL JONES vs. RICKY STEAMBOAT

Mid-Atlantic Heavyweight Title Match
KEN PATERA vs. JOHNNY WEAVER

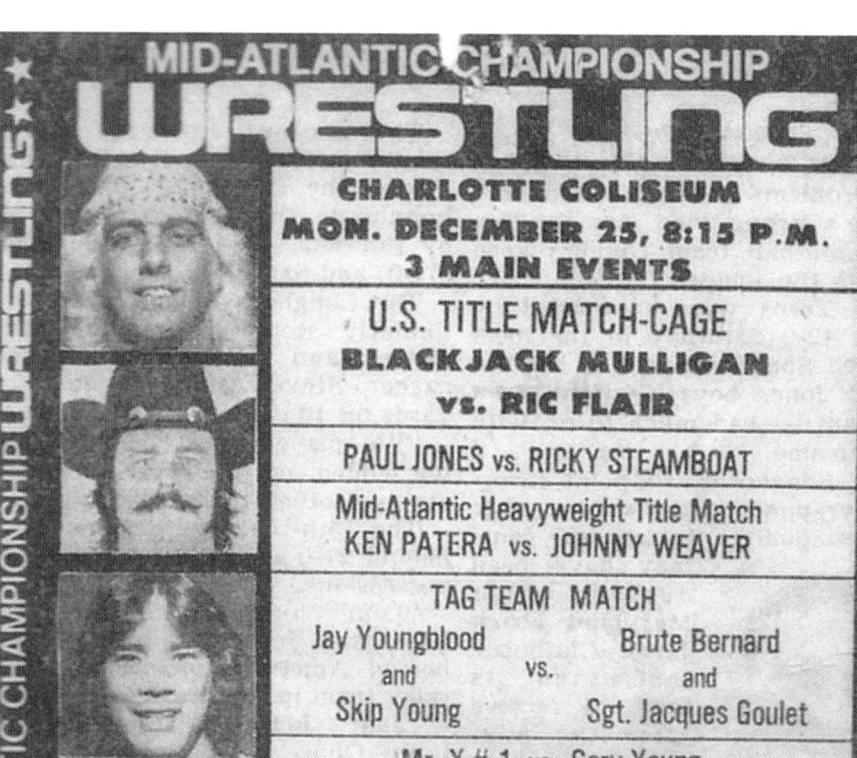

TAG TEAM MATCH
Jay Youngblood and Skip Young vs. Brute Bernard and Sgt. Jacques Goulet

Mr. X #1 vs. Gary Young

Don Kernodle vs. David Patterson

Frank Monte vs. Joe Furr

Klondike Bill vs. Charlie Fulton

RINGSIDE $7.00-RESERVED $6.00 ADULT GENERAL ADM. $5.00 CHILDREN 11 YRS. AND UNDER GENERAL ADM. $2.50 CHRISTMAS DAY - BOX OFFICE AT THE COLISEUM WILL BE OPEN AT 1:00 P.M.

TICKETS AVAILABLE AT COLISEUM BOX OFFICE, NATIONAL HAT SHOP, THE ALAMO - 4447 S. BLVD.

11,303 See Wrestling

A sellout crowd of 11,303 saw the Christmas Night professional wrestling show at the Coliseum, and several hundred others were turned away. Promoter Jim Crockett Jr. said it was the first Charlotte wrestling sellout since 1963.

In the main-event matches, U.S. champ Ric Flair defeated Blackjack Mulligan; televison champ Paul Jones pinned Ricky Steamboat, and Mid-Atlantic titleholder Ken Patera retained his belt as he was disqualified against Johnny Weaver.

Other matches:

Jay Youngblood-Skip Young d. Brute Bernard-Jacques Goulet; Mr. X No. 1 d. Gary Young; Frank Monte d. Joe Furr; Don Kernodle d. Dave Patterson; Klondike Bill d. Charlie Fulton.

MID ATLANTIC CHAMPIONSHIP WRESTLING — NWA — MID ATLANTIC CHAMPIONSHIP WRESTLING

DORTON ARENA • TONIGHT, 8:15 P.M. Dec. 27

RINGSIDE $5.00, GEN. ADM. $4.00, CHILDREN (UNDER 12) $2.00 ADM.
Tickets on sale at Pop-a-Top Beverage in Mission Valley Shopping Center

CAGE MATCH FOR UNITED STATES TITLE
BLACKJACK MULLIGAN vs. RIC FLAIR

PAUL JONES • VERSUS • RICKY STEAMBOAT
JONES' TV TITLE AT STAKE FOR FIRST 15 MINUTES

JAY YOUNGBLOOD & GENE ANDERSON • VERSUS • SKIP YOUNG & JACQUES GOULET

MR. XI vs. STEVE REGAL

JOE PALARDY vs. GARY YOUNG

JIMMY SNUKA • VERSUS • KEN PATERA

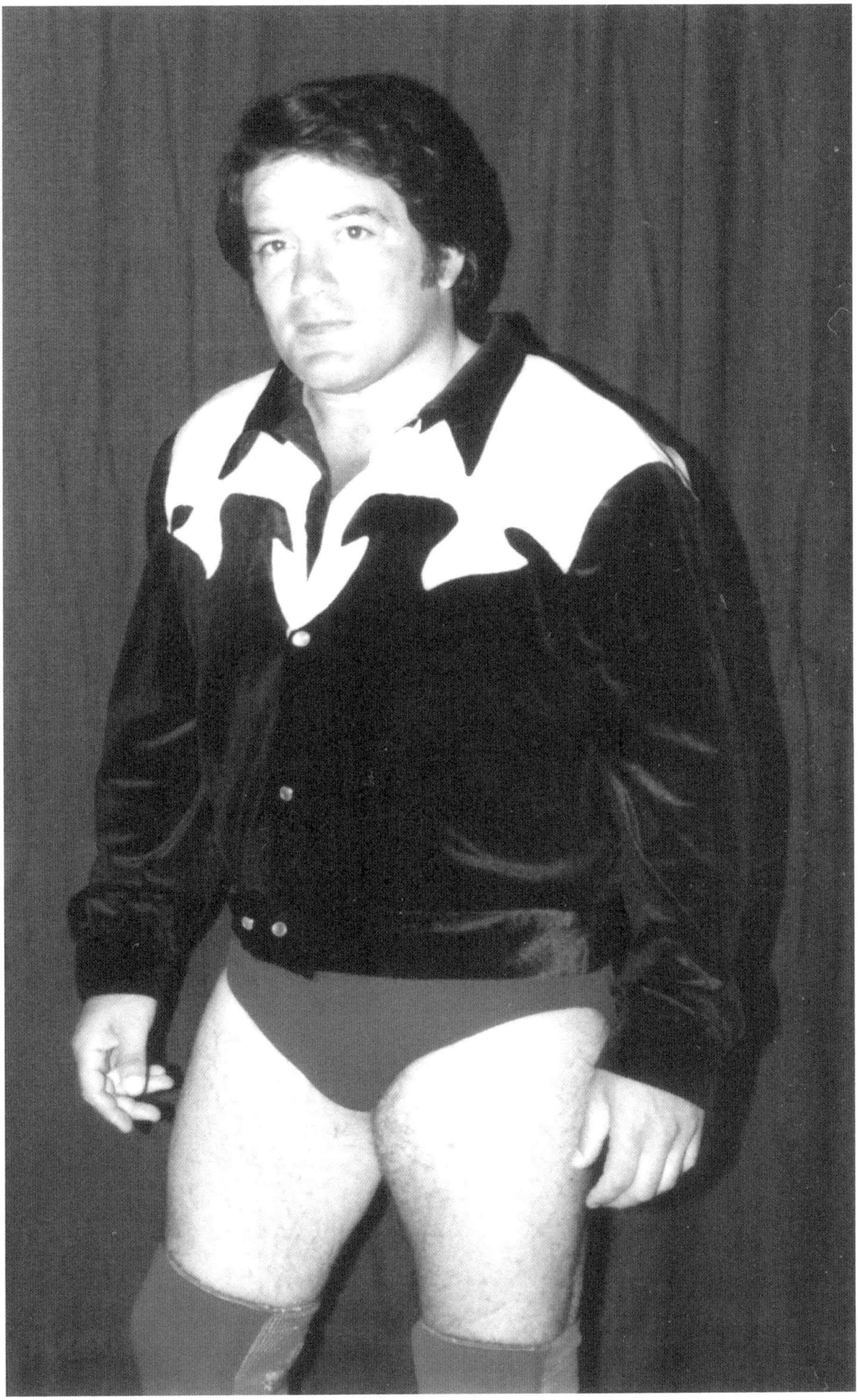

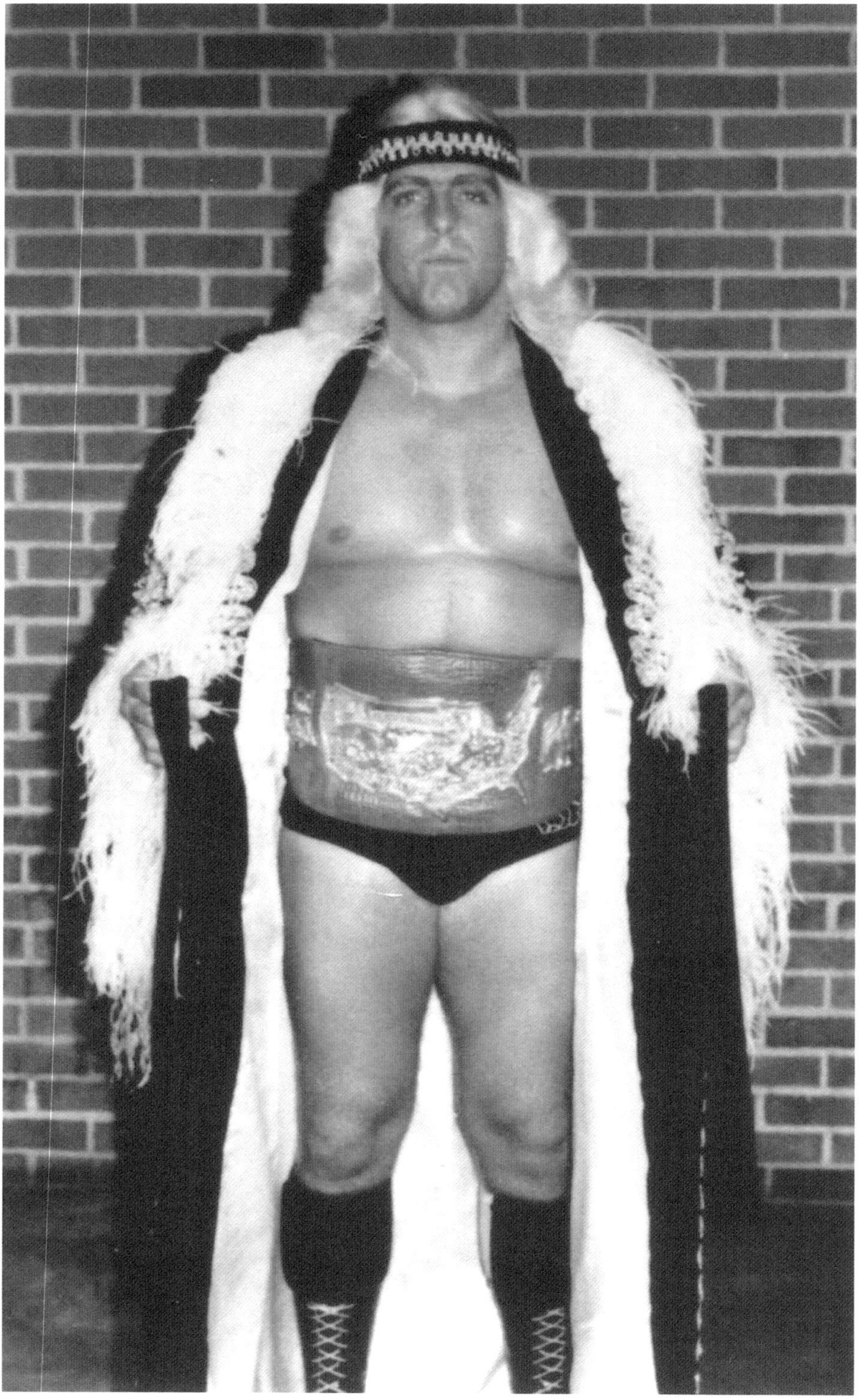

1979

Ads & Results from

Charlotte Coliseum
Dorton Arena
Richmond Coliseum
Asheville Civic Center

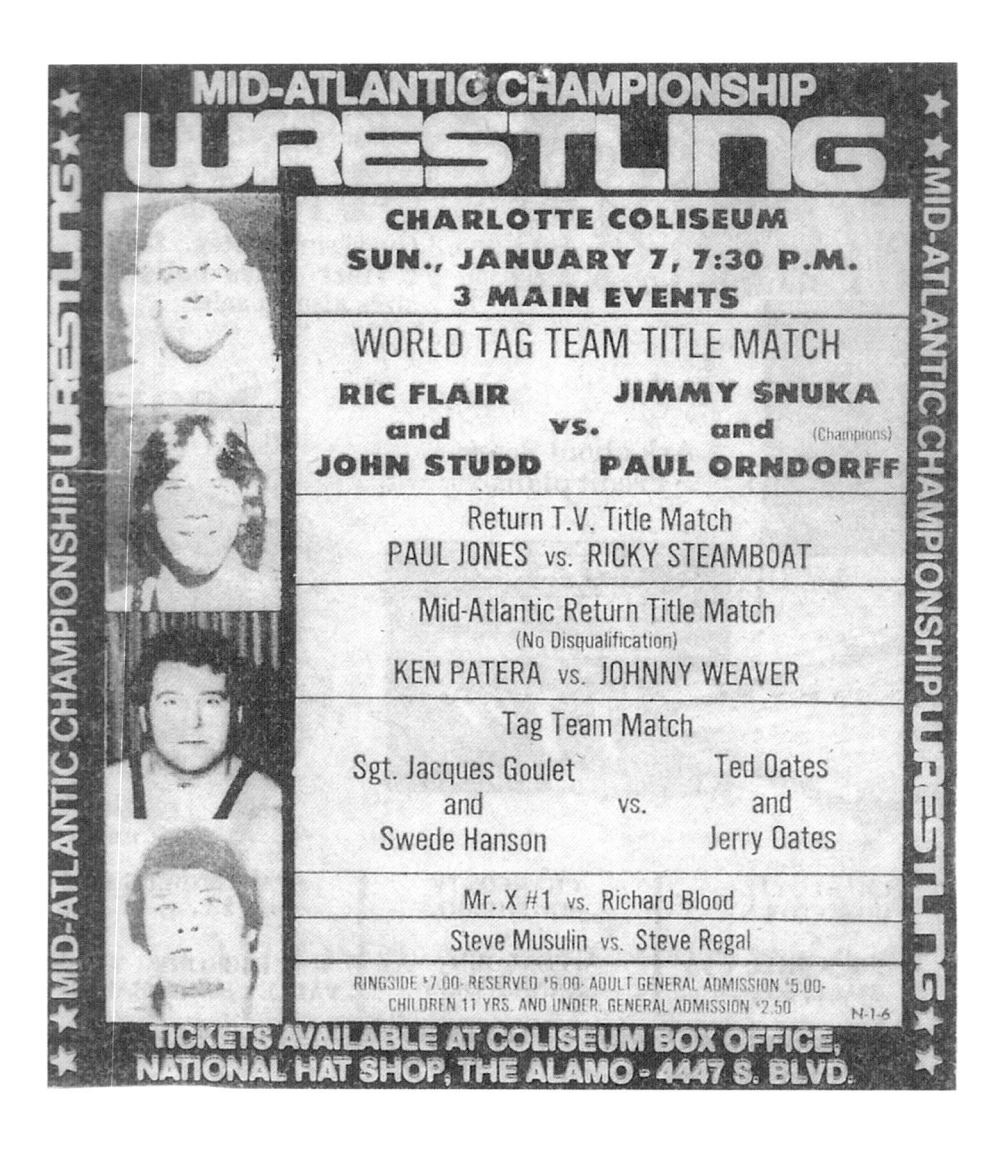

MID-ATLANTIC CHAMPIONSHIP WRESTLING

CHARLOTTE COLISEUM
SUN., JANUARY 7, 7:30 P.M.
3 MAIN EVENTS

WORLD TAG TEAM TITLE MATCH

RIC FLAIR and JOHN STUDD vs. **JIMMY SNUKA and PAUL ORNDORFF** (Champions)

Return T.V. Title Match
PAUL JONES vs. RICKY STEAMBOAT

Mid-Atlantic Return Title Match
(No Disqualification)
KEN PATERA vs. JOHNNY WEAVER

Tag Team Match
Sgt. Jacques Goulet and Swede Hanson vs. Ted Oates and Jerry Oates

Mr. X #1 vs. Richard Blood

Steve Musulin vs. Steve Regal

RINGSIDE $7.00 - RESERVED $6.00 - ADULT GENERAL ADMISSION $5.00 - CHILDREN 11 YRS. AND UNDER, GENERAL ADMISSION $2.50

TICKETS AVAILABLE AT COLISEUM BOX OFFICE, NATIONAL HAT SHOP, THE ALAMO - 4447 S. BLVD.

Titleholders Keep Wrestling Belts

It's status quo among the titleholders following Sunday night's Coliseum professional wrestling card.

Jimmy Snuka and Paul Orndorff topped Ric Flair and John Studd to keep their world tag-team title. Ricky Steamboat kept his U.S. heavyweight crown by defeating Paul Jones; Jones, however, retained his TV belt because the match lasted more than 15 minutes. Ken Patera defeated Johnny Weaver to retain his Mid-Atlantic title.

In other matches, Jacque Goulet-Swede Hansen d. Ted Oates-Jerry Oates; Mr. X No. 1 d. Richard Blood; Steve Regal d. Steve Musilin.

FLAIR MEETS STEAMBOAT

On Sunday January 28, 1979 at 3:00 P.M. at the Charlotte Coliseum in one of three Big Main Events, Ric Flair meets Ricky Steamboat in their long-awaited U.S. Title Match. Also in the Mid-Atlantic Title Match, Ken Patera takes on the "Black Atlas", Tony Atlas. In the third main event, the N.W.A. TV Title Match, Paul Jones meets Paul Orndorff. Four other big matches round out the card.

Paid Advertisement

No Title Change In Pro Wrestling

Champions retained their belts Sunday in a National Wrestling Alliance program at the Charlotte Coliseum.

U.S. champion Ricky Steamboat defeated Ric Flair by disqualification. Ken Patera, the Mid-Atlantic champ, lost by disqualification to Tony Atlas — but he retained the belt, which cannot be lost in a disqualification.

TV champion Paul Jones defeated Paul Orndorff in the other title match.

Other results were Dino Bravo over Greg Valentine, Gene Anderson and Kim Duk over Steve Regal and Gary Young, Jay Youngblood and Skip Young over Moose Mcrowski and Lynn Denton, and The Cobra over David Patterson.

STEAMBOAT vs FLAIR REMATCH

On Sunday, February 11, 1979 at 3:00 P.M. in the Charlotte Coliseum in a special 2 out of 3 falls U.S. Title Match, Ric Flair meets Ricky Steamboat. In the Mid-Atlantic Title Match (Lumberjack Match) Ken Patera goes against Tony Atlas. In other matches John Studd meets Dino Bravo, and Paul Orndorff takes on Greg Valentine. In Tag Team Competition, Johnny Weaver and Rufus R. Jones will meet Swede Hanson and Sgt. Jacques Goulet. Three other bouts round out the card.

Paid Advertisement

Steamboat Disqualified

Ricky Steamboat was disqualified after being counted out outside the ring Sunday afternoon, but he retained his U.S. heavyweight professional wrestling championship in a match against Ric Flair at the Coliseum.

The two had each won a fall in the best-of-three match. Steamboat retains the title because a championship cannot change hands on a disqualification.

In a preliminary feature, Mid-Atlantic champ Ken Patera retained his title with a victory over Tony Atlas in a lumberjack match.

Other results were Dino Bravo over John Studd, Paul Orndorff over Greg Valentine, Jay Youngblood over Lynn Denton, Rufus R. Jones and Johnny Weaver over Swede Hanson and Sgt. Jacques Goulet, and Don Kernodle and Terry Sawyer over Charlie Fulton and David Patterson.

MID-ATLANTIC CHAMPIONSHIP WRESTLING

CHARLOTTE COLISEUM
SATURDAY, MAR. 3 8:15 P.M.

U.S. TITLE MATCH

RICKY STEAMBOAT
(CHAMPION)
VS.
RIC FLAIR

- NO DISQUALIFICATION -
NO COUNT OUT • NO TIME LIMIT

MUST BE A WINNER!

NWA T.V. CHAMPIONSHIP MATCH

PAUL JONES
(CHAMPION)
VS.
DINO BRAVO

ERNIE LADD VS. PAUL ORNDORFF
JIMMY SNUKA VS. BARON VON RASCHKE

BRUTE BERNARD, MOOSE MOROWSKI, & GENE ANDERSON
VS.
JOHNNY WEAVER, SKIP YOUNG, & JAY YOUNGBLOOD — 6 MAN TAG

FRANK MONTE VS. PEDRO MORALES
JOE PALARDY VS. STEVE REGAL

RINGSIDE $7.00 - RESERVED $6.00 - ADULT GENERAL ADMISSION $5.00 - CHILDREN 11 YRS. AND UNDER, GENERAL ADMISSION $2.50

TICKETS AVAILABLE AT COLISEUM BOX OFFICE, NATIONAL HAT SHOP, THE ALAMO - 4447 S. BLVD.

Steamboat Retains U.S. Title

Observer Staff Reports

Ricky Steamboat retained the National Wrestling Alliance U.S. title Saturday night, by defeating Ric Flair at the Charlotte Coliseum. In the other main event, Paul Jones was disqualified in his bout against Dino Bravo.

In other matches, Ernie Ladd decisioned Paul Orndorff; Jimmy Snuka whipped Baron von Raschke; Pedro Morales topped Frank Monte and Steve Regal defeated Joe Palardy.

In the six-man tag match, Johnny Weaver, Skip Young and Jay Youngblood defeated Brute Bernard, Moose Morowski and Gene Anderson.

DORTON ARENA ★ TUE. MAR. 27th

RINGSIDE $5.00. GEN. ADM. $4.00. CHILDREN (Under 12) $2.00 ADM.
Tickets on sale at Pop-a-Top Beverage in Mission Valley Shopping Center

FOR WORLD'S TITLE

JIMMY SNUKA
AND
PAUL ORNDORFF

• VERSUS •

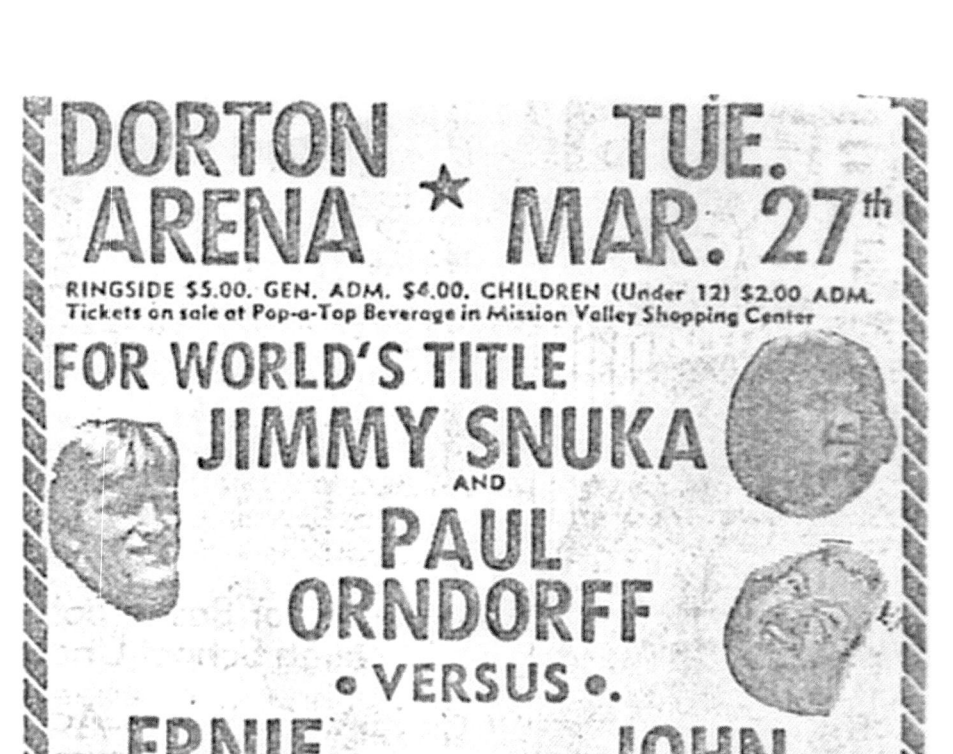

ERNIE LADD & JOHN STUDD

GENE ANDERSON vs. JAY YOUNGBLOOD

PLUS OTHER EXCITING MATCHES

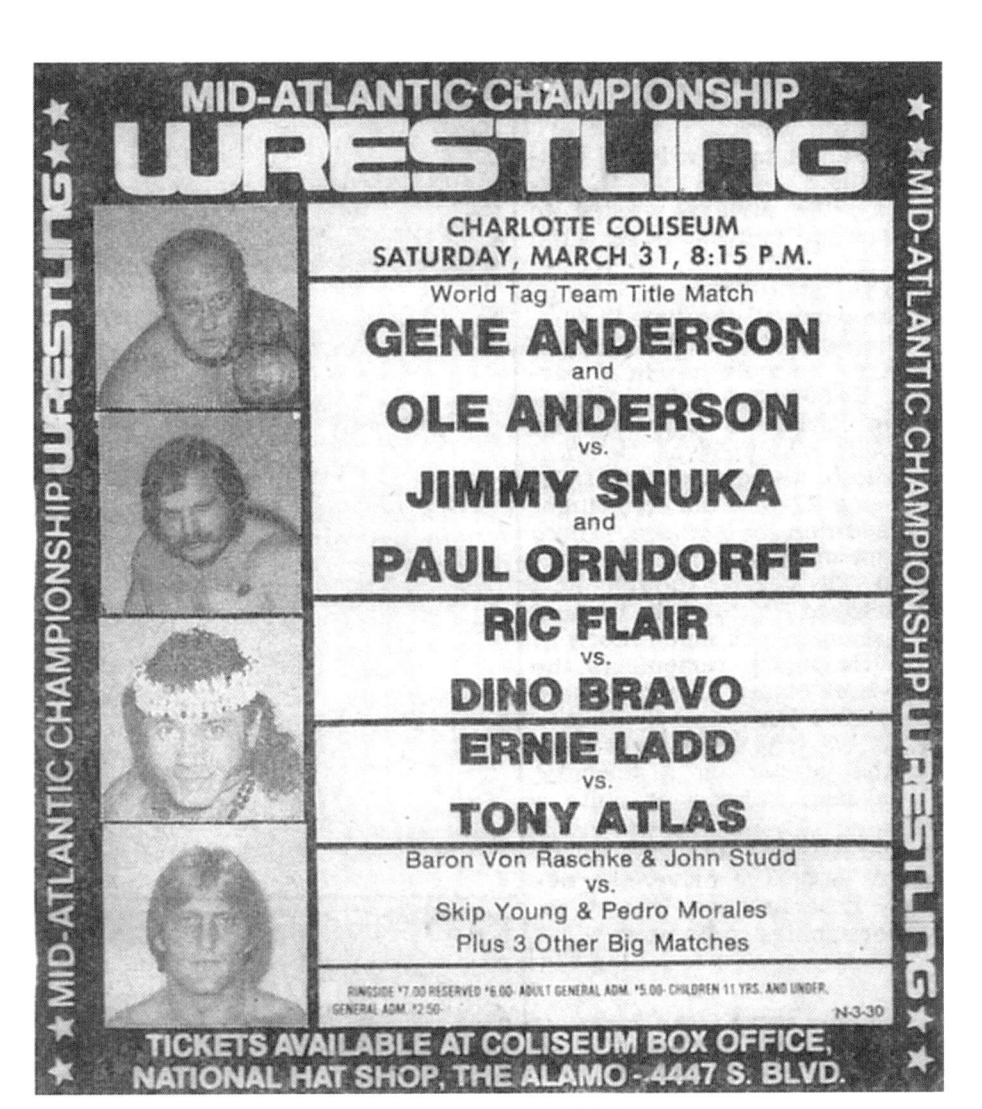

MID-ATLANTIC CHAMPIONSHIP WRESTLING

CHARLOTTE COLISEUM
SATURDAY, MARCH 31, 8:15 P.M.

World Tag Team Title Match

GENE ANDERSON
and
OLE ANDERSON
vs.
JIMMY SNUKA
and
PAUL ORNDORFF

RIC FLAIR
vs.
DINO BRAVO

ERNIE LADD
vs.
TONY ATLAS

Baron Von Raschke & John Studd
vs.
Skip Young & Pedro Morales

Plus 3 Other Big Matches

RINGSIDE $7.00 RESERVED $6.00 ADULT GENERAL ADM. $5.00 CHILDREN 11 YRS. AND UNDER, GENERAL ADM. $2.50

TICKETS AVAILABLE AT COLISEUM BOX OFFICE, NATIONAL HAT SHOP, THE ALAMO - 4447 S. BLVD.

Wrestling Duo Retains Title

Jimmy Snuka and Paul Orndorff retained their world heavyweight title by defeating Ole and Gene Anderson in professional wrestling at the Coliseum Saturday night.

In other matches, Dino Bravo defeated Ric Flair; Tony Atlas was disqualified in his bout against Ernie Ladd, and Baron von Raschke and John Studd decisioned Skip Young and Pedro Morales.

Swede Hansen defeated Joe Palardy; Kim Duk whipped Herb Gallant and Lynn Denton beat Terry Sawyer.

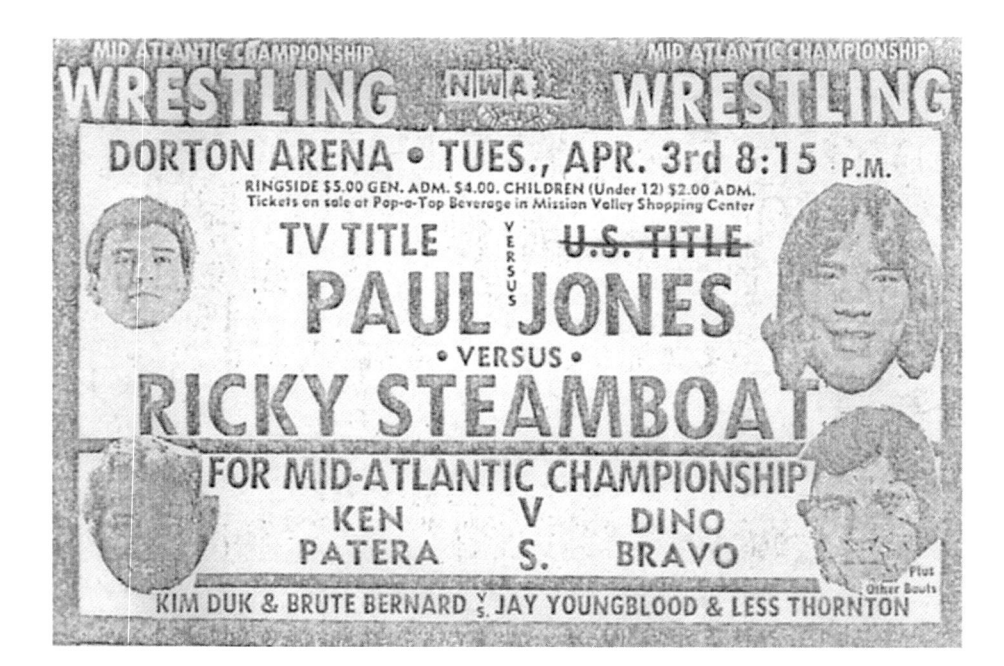

MID ATLANTIC CHAMPIONSHIP WRESTLING — NWA

DORTON ARENA • TUES., APR. 3rd 8:15 P.M.

RINGSIDE $5.00, GEN. ADM. $4.00, CHILDREN (Under 12) $2.00 ADM.
Tickets on sale at Pop-a-Top Beverage in Mission Valley Shopping Center

TV TITLE versus **U.S. TITLE**
PAUL JONES
• VERSUS •
RICKY STEAMBOAT
FOR MID-ATLANTIC CHAMPIONSHIP

KEN PATERA V.S. **DINO BRAVO**

KIM DUK & BRUTE BERNARD vs. JAY YOUNGBLOOD & LESS THORNTON

Plus Other Bouts

MID ATLANTIC CHAMPIONSHIP WRESTLING — NWA

DORTON ARENA • TUES., APR. 10th 8:15 P.M.

RINGSIDE $5.00, GEN. ADM. $4.00, CHILDREN (Under 12) $2.00 ADM.
Tickets on sale at Pop-a-Top Beverage in Mission Valley Shopping Center

For U.S. Title
RIC FLAIR
• VERSUS •
DINO BRAVO

ERNIE LADD
• VERSUS •
BLACKJACK MULLIGAN

MOOSE MOROWSKI & KIM DUK
• VERSUS •
PEDRO MORALES & JOHNNY WEAVER

MR. X No. 1 vs. GARY YOUNG

Plus Other Matches

MID-ATLANTIC CHAMPIONSHIP WRESTLING

CHARLOTTE COLISEUM
SUNDAY, APRIL 15, 7:30 P.M.

U.S. TITLE MATCH
RIC FLAIR
vs.
DINO BRAVO

T.V. TITLE MATCH
RICKY STEAMBOAT
vs.
PAUL JONES

MID-ATLANTIC TITLE MATCH
JIMMY SNUKA
vs.
KEN PATERA

TAG TEAM MATCH
BARON VON RASCHKE & JOHN STUDD
vs.
TONY ATLAS & JOHNNY WEAVER

PLUS 3 OTHER BIG MATCHES

RINGSIDE $7.00 RESERVED $6.00 ADULT GENERAL ADMISSION $5.00 CHILDREN 11 YRS. AND UNDER, GENERAL ADMISSION $2.50

TICKETS AVAILABLE AT COLISEUM BOX OFFICE, NATIONAL HAT SHOP, THE ALAMO - 4447 S. BLVD.

Wrestlers Retain Titles

U.S. wrestling champion Rick Flair, suffering from a torn shoulder muscle, did not wrestle Sunday night, and his substitute, Baron Von Raschke, was defeated by Dino Bravo in the main event at the Coliseum.

In two singles title matches, Ken Patera retained his Mid-Atlantic belt when he and challenger Jimmy Snuka both were counted out of the ring. And, Paul Jones kept his TV title when he ran off with his belt 14 minutes into his match with challenger Ricky Steamboat.

In other matches, Tony Atlas and Johnny Weaver teamed to defeat John Studd and Lynn Denton; Moose Morowski and Jacques Goulet defeated Les Thornton and Don Kernodle; Mr. X No. 1 pinned Herb Gallant and Terry Sawywer was awarded a 15-minute decision over Tony Russo.

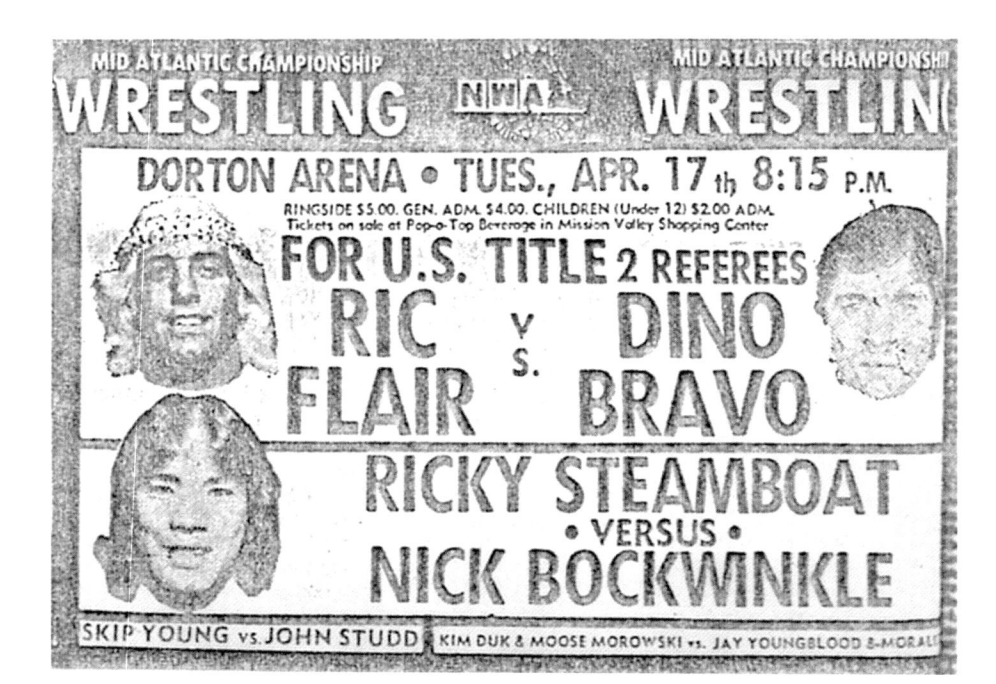

MID ATLANTIC CHAMPIONSHIP WRESTLING — NWA

DORTON ARENA • TUES., APR. 17th 8:15 P.M.

RINGSIDE $5.00, GEN. ADM. $4.00, CHILDREN (Under 12) $2.00 ADM.
Tickets on sale at Pop-o-Top Beverage in Mission Valley Shopping Center

FOR U.S. TITLE — 2 REFEREES

RIC FLAIR vs. DINO BRAVO

RICKY STEAMBOAT versus NICK BOCKWINKLE

SKIP YOUNG vs. JOHN STUDD • KIM DUK & MOOSE MOROWSKI vs. JAY YOUNGBLOOD & MORALES

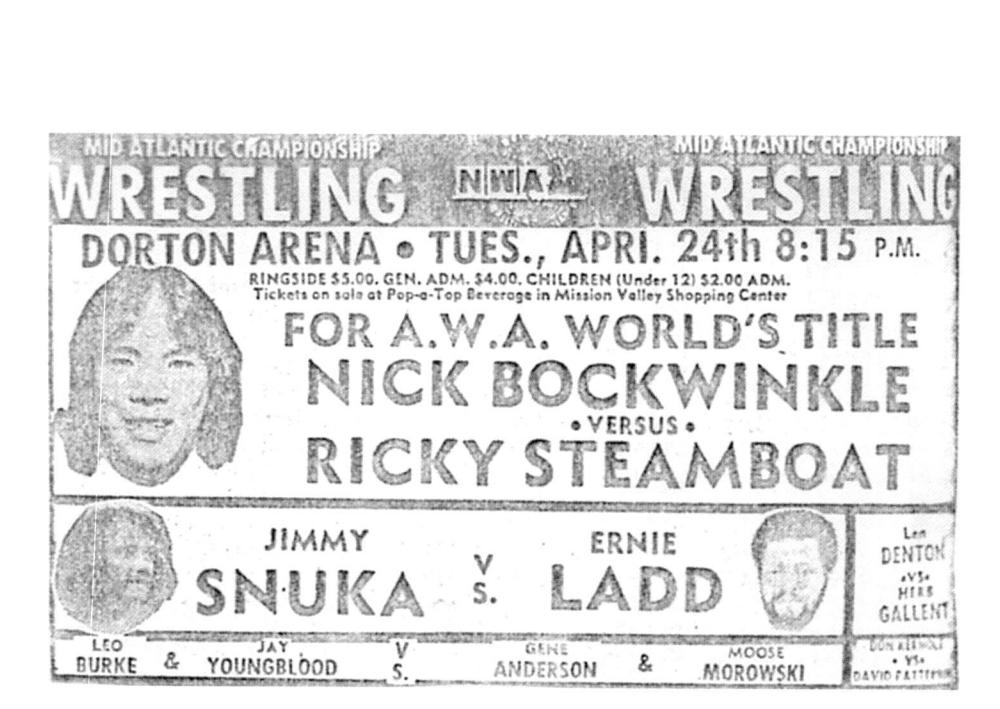

MID ATLANTIC CHAMPIONSHIP WRESTLING — NWA

DORTON ARENA • TUES., APR. 24th 8:15 P.M.

RINGSIDE $5.00, GEN. ADM. $4.00, CHILDREN (Under 12) $2.00 ADM.
Tickets on sale at Pop-o-Top Beverage in Mission Valley Shopping Center

FOR A.W.A. WORLD'S TITLE

NICK BOCKWINKLE versus RICKY STEAMBOAT

JIMMY SNUKA vs. ERNIE LADD

LEN DENTON vs. HERB GALLENT

LEO BURKE & JAY YOUNGBLOOD vs. GENE ANDERSON & MOOSE MOROWSKI

DON KERNODLE vs. DAVID PATTERSON

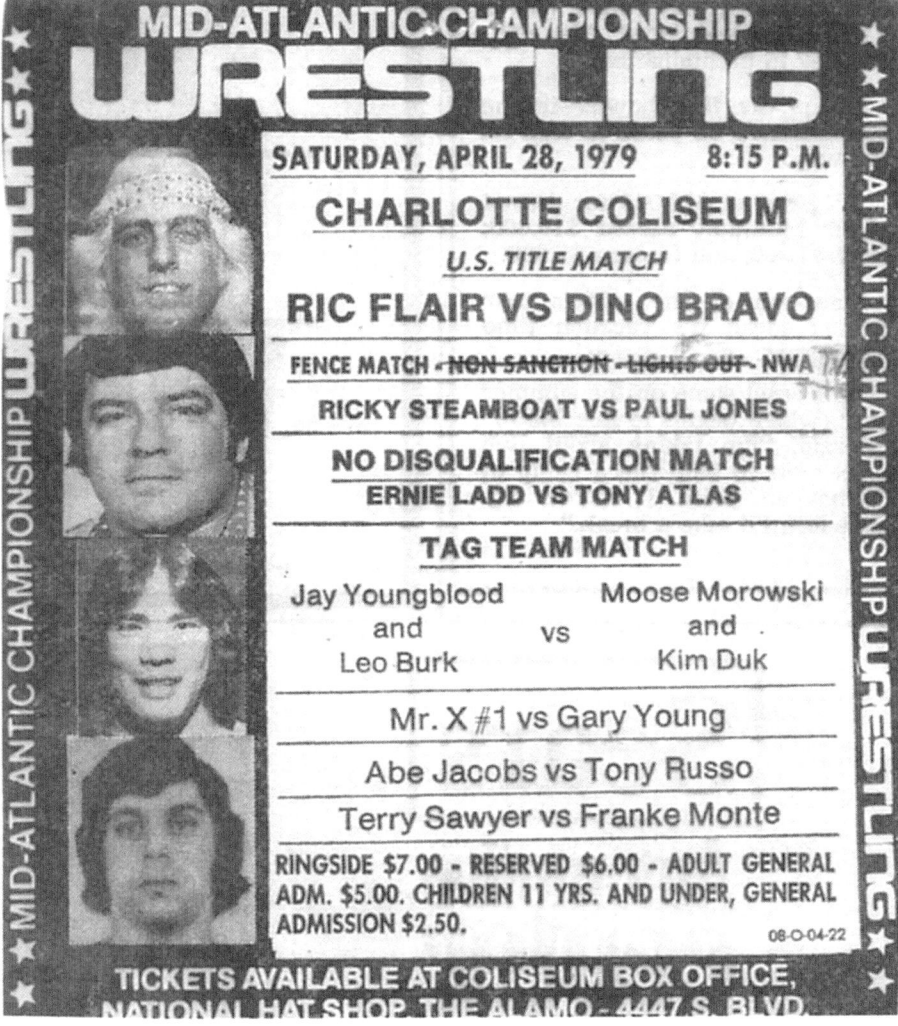

MID-ATLANTIC CHAMPIONSHIP WRESTLING

SATURDAY, APRIL 28, 1979   **8:15 P.M.**

CHARLOTTE COLISEUM

U.S. TITLE MATCH
RIC FLAIR VS DINO BRAVO

FENCE MATCH - ~~NON SANCTION~~ - ~~LIGHTS OUT~~ - NWA

RICKY STEAMBOAT VS PAUL JONES

NO DISQUALIFICATION MATCH
ERNIE LADD VS TONY ATLAS

TAG TEAM MATCH

Jay Youngblood and Leo Burk   vs   Moose Morowski and Kim Duk

Mr. X #1 vs Gary Young

Abe Jacobs vs Tony Russo

Terry Sawyer vs Franke Monte

RINGSIDE $7.00 - RESERVED $6.00 - ADULT GENERAL ADM. $5.00. CHILDREN 11 YRS. AND UNDER, GENERAL ADMISSION $2.50.

08-O-04-22

TICKETS AVAILABLE AT COLISEUM BOX OFFICE, NATIONAL HAT SHOP, THE ALAMO - 4447 S. BLVD.

Flair Beats Bravo, Retains U.S. Title

Ric Flair defeated Dino Bravo and retained his United States heavyweight championship in a professional wrestling program at the Coliseum.

In another feature match, Ricky Steamboat beat Paul Jones, but the match took more than 15 minutes and Jones retained his TV title. Other results:

Ernie Ladd d. Tony Atlas; Jay Youngblood and Leo Burk won by disqualification over Moose Morowski and Kim Duk; Mr. X No. 1 d. Gary Young; Abe Jacobs d. Tony Russo; Frank Monte d. Terry Sawyer.

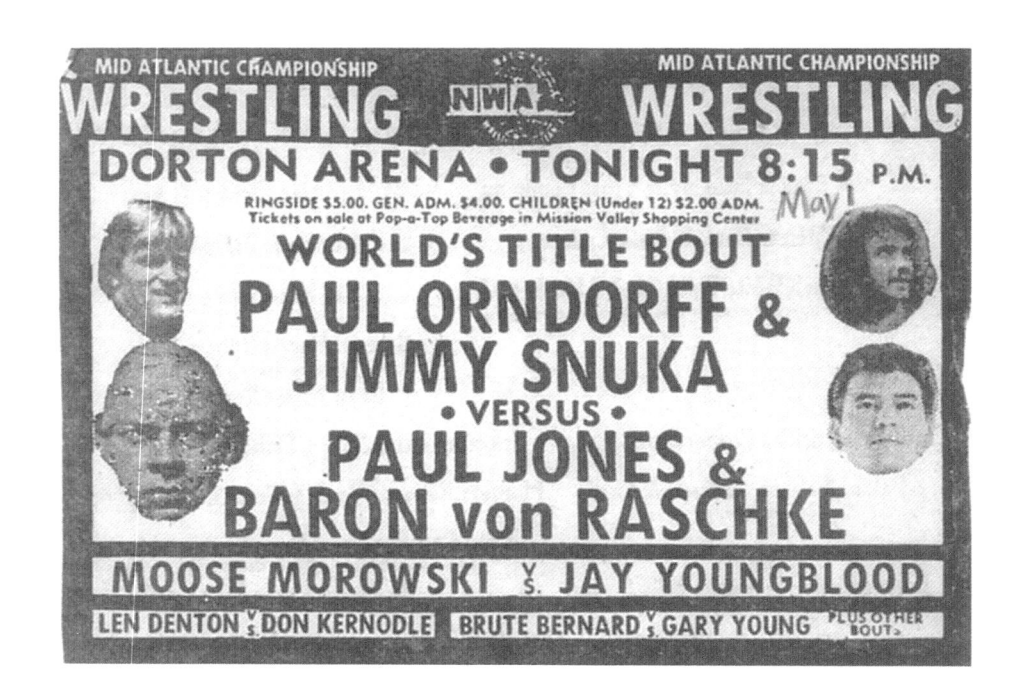

MID ATLANTIC CHAMPIONSHIP WRESTLING — NWA

DORTON ARENA • TONIGHT 8:15 P.M.

RINGSIDE $5.00, GEN. ADM. $4.00, CHILDREN (Under 12) $2.00 ADM.
Tickets on sale at Pop-a-Top Beverage in Mission Valley Shopping Center

May 1

WORLD'S TITLE BOUT
PAUL ORNDORFF & JIMMY SNUKA
• VERSUS •
PAUL JONES & BARON von RASCHKE

MOOSE MOROWSKI vs. JAY YOUNGBLOOD

LEN DENTON vs. DON KERNODLE | BRUTE BERNARD vs. GARY YOUNG | PLUS OTHER BOUTS

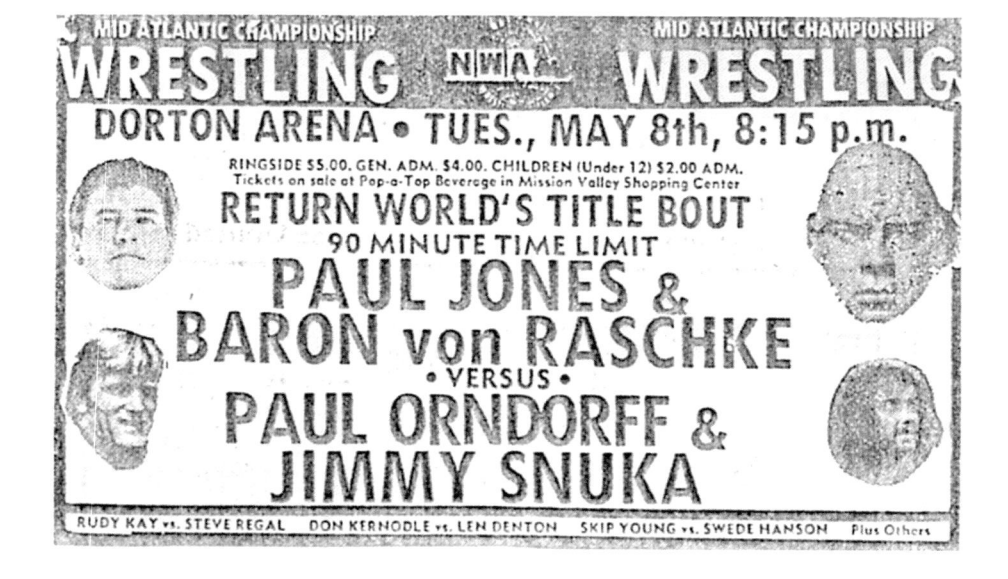

MID ATLANTIC CHAMPIONSHIP WRESTLING — NWA

DORTON ARENA • TUES., MAY 8th, 8:15 p.m.

RINGSIDE $5.00, GEN. ADM. $4.00, CHILDREN (Under 12) $2.00 ADM.
Tickets on sale at Pop-a-Top Beverage in Mission Valley Shopping Center

RETURN WORLD'S TITLE BOUT
90 MINUTE TIME LIMIT
PAUL JONES & BARON von RASCHKE
• VERSUS •
PAUL ORNDORFF & JIMMY SNUKA

RUDY KAY vs. STEVE REGAL | DON KERNODLE vs. LEN DENTON | SKIP YOUNG vs. SWEDE HANSON | Plus Others

MID-ATLANTIC CHAMPIONSHIP WRESTLING

CHARLOTTE COLISEUM
SATURDAY, MAY 12, 8:15 P.M.

U.S. TITLE MATCH
RIC FLAIR
vs.
RICKY STEAMBOAT

MID-ATLANTIC TITLE MATCH
KEN PATERA
vs.
RUFUS R. JONES

ERNIE LADD
vs.
DINO BRAVO

TAG TEAM MATCH
**JOHNNY WEAVER &
JAY YOUNG BLOOD**
vs.
**MOOSE MOROWSKI &
SWEDE HANSON**

PLUS 3 OTHER BIG MATCHES

RINGSIDE $7.00—RESERVED $6.00—ADULT GENERAL ADMISSION $5.00
CHILDREN 11 YRS. AND UNDER, GENERAL ADMISSION $2.50

**TICKETS AVAILABLE AT COLISEUM BOX OFFICE,
NATIONAL HAT SHOP, THE ALAMO - 4447 S. BLVD.**

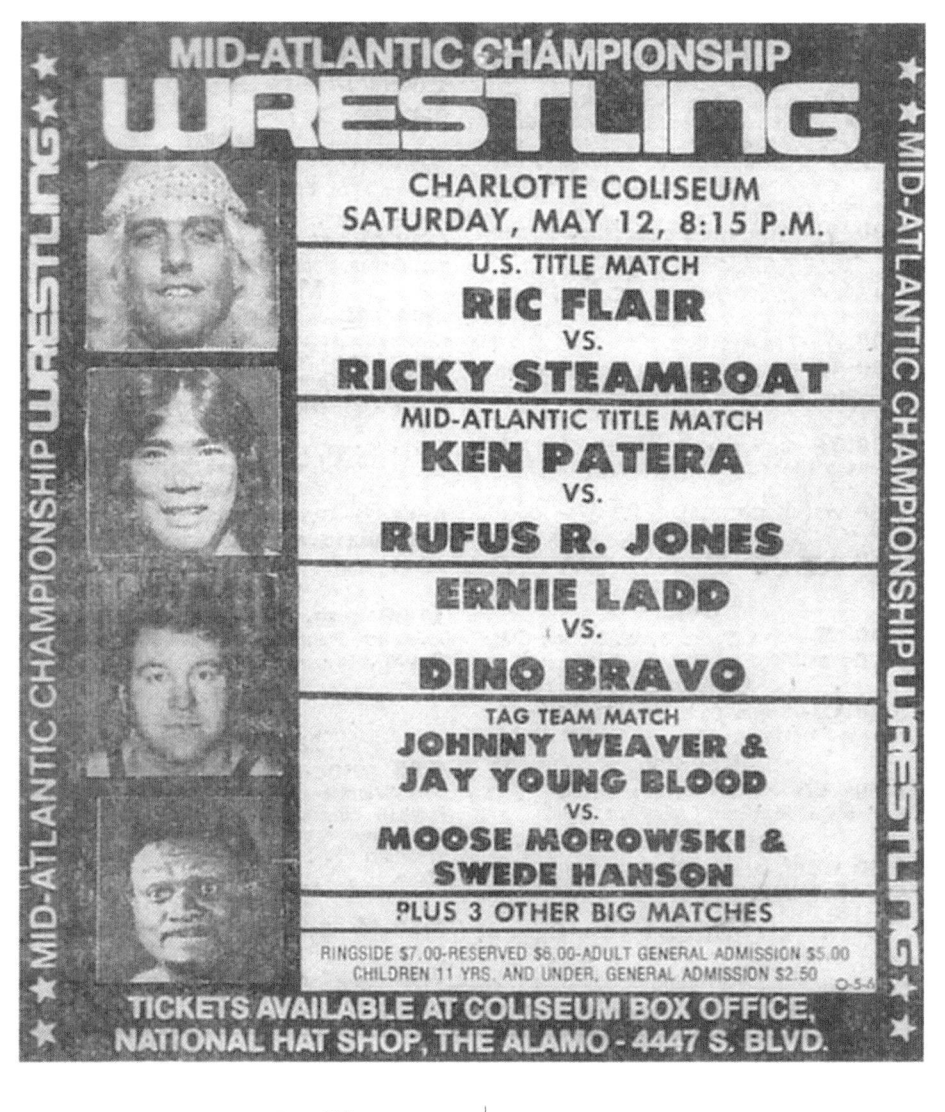

Flair, Patera On Top

Ric Flair defeated Ricky Steamboat and retained his U.S. heavyweight championship in professional wrestling at the Charlotte Coliseum Saturday.

In another title match, Ken Patera kept his Mid-Atlantic title when opponent Rufus R. Jones sustained a severe cut over an eye and the bout was stopped.

In nontitle matches, Dino Bravo beat Ernie Ladd on a disqualification; Johnny Weaver and Jay Youngblood teamed to defeat Moose Morowski and Swede Hansen; Jacque Goulet defeated Skip Young; Len Denton and Leo Burk fought to 20-minute draw, and Abe Jacobs pinned Frank Monte.

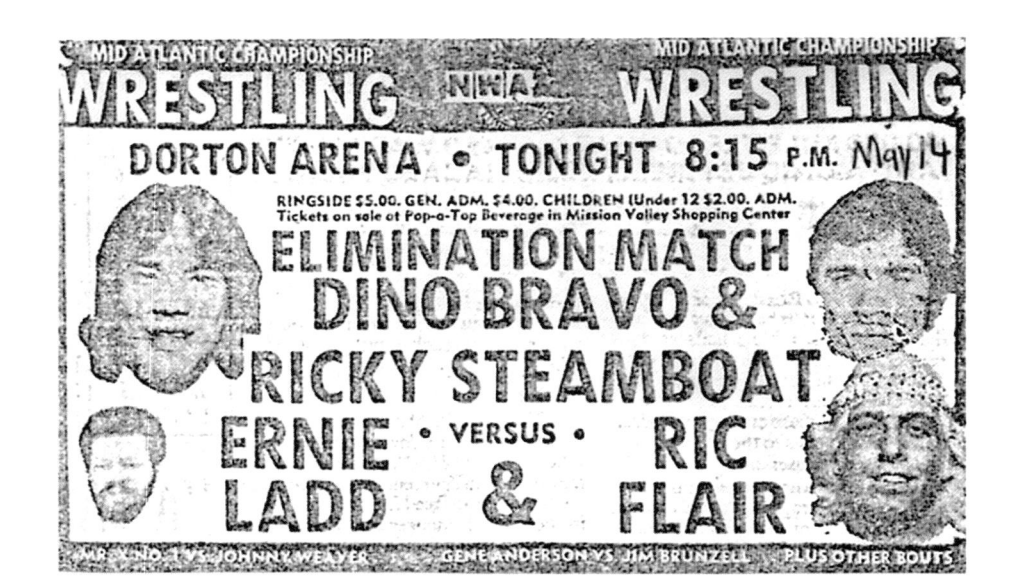

MID ATLANTIC CHAMPIONSHIP WRESTLING

NWA

DORTON ARENA • TONIGHT 8:15 P.M. May 14

RINGSIDE $5.00. GEN. ADM. $4.00. CHILDREN (Under 12) $2.00. ADM.
Tickets on sale at Pop-a-Top Beverage in Mission Valley Shopping Center

ELIMINATION MATCH
DINO BRAVO & RICKY STEAMBOAT
• VERSUS •
ERNIE LADD & RIC FLAIR

MR. X NO. 1 VS. JOHNNY WEAVER • GENE ANDERSON VS JIM BRUNZELL • PLUS OTHER BOUTS

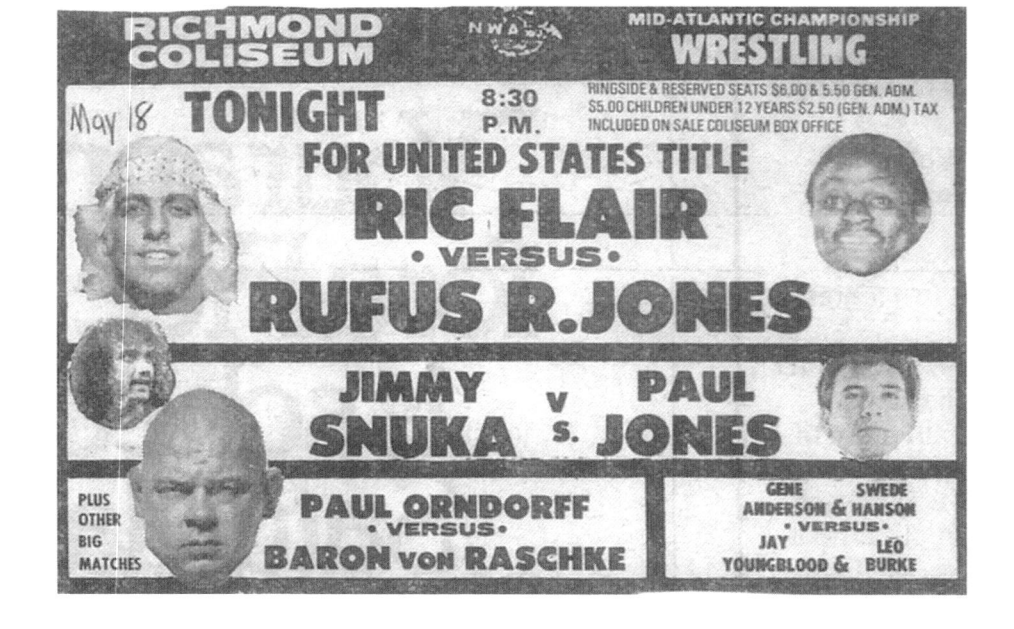

RICHMOND COLISEUM

NWA — MID-ATLANTIC CHAMPIONSHIP WRESTLING

May 18 — TONIGHT 8:30 P.M.

RINGSIDE & RESERVED SEATS $6.00 & 5.50 GEN. ADM.
$5.00 CHILDREN UNDER 12 YEARS $2.50 (GEN. ADM.) TAX
INCLUDED ON SALE COLISEUM BOX OFFICE

FOR UNITED STATES TITLE
RIC FLAIR
• VERSUS •
RUFUS R. JONES

JIMMY SNUKA vs. PAUL JONES

PLUS OTHER BIG MATCHES

PAUL ORNDORFF • VERSUS • **BARON von RASCHKE**

GENE ANDERSON & SWEDE HANSON • VERSUS • JAY YOUNGBLOOD & LEO BURKE

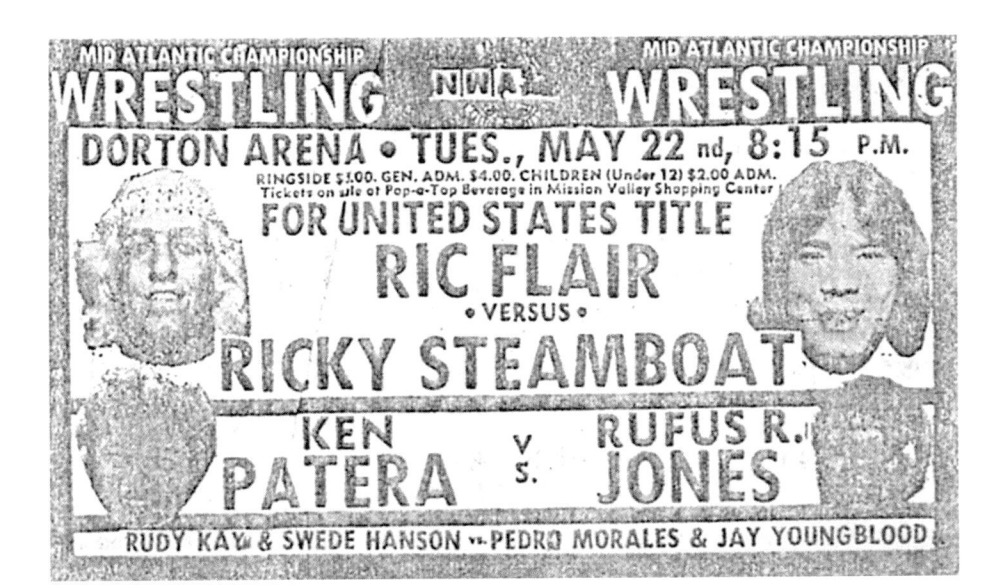

MID ATLANTIC CHAMPIONSHIP WRESTLING — NWA — MID ATLANTIC CHAMPIONSHIP WRESTLING

DORTON ARENA • TUES., MAY 22nd, 8:15 P.M.

RINGSIDE $5.00, GEN. ADM. $4.00, CHILDREN (Under 12) $2.00 ADM.
Tickets on sale at Pop-a-Top Beverage in Mission Valley Shopping Center

FOR UNITED STATES TITLE
RIC FLAIR
• VERSUS •
RICKY STEAMBOAT

KEN PATERA vs. **RUFUS R. JONES**

RUDY KAY & SWEDE HANSON vs. PEDRO MORALES & JAY YOUNGBLOOD

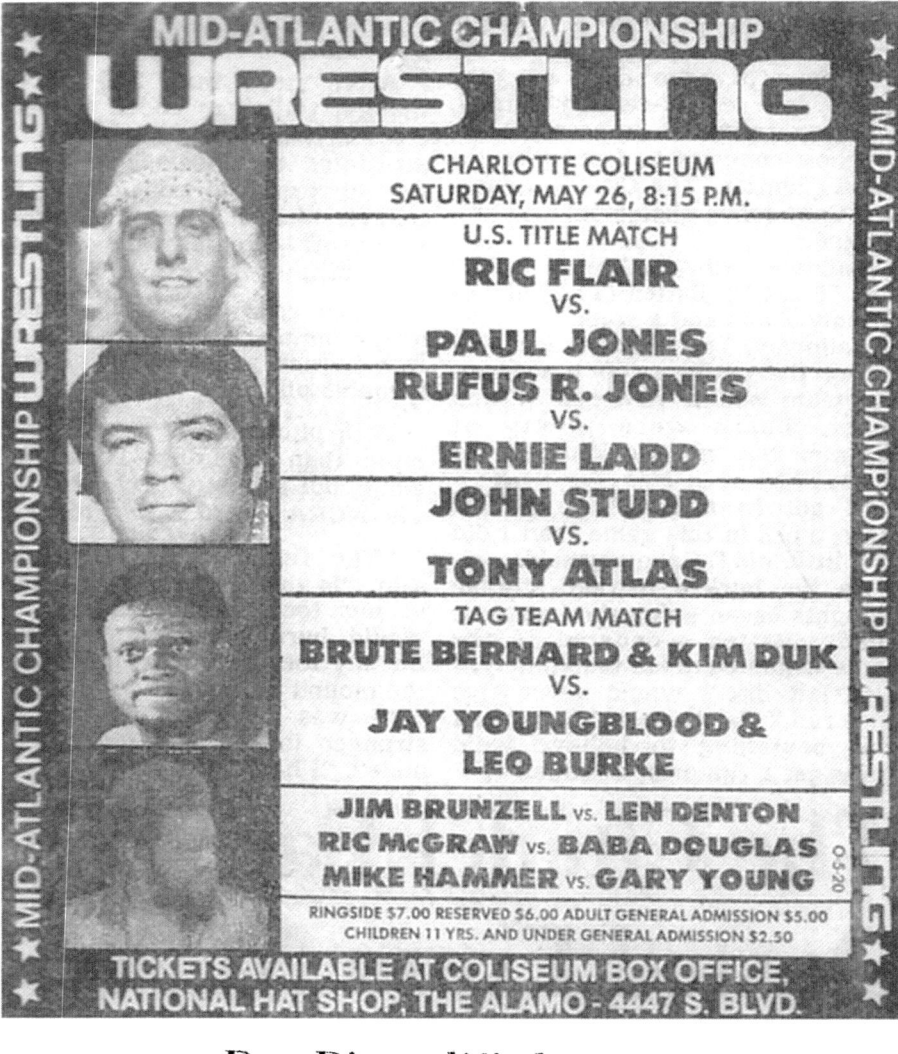

Duo Disqualified

Ric Flair and Paul Jones were disqualified in their bout for the U.S. and TV title belts in wrestling Saturday at the Charlotte Coliseum.

In other matches, Rufus R. Jones defeated Ernie Ladd; Tony Atlas won over John Studd; Jay Youngblood and Leo Burk beat Brute Bernard and Kim Duk; Jim Brunzell beat Lynn Denton; Rick McGraw topped Baba Douglas, and Gary Young won over Mike Hammer.

MID ATLANTIC CHAMPIONSHIP WRESTLING • NWA

DORTON ARENA • TUES., MAY 29th, 8:15 P.M.

RINGSIDE $5.00. GEN. ADM. $4.00. CHILDREN (Under 12) $2.00 ADM.
Tickets on sale at Pop-o-Top Beverage in Mission Valley Shopping Center

FOR MID-ATLANTIC TITLE
KEN PATERA vs. RUFUS R. JONES

ERNIE LADD vs. DINO BRAVO

JIM BRUNZELL • VERSUS • SWEDE HANSON

JAY YOUNGBLOOD AND LEO BURKE v S. GENE ANDERSON AND JACQUES GOULET

BUBBA DOUGLAS • VS • RUDY KAY

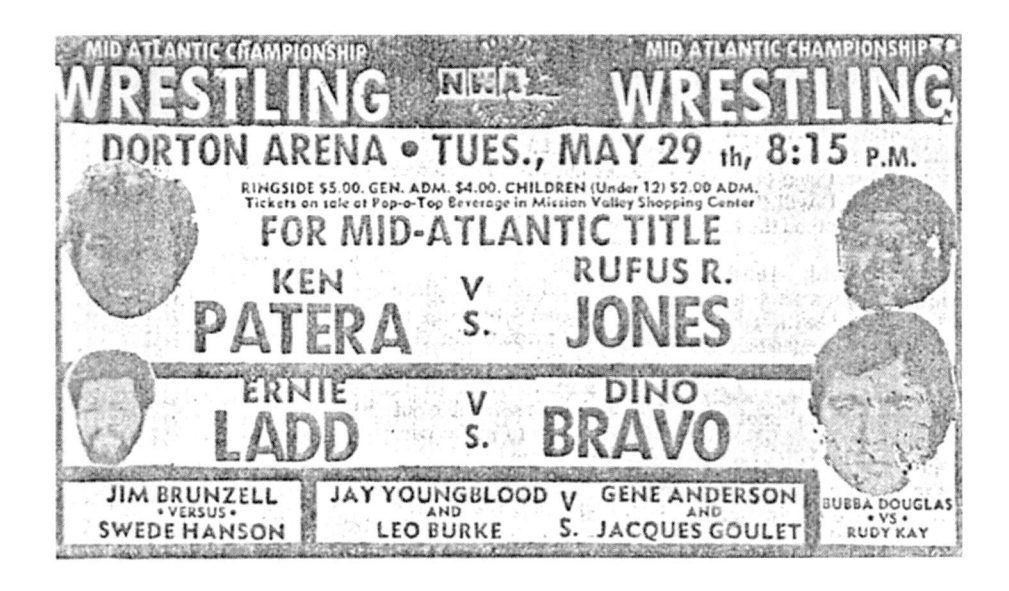

Pro wrestling results

Rufus R. Jones won by disqualification over Ken Patera Tuesday night in professional wrestling at Dorton Arena.

In other matches, Rudy Kay defeated Bubba Douglas, Jim Brunzell was the winner over Swede Hanson, and Dino Bravo stopped Ernie Ladd.

In a tag team match Leo Burke and Jay Youngblood defeated Gene Anderson and Jacques Goulet.

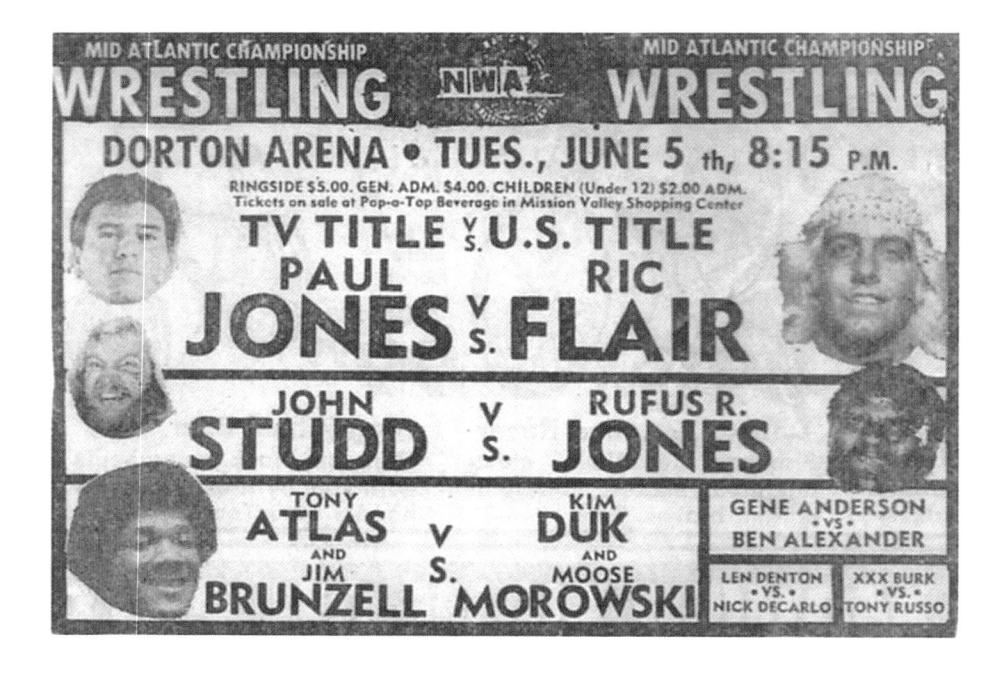

MID ATLANTIC CHAMPIONSHIP WRESTLING NWA

DORTON ARENA • TUES., JUNE 5th, 8:15 P.M.

RINGSIDE $5.00. GEN. ADM. $4.00. CHILDREN (Under 12) $2.00 ADM.
Tickets on sale at Pop-a-Top Beverage in Mission Valley Shopping Center

TV TITLE vs. U.S. TITLE
PAUL JONES vs. RIC FLAIR

JOHN STUDD vs. RUFUS R. JONES

TONY ATLAS AND JIM BRUNZELL v s. KIM DUK AND MOOSE MOROWSKI

GENE ANDERSON vs. BEN ALEXANDER

LEN DENTON vs. NICK DECARLO

XXX BURK vs. TONY RUSSO

Jones, Jones win

Paul Jones and Rufus R. Jones won main events Tuesday night in professional wrestling matches at Dorton Arena.

Paul Jones won by disqualification over Rick Flair, and Rufus R. Jones defeated John Studd.

In other matches, Leo Burke defeated Tony Russo, Len Denton beat Nick DeCarlo and Gene Anderson downed Ben Alexander. In a tag team bout, Tony Atlas and Jim Brunzell won over Kim Duk and Moose Morowski.

MID-ATLANTIC CHAMPIONSHIP WRESTLING

CHARLOTTE COLISEUM
SUNDAY, JUNE 10, 8:00 P.M.

U.S. TITLE VS. ~~T.V. TITLE~~ RETURN
NO DISQUALIFICATION

RIC FLAIR
vs.
PAUL JONES

MID-ATLANTIC TITLE MATCH

KEN PATERA
vs.
DINO BRAVO

TONY ATLAS
vs.
BARON VON RASCHKE

TAG TEAM MATCH
JIMMY SNUKA & PAUL ORNDORFF
vs.
GENE ANDERSON & KIM DUK

PLUS 3 OTHER BIG MATCHES

RINGSIDE $7.00 RESERVED $6.00 ADULT GENERAL ADMISSION $5.00
CHILDREN 11 YRS. AND UNDER GENERAL ADMISSION $2.50

TICKETS AVAILABLE AT COLISEUM BOX OFFICE,
NATIONAL HAT SHOP, THE ALAMO - 4447 S. BLVD.

Flair Holds Title

Ric Flair defeated Paul Jones in pro wrestling Sunday at Charlotte's Coliseum and retained his U.S. Heavyweight title, but Dino Bravo's attempt to take the Mid-Atlantic heavyweight title from Ken Patera was spoiled when both wrestlers were out of the ring for a 10-count. The double disqualification meant the title didn't change hands.

The team of Jimmy Snuka and Paul Orndorff whipped Kim Duk and Gene Anderson in the night's only tag match and Tony Atlas clawed past Baron Von Raschke.

In other matches: Jim Brunzell defeated Jacques Goulet; Jay Youngblood beat Mr. X No. 1 and Gary Young whipped Gordon Nelson.

MID ATLANTIC CHAMPIONSHIP WRESTLING — NWA — **MID ATLANTIC CHAMPIONSHIP WRESTLING**

DORTON ARENA • TUES., JUNE 12th, 8:15 P.M.
RINGSIDE $5.00 GEN. ADM. $4.00. CHILDREN (Under 12) $2.00 ADM.
Tickets on sale at Pop-o-Top Beverage in Mission Valley Shopping Center

NO DISQUALIFICATION
~~TV TITLE~~ vs. U.S. TITLE
PAUL JONES vs. **RIC FLAIR**

FOR MID-ATLANTIC TITLE
DINO BRAVO vs. **KEN PATERA**

JIM BRUNZELL • VERSUS • **BARON von RASCHKE**

JOHNNY WEAVER & JAY YOUNGBLOOD VS. LEN DENTON & RUDY KAY

PLUS OTHER MATCHES

Flair retains belt

Rick Flair retained his United States heavyweight championship by defeating Paul Jones in professional wrestling at Dorton Arena Tuesday night.

In the other main events, Jim Brunzell beat Barron Von Raschke while Dino Bravo won by disqualification over Ken Patera.

In the preliminary bouts, Abe Jacobs pinned Gordon Nelson, Les Thornton won by default over Mr. X No. 1 and Johnny Weaver and Jay Youngblood teamed up to defeat Len Denton and Rudy Kay.

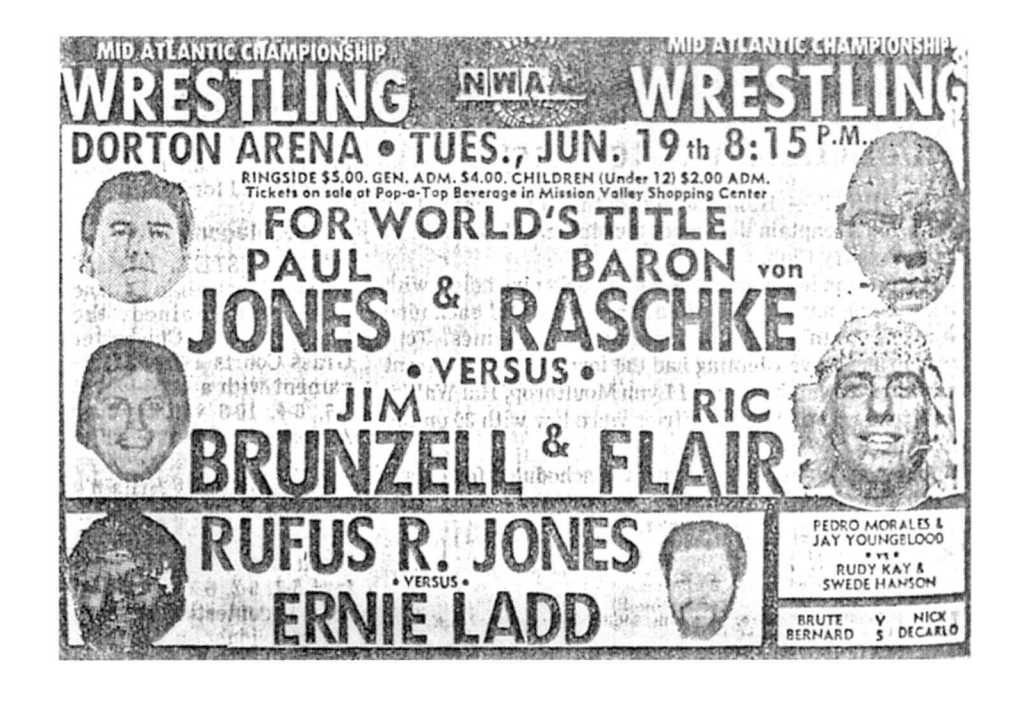

MID ATLANTIC CHAMPIONSHIP WRESTLING
NWA
MID ATLANTIC CHAMPIONSHIP WRESTLING

DORTON ARENA • TUES., JUN. 19th 8:15 P.M.

RINGSIDE $5.00, GEN. ADM. $4.00, CHILDREN (Under 12) $2.00 ADM.
Tickets on sale at Pop-a-Top Beverage in Mission Valley Shopping Center

FOR WORLD'S TITLE
PAUL JONES & BARON von RASCHKE
• VERSUS •
JIM BRUNZELL & RIC FLAIR

RUFUS R. JONES
• versus •
ERNIE LADD

PEDRO MORALES & JAY YOUNGBLOOD
vs
RUDY KAY & SWEDE HANSON

BRUTE BERNARD vs NICK DECARLO

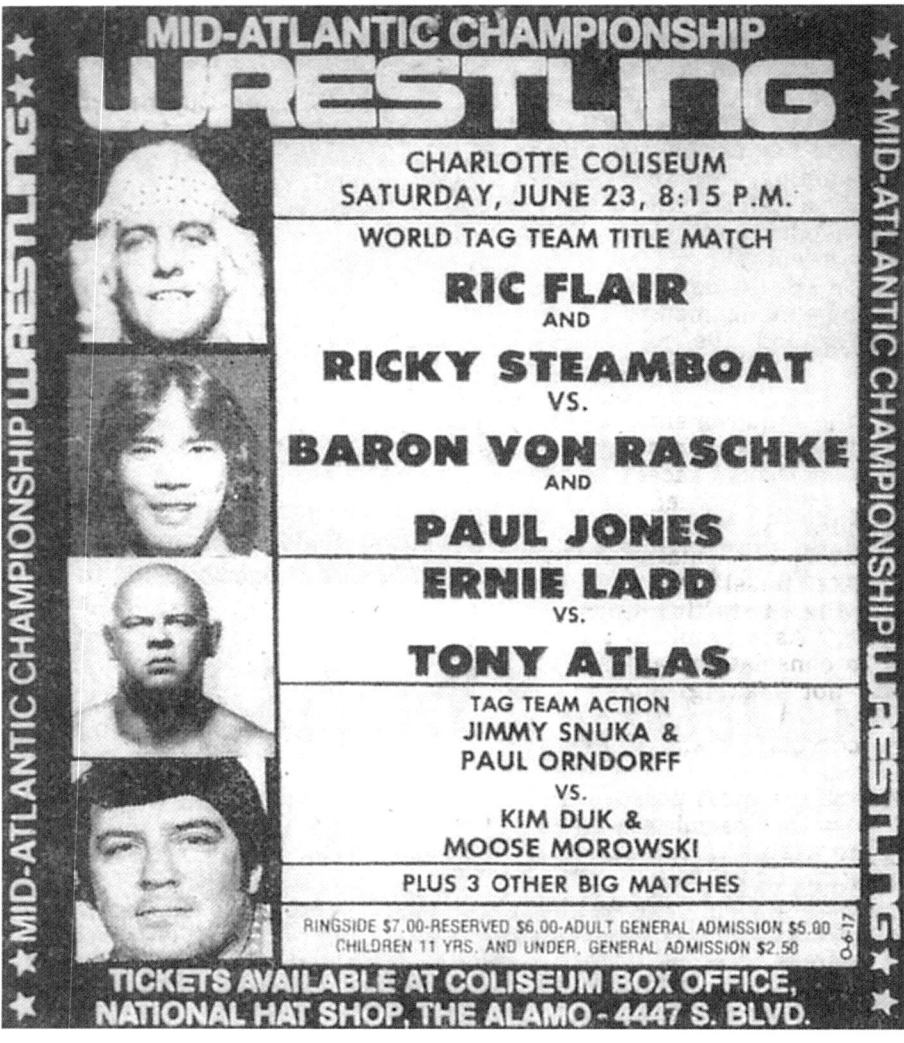

Champs Disqualified, But Don't Lose Title

Ric Flair and Ricky Steamboat defeated defending champs Baron Von Raschke and Paul Jones by disqualification Saturday in a world tag team title match at the Coliseum. However, titles do not change hands by disqualification.

In other action:

Jim Brunzell d. Swede Hanson; Jimmy Snuka-Paul Orndorff d. Kim Duk-Moose Morowski; Les Thornton d. Sgt. Jacque Goulet by disqualification; Tony Atlas d. Ernie Ladd; Bill White-Lynn Denton d. Leo Burke-Don Kernodle.

NWA MID-ATLANTIC CHAMPIONSHIP WRESTLING

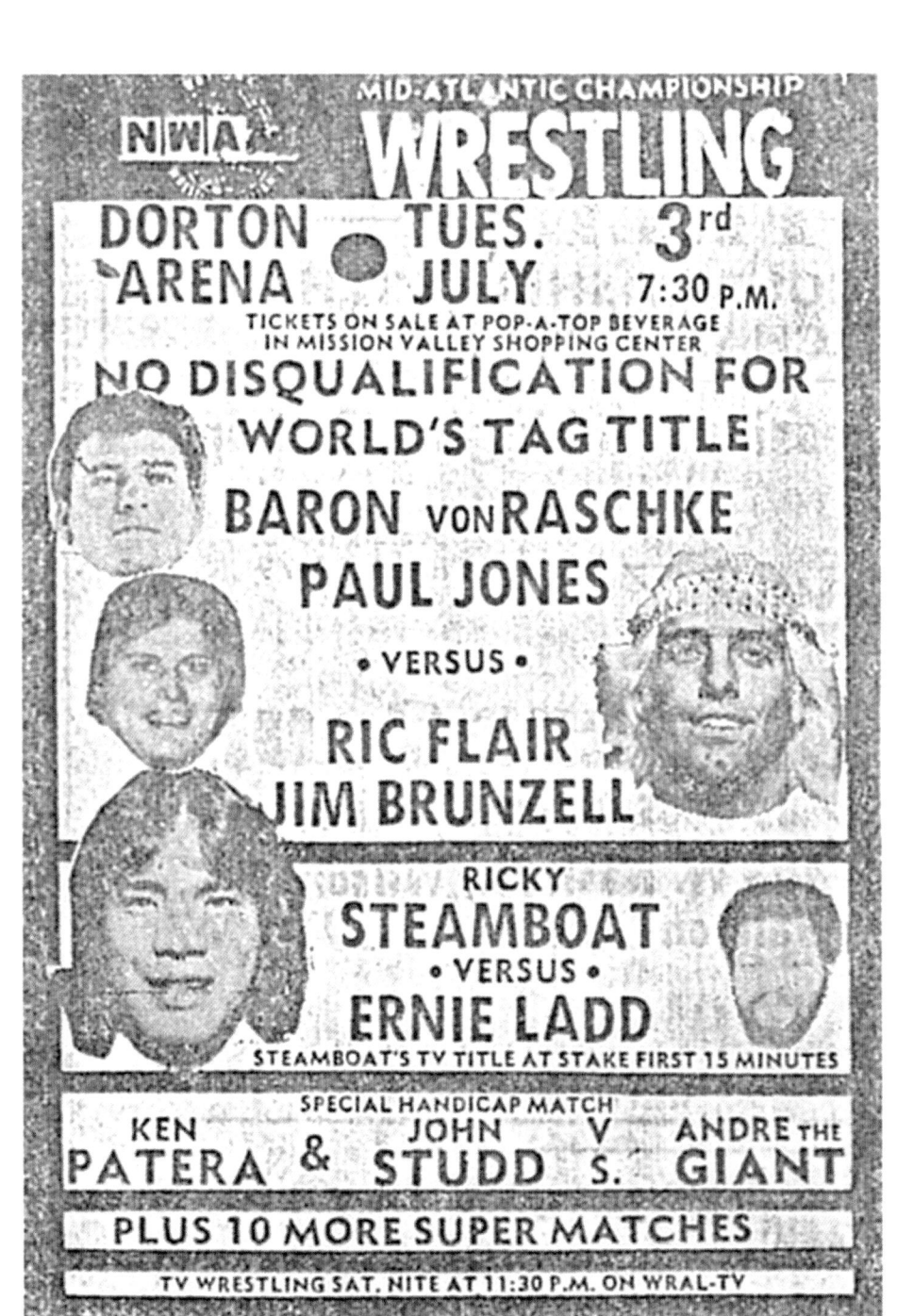

DORTON ARENA • TUES. JULY 3rd 7:30 P.M.

TICKETS ON SALE AT POP-A-TOP BEVERAGE IN MISSION VALLEY SHOPPING CENTER

NO DISQUALIFICATION FOR WORLD'S TAG TITLE

BARON von RASCHKE
PAUL JONES

• VERSUS •

RIC FLAIR
JIM BRUNZELL

RICKY STEAMBOAT
• VERSUS •
ERNIE LADD

STEAMBOAT'S TV TITLE AT STAKE FIRST 15 MINUTES

SPECIAL HANDICAP MATCH

KEN PATERA & JOHN STUDD V.S. ANDRE the GIANT

PLUS 10 MORE SUPER MATCHES

TV WRESTLING SAT. NITE AT 11:30 P.M. ON WRAL-TV

Ladd downs Steamboat

Ernie Ladd defeated Ricky Steamboat before a crowd of more than 6,000 in Tuesday night wrestling action at Dorton Arena.

In other main events, Andre the Giant won by disqualification over Ken Patera and John Studd in a handicap match and Ric Flair and Jim Brunzell were declared the winners when Paul Jones and Baron von Raschke were counted out of the ring.

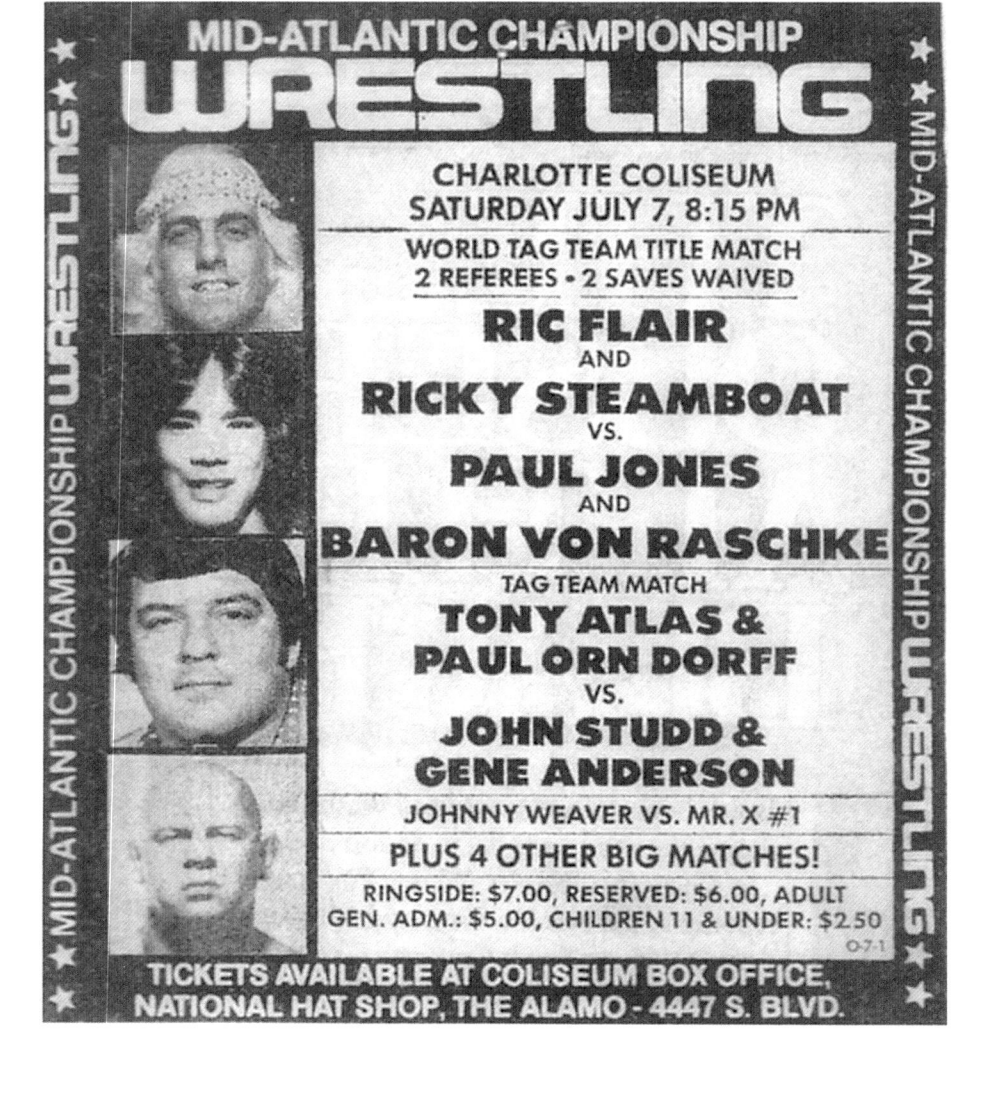

MID-ATLANTIC CHAMPIONSHIP WRESTLING

CHARLOTTE COLISEUM
SATURDAY JULY 7, 8:15 PM

WORLD TAG TEAM TITLE MATCH
2 REFEREES • 2 SAVES WAIVED

RIC FLAIR
AND
RICKY STEAMBOAT
VS.
PAUL JONES
AND
BARON VON RASCHKE

TAG TEAM MATCH
TONY ATLAS & PAUL ORN DORFF
VS.
JOHN STUDD & GENE ANDERSON

JOHNNY WEAVER VS. MR. X #1

PLUS 4 OTHER BIG MATCHES!

RINGSIDE: $7.00, RESERVED: $6.00, ADULT GEN. ADM.: $5.00, CHILDREN 11 & UNDER: $2.50

TICKETS AVAILABLE AT COLISEUM BOX OFFICE, NATIONAL HAT SHOP, THE ALAMO - 4447 S. BLVD.

Pro Wrestling Card

Ric Flair and Ricky Steamboat defeated world tag team champions Paul Jones and Baron Von Raschke on a disqualification when the champs ran out of the ring Saturday night in the Coliseum. But Flair and Steamboat did not win the titles because the belts cannot change hands on a disqualification.

In other action: John Studd and Gene Anderson defeated Tony Atlas and Paul Orndorff; Jay Youngblood defeated Lynn Denton; Johnny Weaver defeated Mr. X No. 1; Leo Burke defeated Charlie Fulton; Nick De Carlo defeated Don Moore; and Abe Jacobs battled Les Thornton to a draw.

MID-ATLANTIC CHAMPIONSHIP WRESTLING — NWA

DORTON ARENA • TUES., July 10th 8:15 P.M.

RINGSIDE $5.00. GEN. ADM. $4.00. CHILDREN (Under 12) $2.00 ADM.
Tickets on sale at Pop-a-Top Beverage in Mission Valley Shopping Center

FALLS COUNT ANYWHERE IN BUILDING
WORLD'S TAG TITLE
PAUL JONES AND BARON von RASCHKE
• VERSUS •
RIC FLAIR AND JIM BRUNZELL

TONY ATLAS vs. GENE ANDERSON
JAY YOUNGBLOOD vs. BILL WHITE
PLUS OTHERS
TV Wrestling Starts at 11:30 WRAL-TV

Jones, von Raschke retain title

Paul Jones and Baron von Raschke retained their world's tag-team championship by defeating Ric Flair and Jim Brunzell in the wrestling main event Tuesday night at Dorton Arena.

In other matches, Don Kernodle defeated Charlie Fulton, Tony Garea defeated Frank Monte, Jay Youngblood defeated Bill White and Tony Atlas defeated Gene Anderson.

MID-ATLANTIC CHAMPIONSHIP WRESTLING — NWA

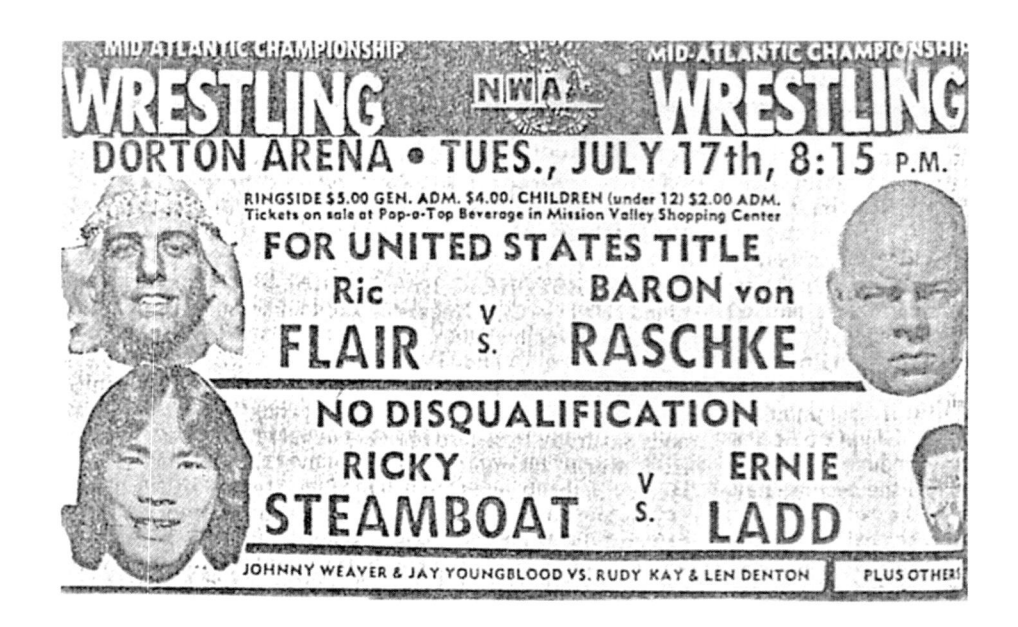

DORTON ARENA • TUES., JULY 17th, 8:15 P.M.

RINGSIDE $5.00 GEN. ADM. $4.00. CHILDREN (under 12) $2.00 ADM.
Tickets on sale at Pop-a-Top Beverage in Mission Valley Shopping Center

FOR UNITED STATES TITLE
Ric **FLAIR** vs. **BARON** von **RASCHKE**

NO DISQUALIFICATION
RICKY **STEAMBOAT** vs. ERNIE **LADD**

JOHNNY WEAVER & JAY YOUNGBLOOD VS. RUDY KAY & LEN DENTON — PLUS OTHERS

Steamboat, Flair win

Ric Flair defeated Baron von Raschke and Ricky Steamboat beat Ernie Ladd Tuesday night in the feature matches on a professional wrestling card at Dorton Arena.

In other matches, Les Thornton and Charlie Fulton battled to a draw, Tony Garea defeated Mr. X and, in a tag-team bout, Johnny Weaver and Jay Youngblood defeated Len Denton and Rudy Kay.

No Titles Change

Paul Jones and Baron Von Raschke retained their National Wrestling Alliance world tag-team belts Saturday by defeating Ricky Steamboat and Ric Flair in the main event at professional wrestling at the Coliseum.

In other top matches, Blackjack Mulligan and John Studd both were counted out of the ring, a double disqualification, and Jim Brunzell and Rufus R. Jones teamed to defeat Buddy Rogers and Gene Anderson.

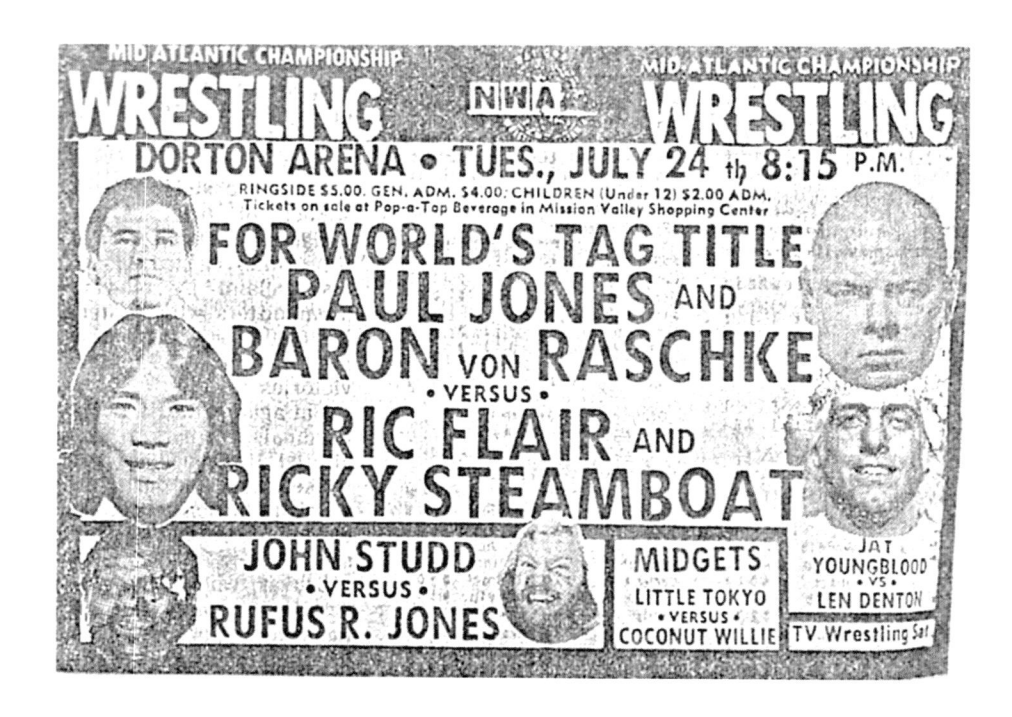

MID ATLANTIC CHAMPIONSHIP WRESTLING
NWA
MID ATLANTIC CHAMPIONSHIP WRESTLING

DORTON ARENA • TUES., JULY 24 th 8:15 P.M.

RINGSIDE $5.00, GEN. ADM. $4.00, CHILDREN (Under 12) $2.00 ADM.
Tickets on sale at Pop-a-Top Beverage in Mission Valley Shopping Center

FOR WORLD'S TAG TITLE
PAUL JONES AND BARON von RASCHKE
• VERSUS •
RIC FLAIR AND RICKY STEAMBOAT

JOHN STUDD • VERSUS • **RUFUS R. JONES**

MIDGETS LITTLE TOKYO • VERSUS • COCONUT WILLIE

JAY YOUNGBLOOD vs LEN DENTON

TV Wrestling Sat.

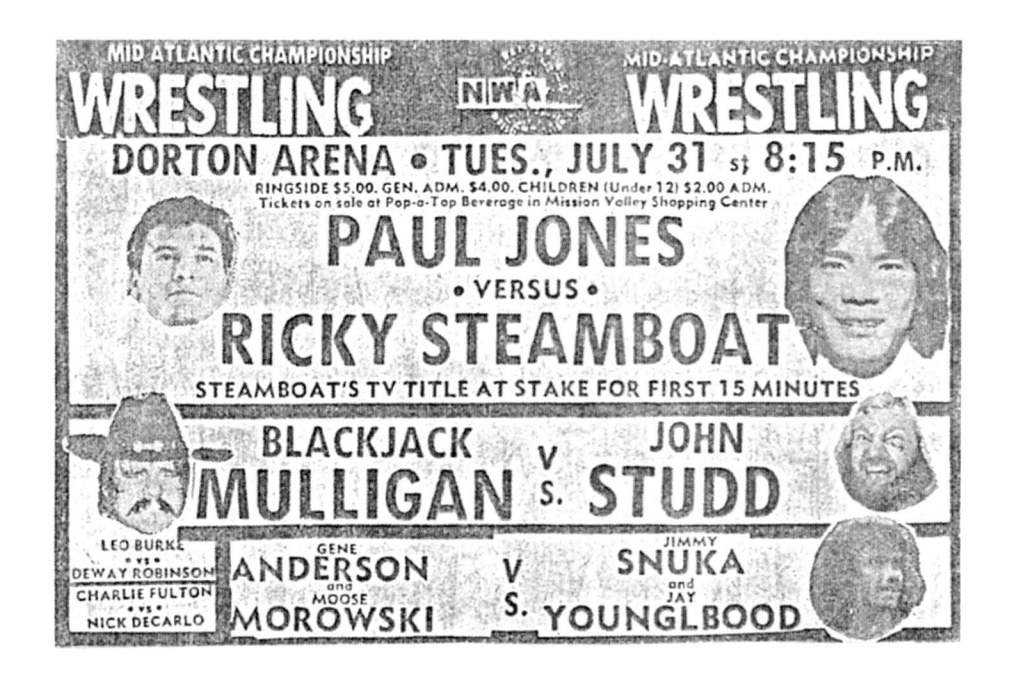

MID-ATLANTIC CHAMPIONSHIP WRESTLING — NWA — **MID-ATLANTIC CHAMPIONSHIP WRESTLING**

DORTON ARENA • TUES., JULY 31 at 8:15 P.M.

RINGSIDE $5.00, GEN. ADM. $4.00, CHILDREN (Under 12) $2.00 ADM.
Tickets on sale at Pop-a-Top Beverage in Mission Valley Shopping Center

PAUL JONES • VERSUS • RICKY STEAMBOAT

STEAMBOAT'S TV TITLE AT STAKE FOR FIRST 15 MINUTES

BLACKJACK MULLIGAN vs. JOHN STUDD

LEO BURKE vs DEWAY ROBINSON
CHARLIE FULTON vs NICK DECARLO

GENE ANDERSON and MOOSE MOROWSKI vs. JIMMY SNUKA and JAY YOUNGBLOOD

Steamboat wins

Ricky Steamboat defeated Paul Jones and Blackjack Mulligan was a winner over John Studd in the featured wrestling matches Tuesday night at Dorton Arena.

In other matches, Charlie Fulton fought to a draw with Nick DeCarlo, Coco Somoa defeated Tony Russo, and the tage team of Jimmy Snuka and Jay Youngblood defeated Gene Anderson and Moose Morowski.

MID-ATLANTIC CHAMPIONSHIP WRESTLING

CHARLOTTE COLISEUM
SATURDAY, AUG. 4, 8:15 P.M.

SIX MAN TAG TEAM MATCH

RIC FLAIR
RICKY STEAMBOAT
BLACKJACK MULLIGAN

vs.

BARON VON RASCHKE
PAUL JONES
JOHN STUDD

JIM BRUNZELL
vs.
BRUTE BERNARD

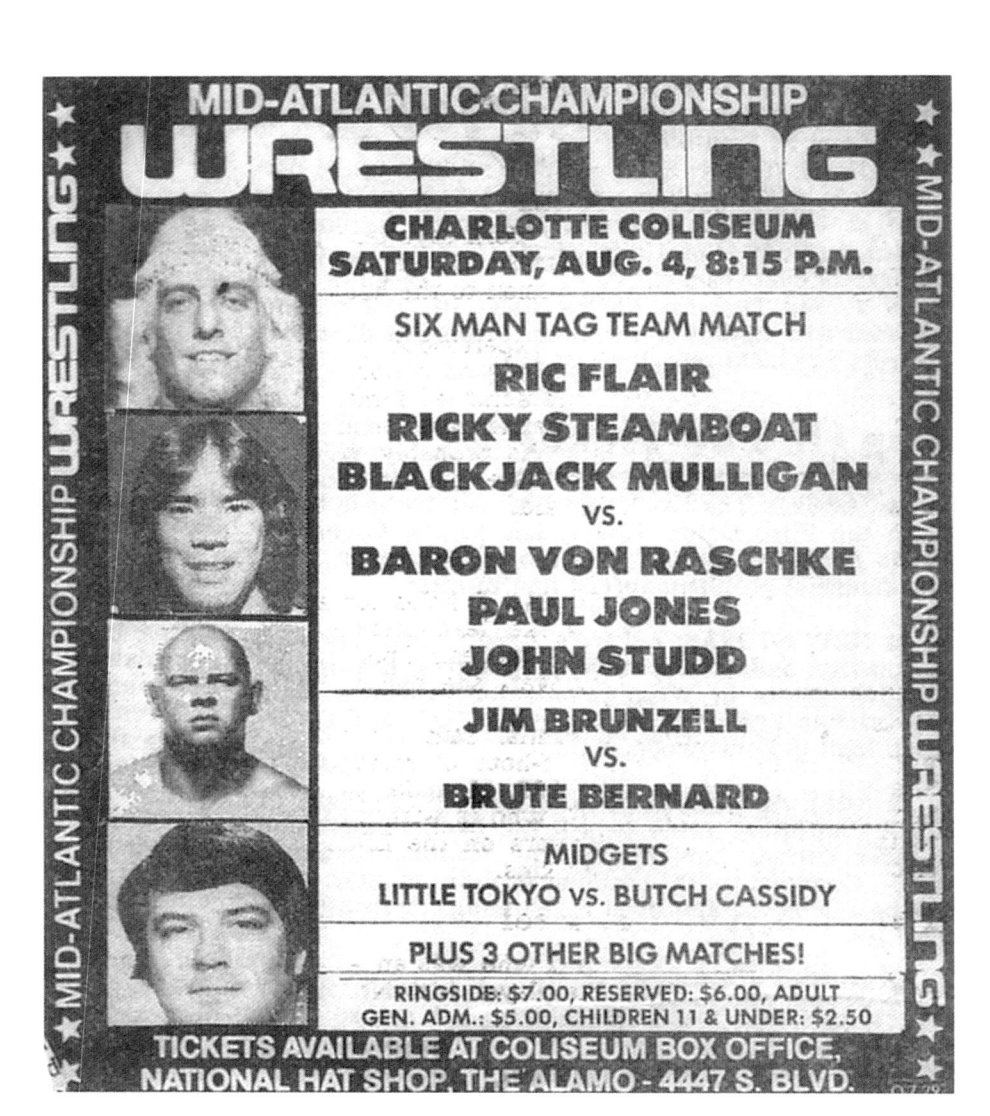

MIDGETS
LITTLE TOKYO vs. **BUTCH CASSIDY**

PLUS 3 OTHER BIG MATCHES!

RINGSIDE: $7.00, RESERVED: $6.00, ADULT
GEN. ADM.: $5.00, CHILDREN 11 & UNDER: $2.50

TICKETS AVAILABLE AT COLISEUM BOX OFFICE,
NATIONAL HAT SHOP, THE ALAMO - 4447 S. BLVD.

Pro Wrestling Card

Ric Flair, Blackjack Mulligan and Ricky Steamboat teamed to beat Baron von Raschke, Paul Jones and John Studd in the main event of Saturday's professional wrestling at the Coliseum. The victory came when Mulligan pinned Studd late in the match.

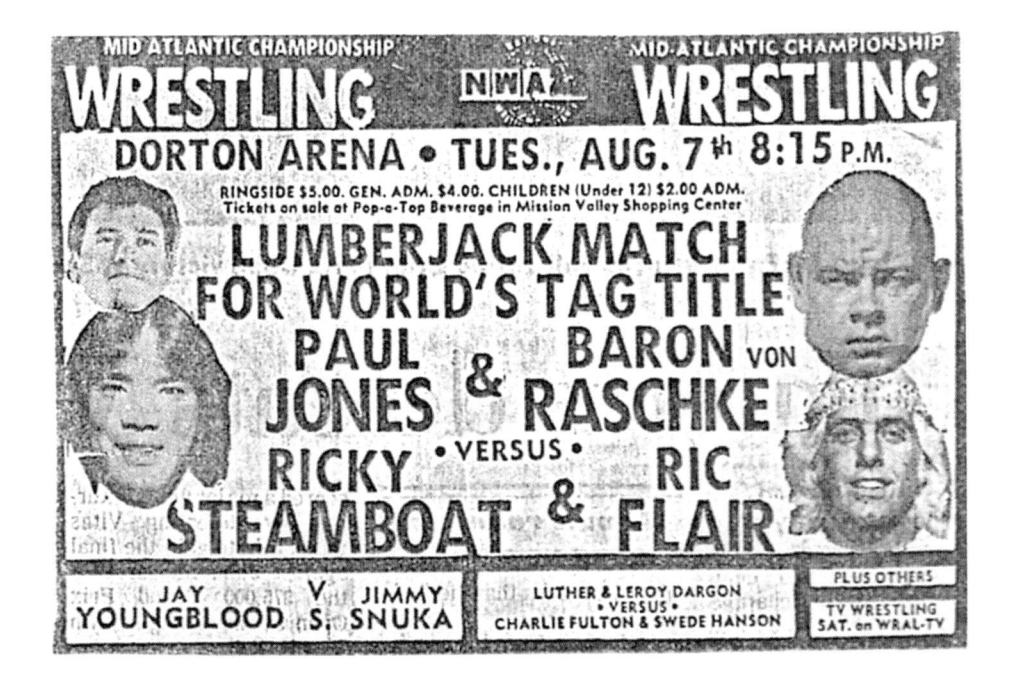

MID-ATLANTIC CHAMPIONSHIP WRESTLING
NWA
MID-ATLANTIC CHAMPIONSHIP WRESTLING

DORTON ARENA • TUES., AUG. 7th 8:15 P.M.

RINGSIDE $5.00. GEN. ADM. $4.00. CHILDREN (Under 12) $2.00 ADM.
Tickets on sale at Pop-a-Top Beverage in Mission Valley Shopping Center

LUMBERJACK MATCH
FOR WORLD'S TAG TITLE

PAUL JONES & BARON VON RASCHKE

• VERSUS •

RICKY STEAMBOAT & RIC FLAIR

| JAY YOUNGBLOOD VS. JIMMY SNUKA | LUTHER & LEROY DARGON • VERSUS • CHARLIE FULTON & SWEDE HANSON | PLUS OTHERS — TV WRESTLING SAT. on WRAL-TV |

WIDE WORLD WRESTLING

TOMORROW AUGUST 12th 3:00 P.M.

TRIPLE MAIN EVENT

U.S. TITLE MATCH

U.S. CHAMP
(NATURE BOY)
RIC FLAIR
-VS-
(THE CAT)
ERNIE LADD

RIC | ERNIE

2ND MAIN EVENT
($1,000 IF PATERA IS BEATEN)
(MID ATL. CHAMP)
KEN PATERA
-VS-
JIM BRUNZELL

1ST MAIN EVENT
(FREIGHT TRAIN)
RUFUS R. JONES
-VS-
JIMMY SNUKA

KEN  | JIM

TAG TEAM MATCH

BRUTE BERNARD & THE SCORPION -vs- JAY YOUNGBLOOD & PEDRO MORALES

PLUS 2 SINGLE MATCHES

Box Office-255-5771. Ringside-$5.00, Center Balcony-$4.00
Other Balcony: Adults-$4.00, Children under 12-$2.00
Box Office Open Mon.-Fri. 10:00-5:30, Sat. 11:00-4:00, Day of Match. 1:00 PM NO CHECKS OR CREDIT CARDS DAY OF MATCH.

SEE NWA WORLD WIDE WRESTLING SATURDAY
ON WLOS-TV CHANNEL 13 11:30 PM-12:30 AM

Asheville Civic Center

MID ATLANTIC CHAMPIONSHIP WRESTLING - NWA

DORTON ARENA • TUES., AUG. 14 - 8:

RINGSIDE $5.00, GEN. ADM. $4.00, CHILDREN (Under 12) $2.00
Tickets on sale at Pop-a-Top Beverage in Mission Valley Shopping Cen

6-MAN TAG TEAM MATCH

BARON VON RASCHKE
PAUL JONES
JIMMY SNUKA

• VERSUS •

RICK FLAIR
RICKY STEAMBOAT
BLACKJACK MULLIGAN

GENE ANDERSON vs JOHNNY WEAVER • PLUS OTHERS • TV WRE

Pro wrestling

In a featured six-man, tag-team wrestling match Tuesday night at Dorton arena, Ric Flair, Ricky Steamboat and Black Jack Mulligan defeated the threesome of Paul Jones, Baron Von Raschke and Jimmy Snuka.

In other matches, Tony Garea won by a referee's decision over Brute Bernard, Abe Jacobs defeated Rudy Kay, Dewey Robertson defeated Don Kernodle and Johnny Weaver was a winner over Gene Anderson.

MID-ATLANTIC CHAMPIONSHIP WRESTLING

CHARLOTTE COLISEUM
SATURDAY, AUGUST 18, 8:15 P.M.

SIX MAN TAG TEAM MATCH

ERNIE LADD
BARON VON RASCHKE
PAUL JONES

VS.

RIC FLAIR
RICKY STEAMBOAT
BLACKJACK MULLIGAN

RUFUS R. JONES
VS.
JIMMY SNUKA

JAY YOUNGBLOOD VS. THE SCORPION

PLUS 3 MORE BIG MATCHES!

RINGSIDE $7.00 - RESERVED $6.00 - ADULT GENERAL ADMISSION $5.00 CHILDREN 11 YRS. AND UNDER, GENERAL ADMISSION $2.50

TICKETS AVAILABLE AT COLISEUM BOX OFFICE, NATIONAL HAT SHOP, THE ALAMO - 4447 S. BLVD.

Flair Pins Jones

Ric Flair pinned Paul Jones with a figure-4 leglock, as he and teammates Ricky Steamboat and Blackjack Mulligan defeated Jones, Baron Von Raschke and Ernie Ladd in the feature triple tag team pro wrestling match at the Coliseum.

Earlier, Rufus R. Jones defeated Jimmy Snuka; Jay Youngblood downed the Scorpion; Swede Hansen and Dewey Robertson rolled over Pedro Morales and Abe Jacobs; Rick McGraw beat Frank Monte; and Mr. X No. 1 defeated Tony Russo.

MID-ATLANTIC CHAMPIONSHIP WRESTLING

NWA

DORTON ARENA • TUES., AUG. 21st, 8:15 P.M.

RINGSIDE $5.00, GEN. ADM. $4.00, CHILDREN (Under 12) $2.00 ADM.
Tickets on sale at Pop-o-Top Beverage in Mission Valley Shopping Center

BLACKJACK MULLIGAN vs. PAUL JONES

$1,000.00 MATCH
JIM BRUNZELL vs. KEN PATERA

FOR WOMAN'S WORLD TITLE
THE FABULOUS MOOLA v WINDA S. LITTLEHEART

GENE ANDERSON & DEWEY ROBERTSON
• VERSUS •
DON KERNODLE & COCO SOMOA

JAY YOUNGBLOOD
• VS •
RUDY KAY

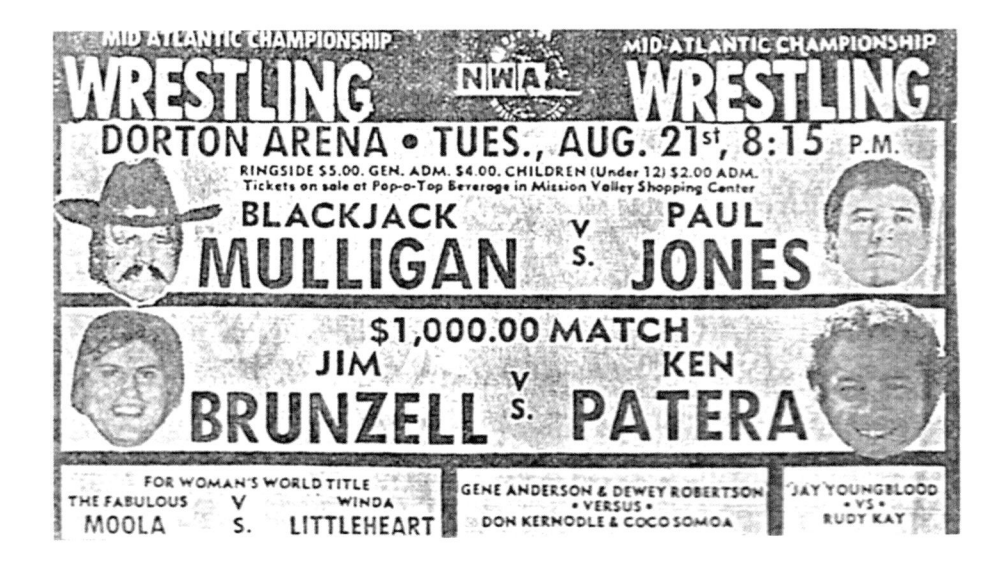

Brunzell wins

Jim Brunzell won $1,000 Tuesday night by defeating Ken Patera in the main event at Dorton Arena. In the second main event, Black Jack Mulligan defeated Paul Jones.

In other action, Jay Youngblood defeated Rudy Kay and Gene Anderson and Dewey Robertson defeated Don Kernodle and Coco Somoa in a tag-team match.

In a women's match, The Fabulous Moola retained her world's title by defeating Winoa Littleheart.

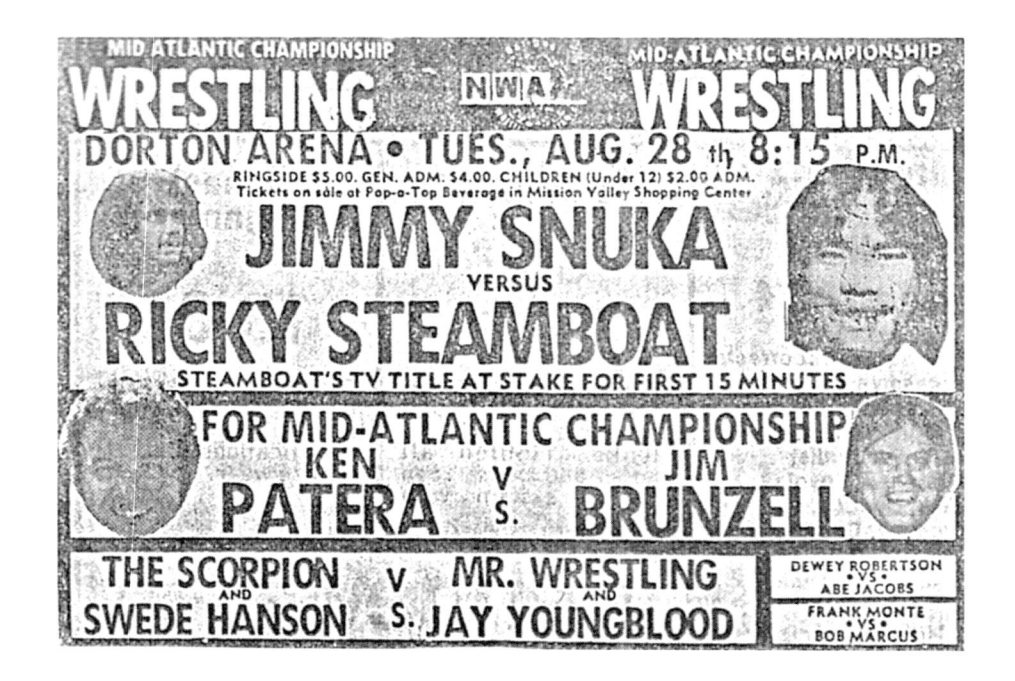

MID-ATLANTIC CHAMPIONSHIP WRESTLING — NWA

DORTON ARENA • TUES., AUG. 28th 8:15 P.M.

RINGSIDE $5.00. GEN. ADM. $4.00. CHILDREN (Under 12) $2.00 ADM.
Tickets on sale at Pop-a-Top Beverage in Mission Valley Shopping Center

JIMMY SNUKA VERSUS RICKY STEAMBOAT
STEAMBOAT'S TV TITLE AT STAKE FOR FIRST 15 MINUTES

FOR MID-ATLANTIC CHAMPIONSHIP
KEN PATERA vs. JIM BRUNZELL

THE SCORPION AND SWEDE HANSON vs. MR. WRESTLING AND JAY YOUNGBLOOD

DEWEY ROBERTSON vs. ABE JACOBS
FRANK MONTE vs. BOB MARCUS

Steamboat downs Snuka

Ricky Steamboat defeated Jimmy Snuka and Jim Brunzell wpm by disqualification over Ken Patera in the main events on the wrestling card Tuesday night at Dorton Arena.

In other events, Bob Marcus defeated Frank Monte, Dewey Robertson downed Abe Jacobs, and Mr. Wrestling and Jay Youngblood defeated Swede Hanson and The Scorpion in a tag-team match.

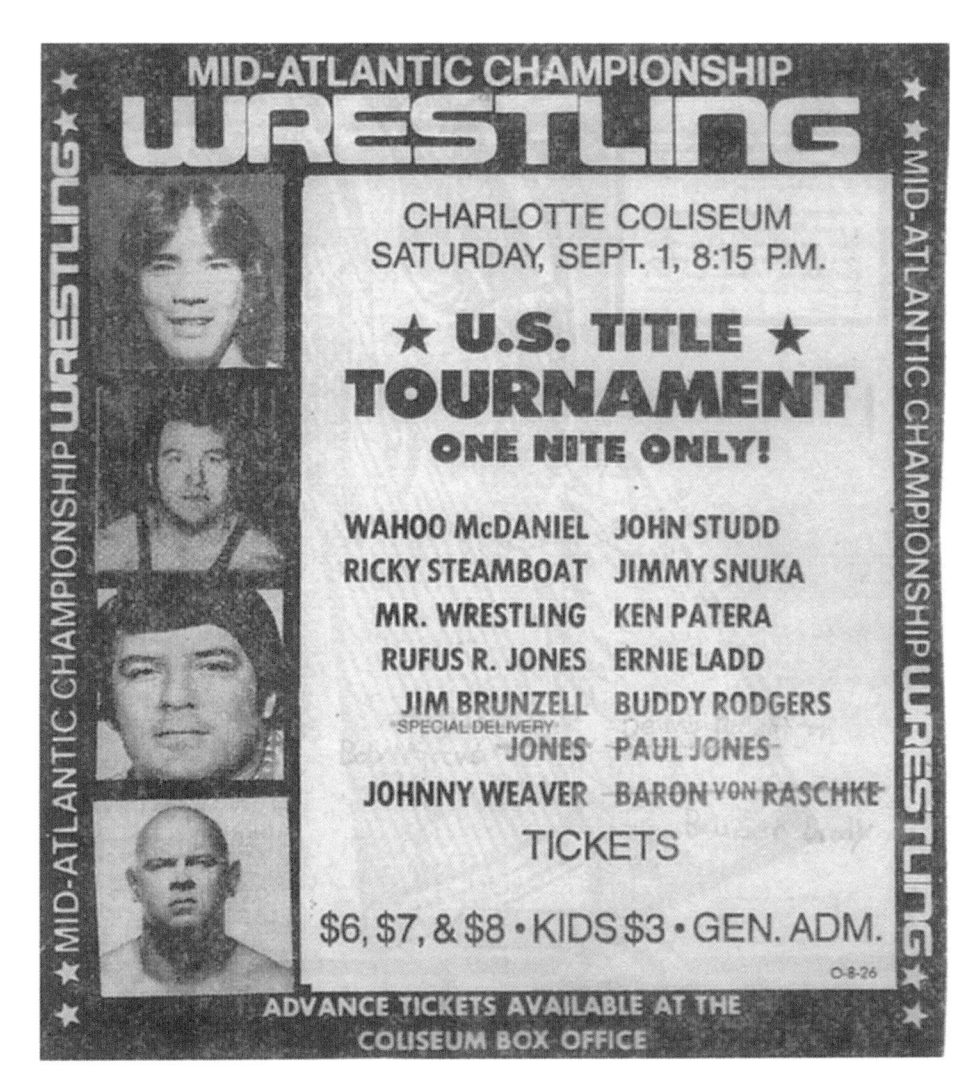

MID-ATLANTIC CHAMPIONSHIP WRESTLING

CHARLOTTE COLISEUM
SATURDAY, SEPT. 1, 8:15 P.M.

★ U.S. TITLE ★ TOURNAMENT
ONE NITE ONLY!

WAHOO McDANIEL	JOHN STUDD
RICKY STEAMBOAT	JIMMY SNUKA
MR. WRESTLING	KEN PATERA
RUFUS R. JONES	ERNIE LADD
JIM BRUNZELL	BUDDY RODGERS
SPECIAL DELIVERY JONES	PAUL JONES
JOHNNY WEAVER	BARON VON RASCHKE

TICKETS
$6, $7, & $8 • KIDS $3 • GEN. ADM.

ADVANCE TICKETS AVAILABLE AT THE COLISEUM BOX OFFICE

Snuka Wins Wrestling

Jimmy Snuka pinned Ricky Steamboat and captured the U.S. heavyweight wrestling championship before 5,352 fans at the Coliseum. Snuka advanced with a victory over Jim Brunzell in the semifinals. Steamboat defeated Ken Patera in his semifinal.

Tournament results:

First Round—Ricky Steamboat pinned Ernie Ladd; Wahoo McDaniel and John Studd, double disqualification; Ken Patera pinned Rufus R. Jones; Buddy Rogers d. John Marcus, submission; Jimmy Snuka d. Tim Woods, referee's decision; Bruiser Brodie pinned Johnny Weaver; Jim Brunzell d. Dewey Robertson, referee's decision.

Second Round—Steamboat d. Rogers, countout; Brunzell pinned Brodie.

Semifinals—Steamboat pinned Patera, Snuka pinned Brunzell.

Finals—Snuka pinned Steamboat.

Snuka Retains Crown

Jimmy Snuka pinned Ric Flair, retaining his National Wrestling Alliance U.S. heavyweight belt in the feature professional wrestling match Saturday at the Coliseum.

In another title bout, Ricky Steamboat kept his TV title by defeating Ken Patera. Patera's Mid-Atlantic title was to have been on the line, too, but he lost it Friday to Jim Brunzell in a match at Richmond.

In other matches, Rufus R. Jones won on disqualification over Baron von Raschke; Jay Youngblood and Special Delivery Jones defeated Swede Hanson and Jacque Goulet; Dewey Robertson topped Pedro Morales; Nick DeCarlo and Bob Marcus defeated Tony Russo and Frank Monte, and Don Kernodle was awarded a referee's decision over The Scorpion.

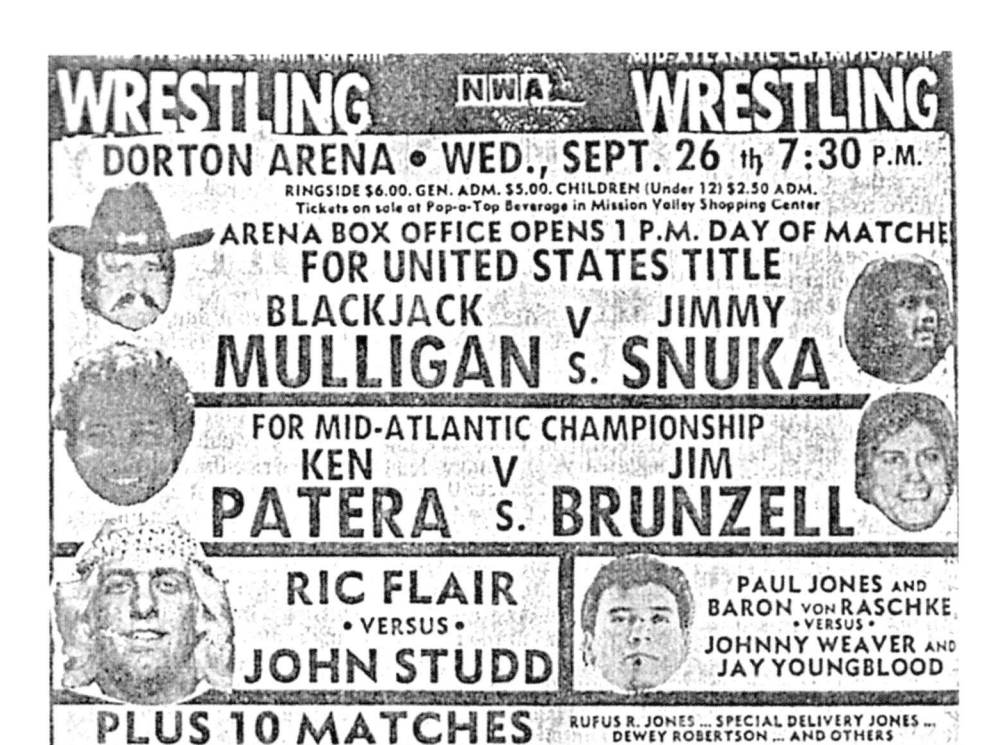

MID ATLANTIC CHAMPIONSHIP WRESTLING
NWA
DORTON ARENA • TUES., SEPT. 18th, 8:15 P.M.

RINGSIDE $5.00, GEN. ADM. $4.00, CHILDREN (Under 12) $2.00 ADM.
Tickets on sale at Pop-a-Top Beverage in Mission Valley Shopping Center

FOR UNITED STATES TITLE
JIMMY SNUKA vs. **RIC FLAIR**

A.W.A. WORLD'S TITLE vs. TV TITLE
NICK BOCKWINKLE • VERSUS • **RICKY STEAMBOAT**

BRUTE BERNARD & JACQUES GOULET vs. DON KERNODLE & JAY YOUNGBLOOD

TV WRESTLING SAT. WRAL-TV

MID ATLANTIC CHAMPIONSHIP WRESTLING
NWA
DORTON ARENA • WED., SEPT. 26th 7:30 P.M.

RINGSIDE $6.00, GEN. ADM. $5.00, CHILDREN (Under 12) $2.50 ADM.
Tickets on sale at Pop-a-Top Beverage in Mission Valley Shopping Center
ARENA BOX OFFICE OPENS 1 P.M. DAY OF MATCH

FOR UNITED STATES TITLE
BLACKJACK MULLIGAN vs. **JIMMY SNUKA**

FOR MID-ATLANTIC CHAMPIONSHIP
KEN PATERA vs. **JIM BRUNZELL**

RIC FLAIR • VERSUS • **JOHN STUDD**

PAUL JONES AND BARON von RASCHKE • VERSUS • **JOHNNY WEAVER AND JAY YOUNGBLOOD**

PLUS 10 MATCHES — RUFUS R. JONES ... SPECIAL DELIVERY JONES ... DEWEY ROBERTSON ... AND OTHERS

SNUKA BATTLES STEAMBOAT!

At 8:00 PM Sunday, September 30, 1979 at the Charlotte Coliseum in the first of 3 Main Events, U.S. Champion Jimmy Snuka battles T.V. Champion Ricky Steamboat for the U.S. Title belt. In two other big main events Paul Jones takes on Blackjack Mulligan and John Studd meets Ric Flair. Two tag team matches and two other big bouts round out the card. Don't miss a minute of the action - Sunday September 30, 8 PM at the Charlotte Coliseum.

Pro Wrestling Card

Ricky Steamboat won the feature match on Sunday's pro wrestling card at the Charlotte Coliseum, defeating Jimmy Snuka on a disqualification. But Steamboat cannot claim Snuka's heavyweight title because National Wrestling Alliance rules prohibit winning a title on a disqualification.

In other matches, Blackjack Mulligan defeated Paul Jones; Ric Flair defeated John Studd; Johnny Weaver and Jay Youngblood conquered Brute Bernard and Gene Anderson; Dewey Robertson beat Bob Marcus; Pedro Morales edged David Patterson; and Leroy and Luter Dargan defeated Doug Summers and Frank Monte.

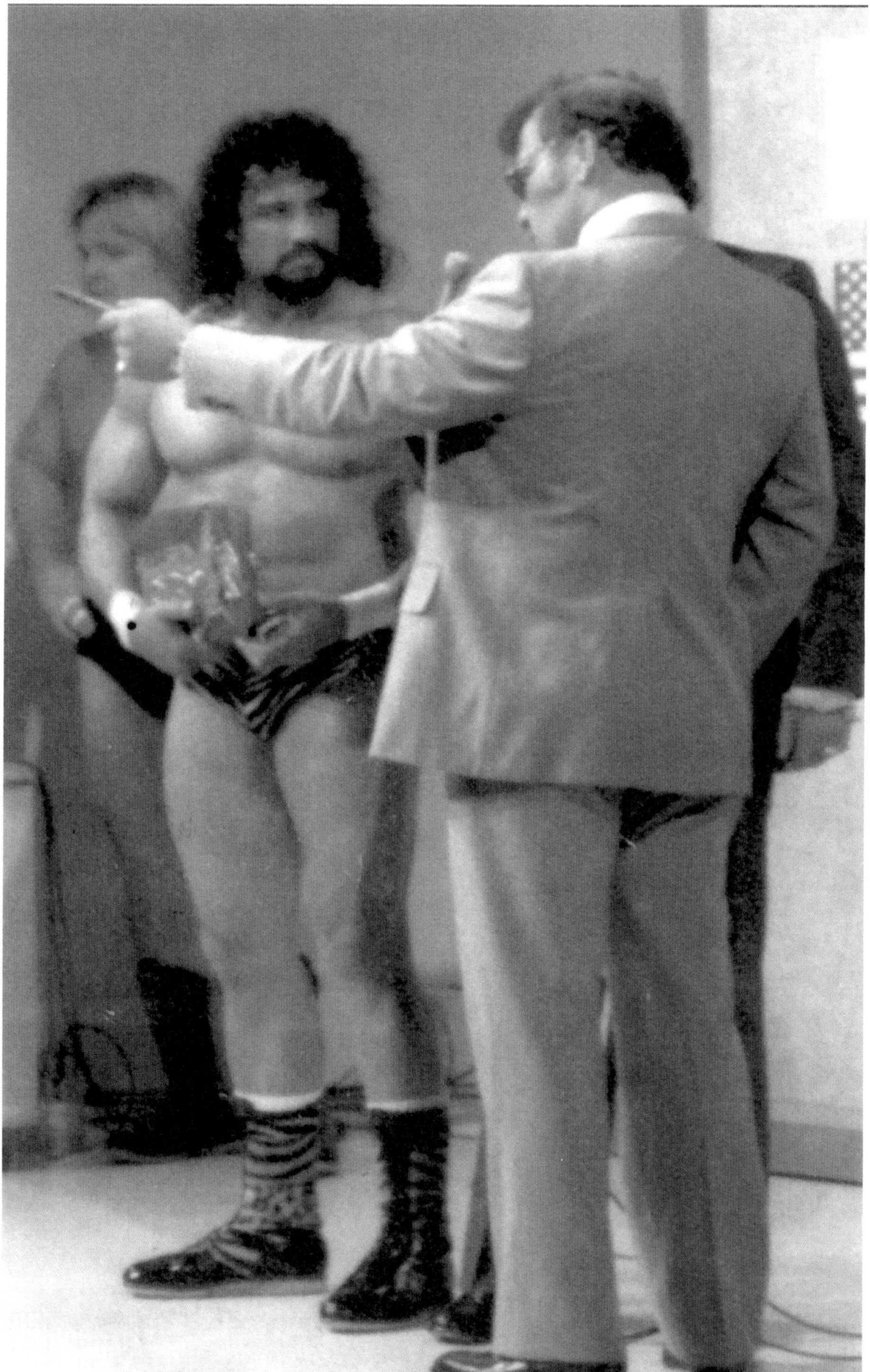

MID-ATLANTIC CHAMPIONSHIP WRESTLING

NWA

DORTON ARENA • TUES., OCT. 2nd, 8:15 P.M.

RINGSIDE $5.00 GEN. AMD. $4.00 CHILDREN (Under 12) $2.00 ADM.
Tickets on sale at Pop-a-To Beverage in Mission Valley Shopping Center.

RETURN MACH
FOR UNITED STATES TITLE
BLACK JACK MULLIGAN vs. JIMMY SNUKA

FOR MID-ATLANTIC CHAMPIONSHIP
JIM BRUNZELL vs. DEWEY ROBERTSON

JOHNNY WEAVER AND SPECIAL DELIVERY JONES vs. MR. X NO. 1 AND THE SCORPION

RICK McGRAW vs. DON KERNODLE

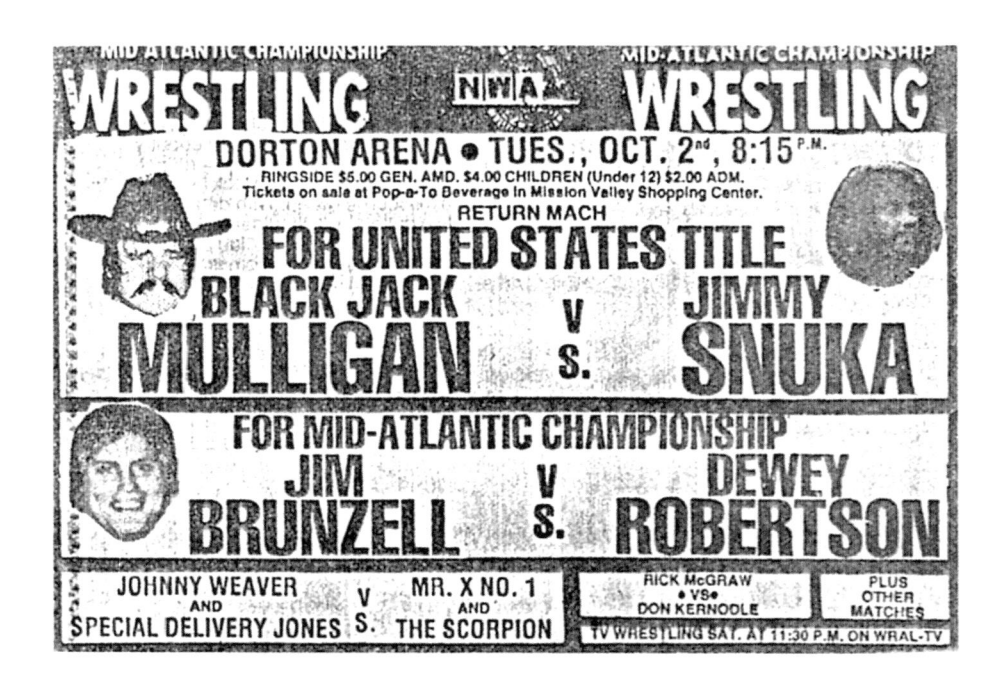

PLUS OTHER MATCHES

TV WRESTLING SAT. AT 11:30 P.M. ON WRAL-TV

Snuka, Brunzell win

Jimmy Snuka retain his U.S. title, defeating Black Jack Mulligan, and Jim Brunzell successfully defended his Mid-Atlantic title, beating Dooley Robertson, in pro wrestling matches at Dorton Arena Tuesday night.

In other matches, Johnny Weaver and Special Delivery Jones beat The Scorpion and Mr. X in a tag-team bout, Rick McGraw and Don Kernodle wrestled to a draw, and Frank Monte beat John Condroy.

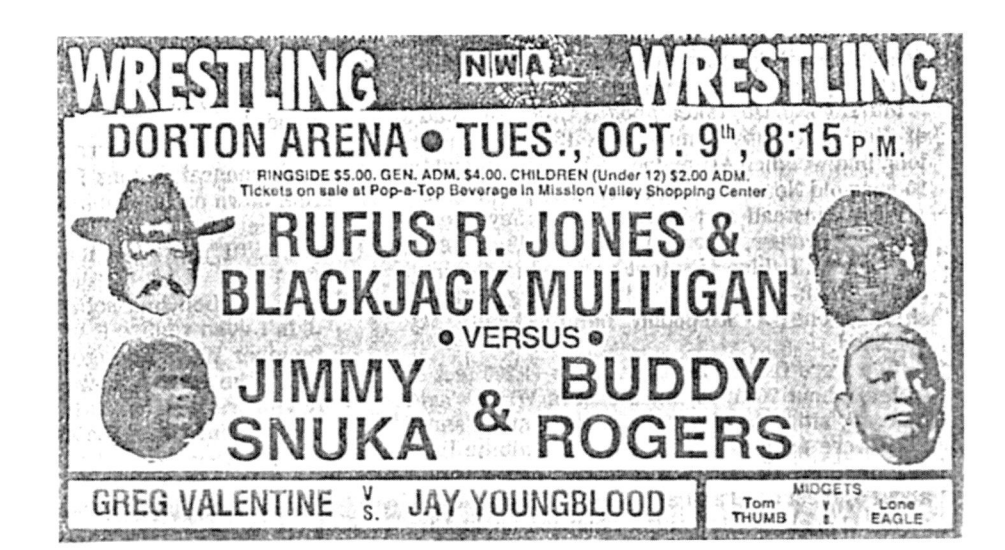

WRESTLING NWA WRESTLING

DORTON ARENA • TUES., OCT. 9th, 8:15 P.M.

RINGSIDE $5.00, GEN. ADM. $4.00, CHILDREN (Under 12) $2.00 ADM.
Tickets on sale at Pop-a-Top Beverage in Mission Valley Shopping Center

RUFUS R. JONES & BLACKJACK MULLIGAN
• VERSUS •
JIMMY SNUKA & BUDDY ROGERS

| GREG VALENTINE vs. JAY YOUNGBLOOD | MIDGETS: Tom THUMB vs. Lone EAGLE |

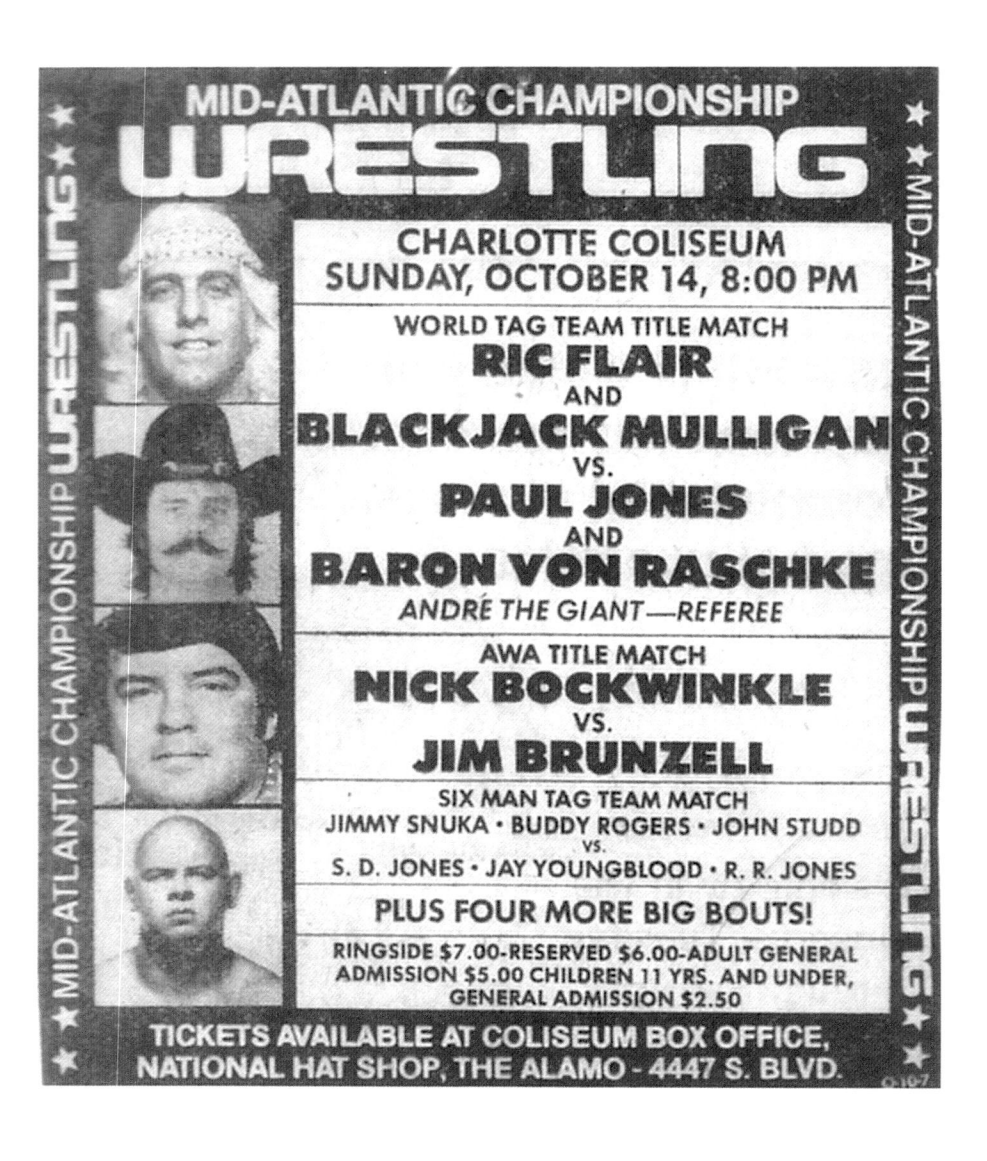

MID-ATLANTIC CHAMPIONSHIP WRESTLING

CHARLOTTE COLISEUM
SUNDAY, OCTOBER 14, 8:00 PM

WORLD TAG TEAM TITLE MATCH
RIC FLAIR
AND
BLACKJACK MULLIGAN
VS.
PAUL JONES
AND
BARON VON RASCHKE
ANDRÉ THE GIANT—REFEREE

AWA TITLE MATCH
NICK BOCKWINKLE
VS.
JIM BRUNZELL

SIX MAN TAG TEAM MATCH
JIMMY SNUKA • BUDDY ROGERS • JOHN STUDD
VS.
S. D. JONES • JAY YOUNGBLOOD • R. R. JONES

PLUS FOUR MORE BIG BOUTS!

RINGSIDE $7.00-RESERVED $6.00-ADULT GENERAL ADMISSION $5.00 CHILDREN 11 YRS. AND UNDER, GENERAL ADMISSION $2.50

TICKETS AVAILABLE AT COLISEUM BOX OFFICE, NATIONAL HAT SHOP, THE ALAMO - 4447 S. BLVD.

Champions Retain Titles

Paul Jones and Baron Von Raschke were disqualified but retained their world tag team title in a pro wrestling program Sunday at the Coliseum. They were counted out of the ring in a match against Blackjack Mulligan and Ric Flair.

In another title match, Jim Brunzell won on a disqualification against Nick Bockwinkle — but Bockwinkle retained his American Wrestling Alliance crown.

Jimmy Snuka, Buddy Rodgers and John Studd defeated Jay Youngblood, Rufus R. Jones and Special Delivery Jones in a triple tag team event. In other matches, Dewey Robertson defeated Rick McGraw, Lone Eagle beat Tiny Thumb, Brute Bernard defeated Pedro Morales, Mr. X No. 1 beat Frank Monte, and Billy Starr defeated David Patterson.

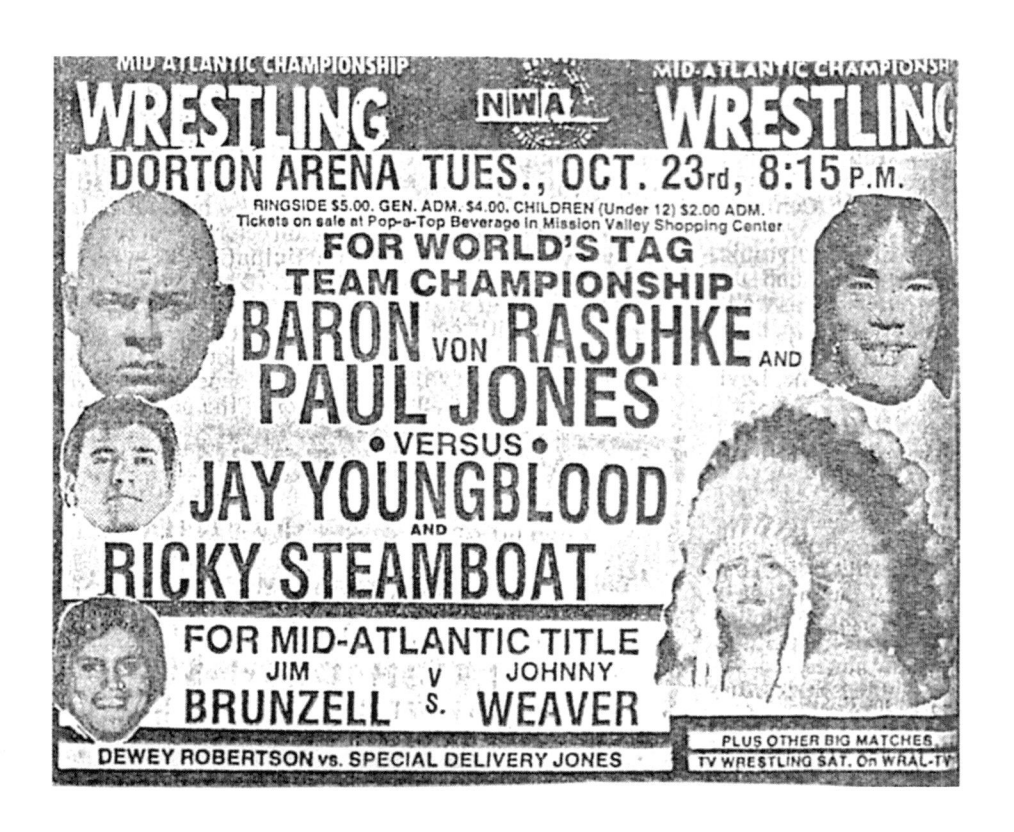

MID-ATLANTIC CHAMPIONSHIP WRESTLING — NWA

DORTON ARENA TUES., OCT. 23rd, 8:15 P.M.

RINGSIDE $5.00. GEN. ADM. $4.00. CHILDREN (Under 12) $2.00 ADM.
Tickets on sale at Pop-a-Top Beverage in Mission Valley Shopping Center

FOR WORLD'S TAG TEAM CHAMPIONSHIP
BARON VON RASCHKE AND PAUL JONES
• VERSUS •
JAY YOUNGBLOOD AND RICKY STEAMBOAT

FOR MID-ATLANTIC TITLE
JIM BRUNZELL vs. **JOHNNY WEAVER**

DEWEY ROBERTSON vs. SPECIAL DELIVERY JONES

PLUS OTHER BIG MATCHES
TV WRESTLING SAT. On WRAL-TV

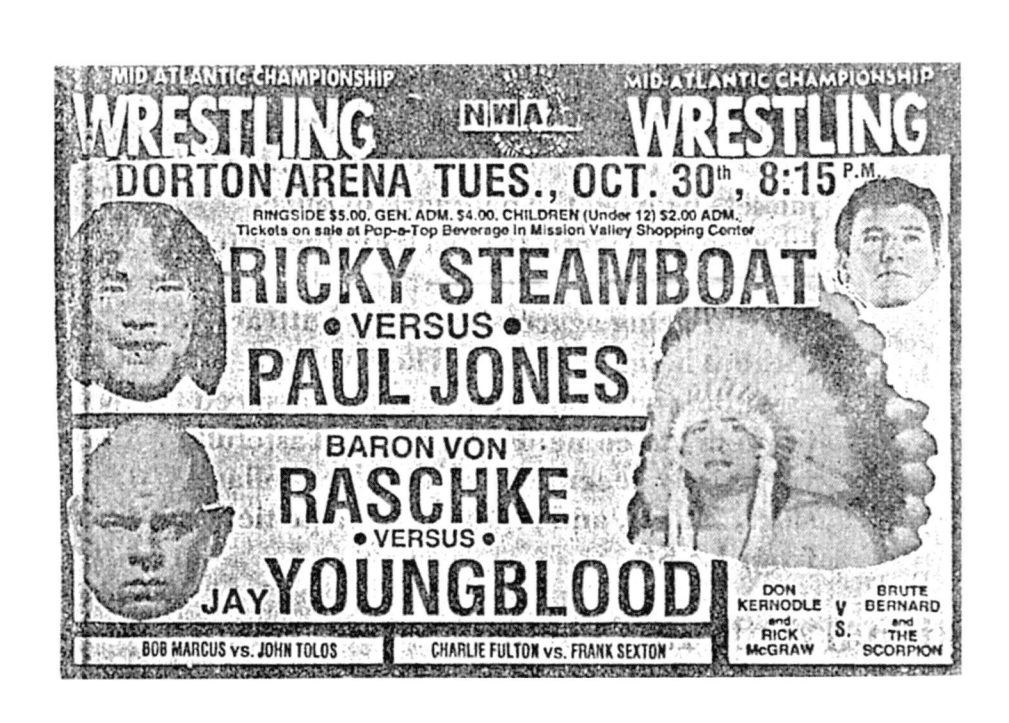

MID-ATLANTIC CHAMPIONSHIP WRESTLING — NWA

DORTON ARENA TUES., OCT. 30th, 8:15 P.M.

RINGSIDE $5.00. GEN. ADM. $4.00. CHILDREN (Under 12) $2.00 ADM.
Tickets on sale at Pop-a-Top Beverage in Mission Valley Shopping Center

RICKY STEAMBOAT
• VERSUS •
PAUL JONES

BARON VON RASCHKE
• VERSUS •
JAY YOUNGBLOOD

DON KERNODLE and RICK McGRAW vs. BRUTE BERNARD and THE SCORPION

BOB MARCUS vs. JOHN TOLOS   CHARLIE FULTON vs. FRANK SEXTON

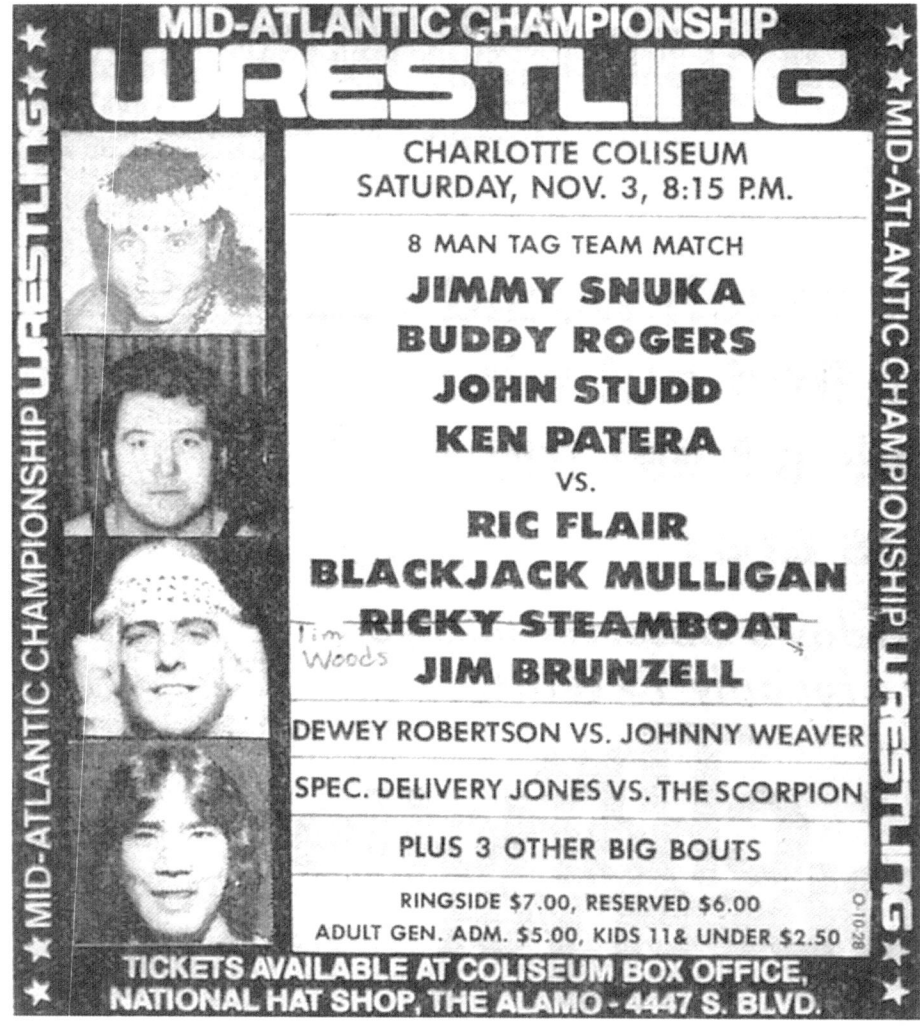

MID-ATLANTIC CHAMPIONSHIP WRESTLING

CHARLOTTE COLISEUM
SATURDAY, NOV. 3, 8:15 P.M.

8 MAN TAG TEAM MATCH

JIMMY SNUKA
BUDDY ROGERS
JOHN STUDD
KEN PATERA

VS.

RIC FLAIR
BLACKJACK MULLIGAN
~~RICKY STEAMBOAT~~ (Tim Woods)
JIM BRUNZELL

DEWEY ROBERTSON VS. JOHNNY WEAVER

SPEC. DELIVERY JONES VS. THE SCORPION

PLUS 3 OTHER BIG BOUTS

RINGSIDE $7.00, RESERVED $6.00
ADULT GEN. ADM. $5.00, KIDS 11 & UNDER $2.50

TICKETS AVAILABLE AT COLISEUM BOX OFFICE, NATIONAL HAT SHOP, THE ALAMO - 4447 S. BLVD.

Pro Wrestling

Blackjack Mulligan, Ric Flair, Tim Woods and Jim Brunzell defeated Jimmy Snuka, Buddy Rodgers, John Studd and Ken Patera in an 8-man tag-team feature at Saturday's Coliseum professional wrestling card.

Mulligan pinned Patera, giving his team the victory. Woods, also known as Mr. Wrestling, replaced Ricky Steamboat, who could not wrestle because of an injury.

In other matches, Johnny Weaver defeated Dewey Robertson on a disqualification; Special Delivery Jones downed the Scorpion; Bob Marcus conquered Jaque Goulet (substituting for John Tolas); Tony Garea downed Doug Sommers and veteran Abe Jacobs defeated David Patterson.

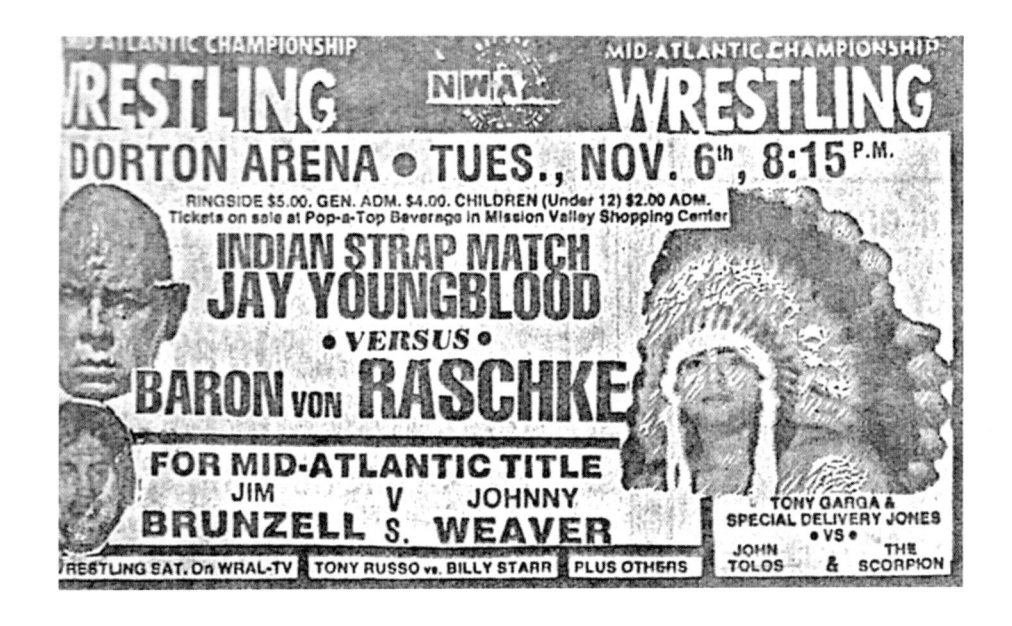

Youngblood, Brunzell win

Jay Youngblood defeated Baron von Raschke and Jim Brunzell beat Johnny Weaver in the main wrestling events here Tuesday night at Dorton Arena.

In other matches, S.D. Jones and Tony Gerea defeated David Patterson and the Scorpion, Billy Starr defeated Tony Russo and Joe Furr defeated John Condroy.

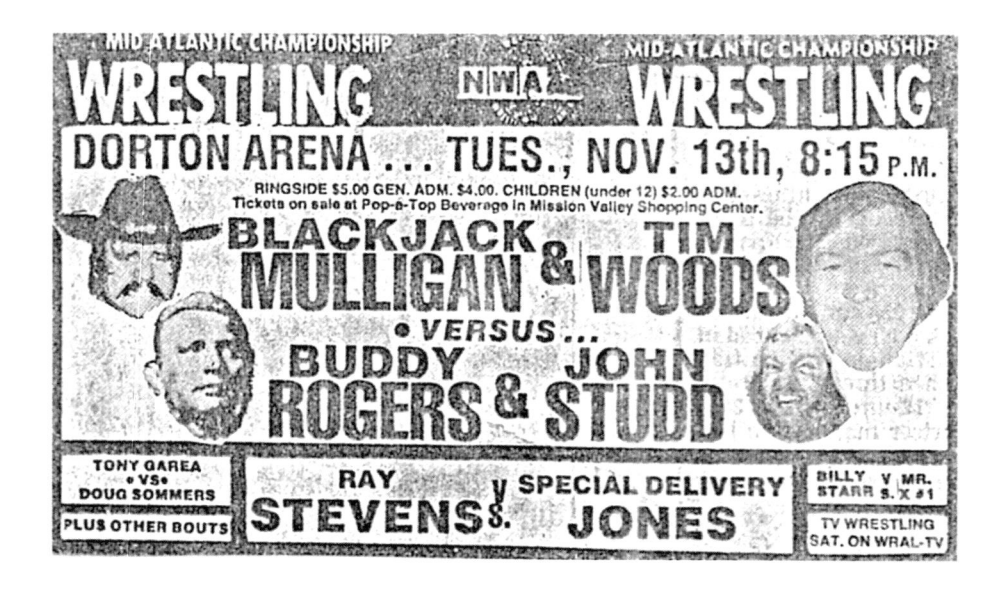

MID-ATLANTIC CHAMPIONSHIP WRESTLING — NWA

DORTON ARENA ... TUES., NOV. 13th, 8:15 P.M.

RINGSIDE $5.00 GEN. ADM. $4.00 CHILDREN (under 12) $2.00 ADM.
Tickets on sale at Pop-a-Top Beverage in Mission Valley Shopping Center.

BLACKJACK MULLIGAN & TIM WOODS
VERSUS...
BUDDY ROGERS & JOHN STUDD

- TONY GAREA vs DOUG SOMMERS
- PLUS OTHER BOUTS
- RAY STEVENS vs SPECIAL DELIVERY JONES
- BILLY STARR vs MR. X #1
- TV WRESTLING SAT. ON WRAL-TV

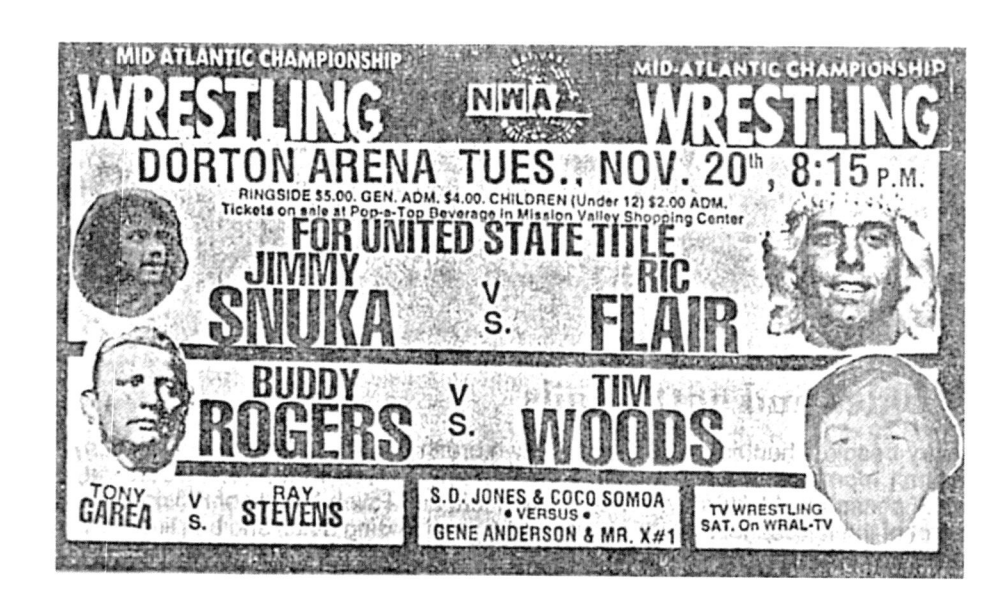

MID-ATLANTIC CHAMPIONSHIP WRESTLING — NWA

DORTON ARENA TUES., NOV. 20th, 8:15 P.M.

RINGSIDE $5.00. GEN. ADM. $4.00. CHILDREN (Under 12) $2.00 ADM.
Tickets on sale at Pop-a-Top Beverage in Mission Valley Shopping Center

FOR UNITED STATES TITLE
JIMMY SNUKA vs. RIC FLAIR

BUDDY ROGERS vs. TIM WOODS

- TONY GAREA vs. RAY STEVENS
- S.D. JONES & COCO SAMOA VERSUS GENE ANDERSON & MR. X #1
- TV WRESTLING SAT. On WRAL-TV

MID-ATLANTIC CHAMPIONSHIP WRESTLING

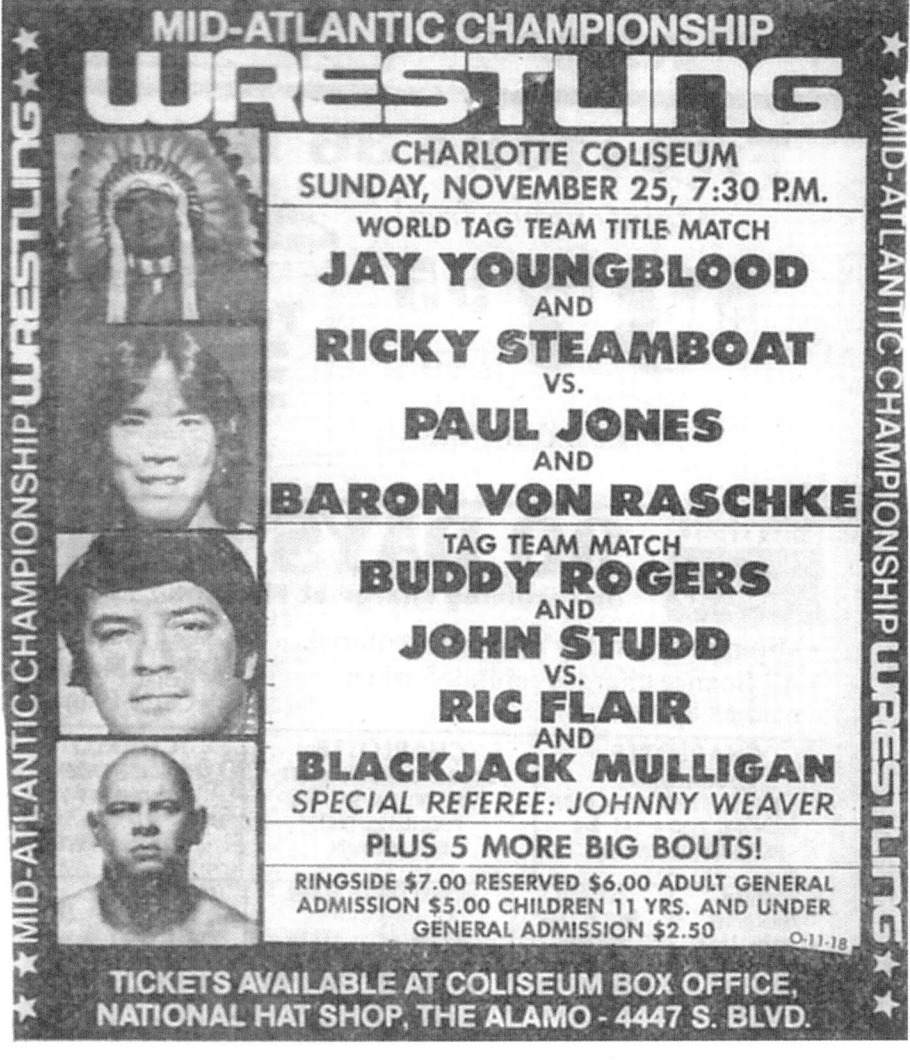

CHARLOTTE COLISEUM
SUNDAY, NOVEMBER 25, 7:30 P.M.

WORLD TAG TEAM TITLE MATCH

JAY YOUNGBLOOD
AND
RICKY STEAMBOAT
VS.
PAUL JONES
AND
BARON VON RASCHKE

TAG TEAM MATCH
BUDDY ROGERS
AND
JOHN STUDD
VS.
RIC FLAIR
AND
BLACKJACK MULLIGAN

SPECIAL REFEREE: JOHNNY WEAVER

PLUS 5 MORE BIG BOUTS!

RINGSIDE $7.00 RESERVED $6.00 ADULT GENERAL ADMISSION $5.00 CHILDREN 11 YRS. AND UNDER GENERAL ADMISSION $2.50

TICKETS AVAILABLE AT COLISEUM BOX OFFICE, NATIONAL HAT SHOP, THE ALAMO - 4447 S. BLVD.

Pro Wrestling Card

Jay Youngblood and Ricky Steamboat defeated Paul Jones and Baron Von Raschke in the professional wrestling feature match at the Coliseum.

The victory allowed Youngblood and Steamboat to retain their tag team championship belts.

Ric Flair and Blackjack Mulligan were also winners, gaining a decision over Buddy Rogers and John Studd. Rogers and Studd left the ring and refused to return.

In other matches, Ray Stevens defeated Special Delivery Jones, Dewey Robinson beat Don Kernodle, Brute Bernard defeated Billy Starr, Gene Anderson beat Abe Jacobs, and Bob Marcus and Mr. X No.1 battled to a draw.

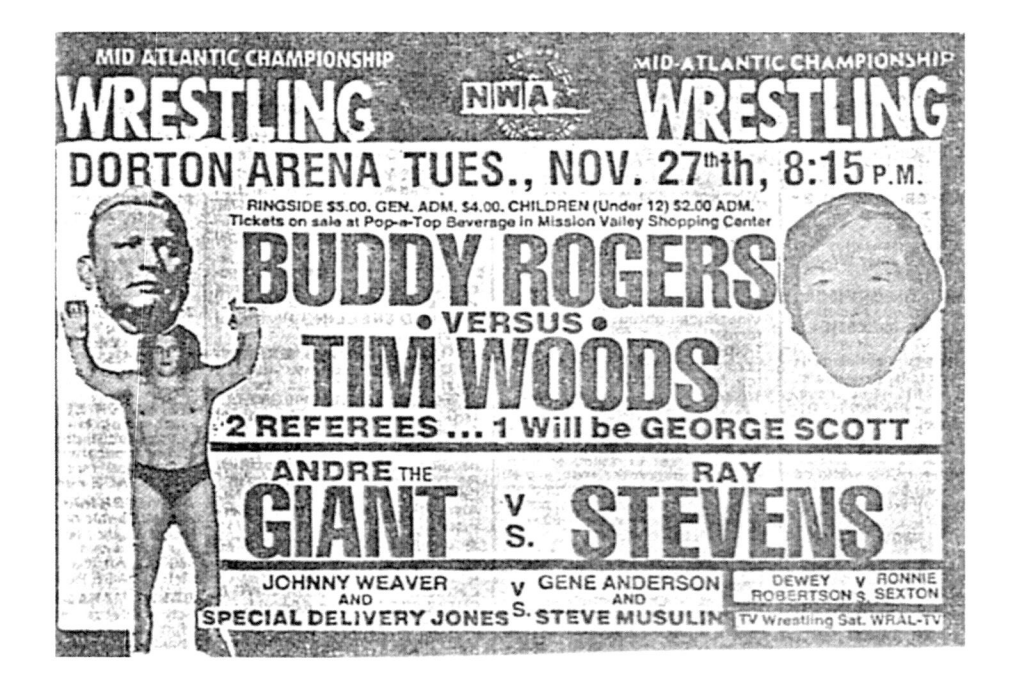

Woods, Andre win

Tim Woods defeated Buddy Rogers and Andre the Giant was the winner over Ray Stevens in the main events Tuesday night in the professional wrestling card at Dorton Arena.

In other matches, Luther Dargon defeated Mr. X and Dewey Robertson beat Ronnie Sexton. Johnny Weaver and S.D. Jones defeated Gene Anderson and Steve Muslin in a tag-team bout.

MID-ATLANTIC CHAMPIONSHIP WRESTLING

CHARLOTTE COLISEUM
SUNDAY, DEC. 9, 7:30 P.M.

2 OUT OF 3 FALL WORLD TAG TEAM TITLE MATCH

PAUL JONES
AND
BARON VON RASCHKE
VERSUS
RICKY STEAMBOAT
AND
JAY YOUNGBLOOD

TEXAS STREET FIGHT
BLACKJACK MULLIGAN
VS.
JOHN STUDD

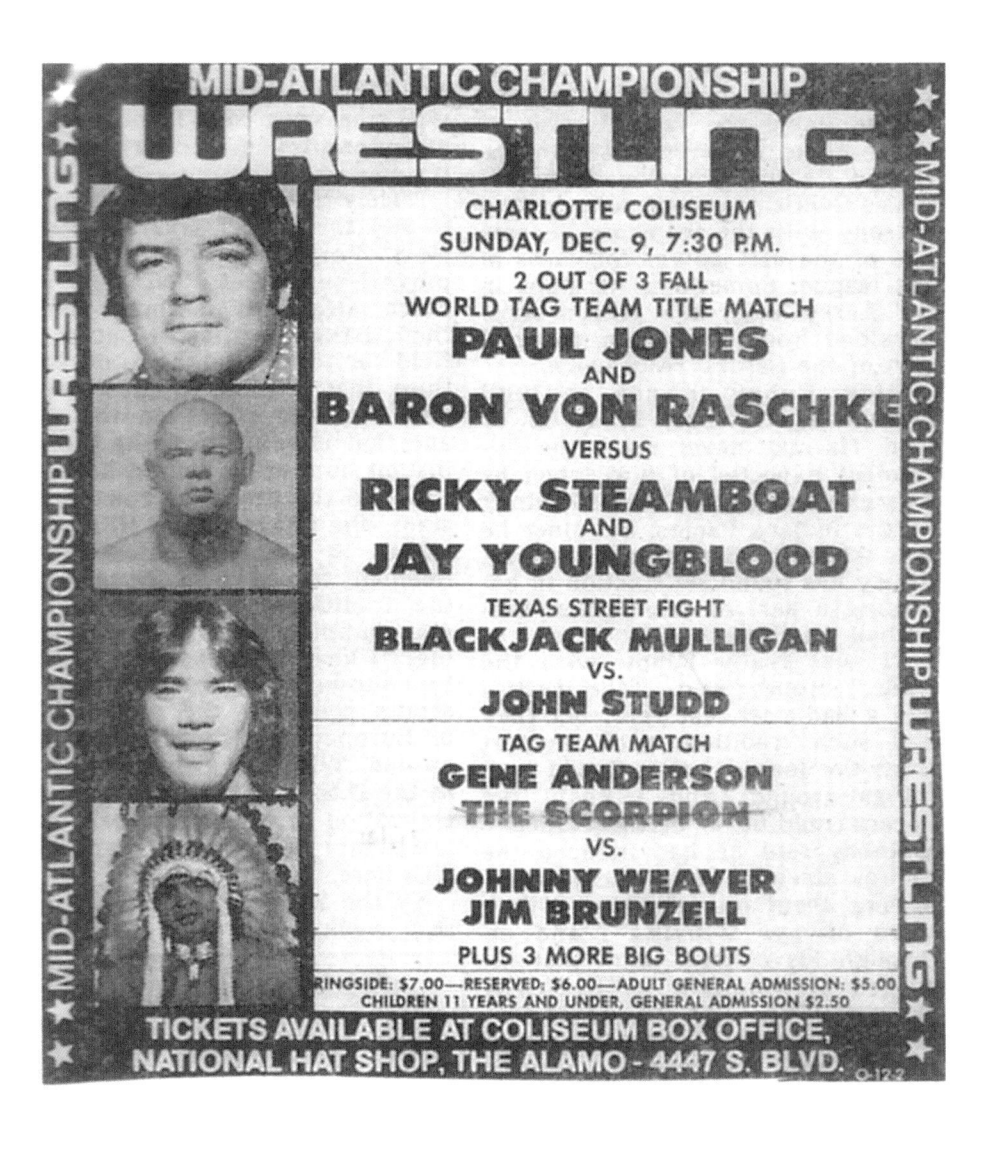

TAG TEAM MATCH
GENE ANDERSON
~~THE SCORPION~~
VS.
JOHNNY WEAVER
JIM BRUNZELL

PLUS 3 MORE BIG BOUTS

RINGSIDE: $7.00 — RESERVED: $6.00 — ADULT GENERAL ADMISSION: $5.00
CHILDREN 11 YEARS AND UNDER, GENERAL ADMISSION $2.50

TICKETS AVAILABLE AT COLISEUM BOX OFFICE, NATIONAL HAT SHOP, THE ALAMO - 4447 S. BLVD.

Professional Wrestling

Jay Youngblood and Ricky Steamboat retained their world championship tag team belts Sunday night on a disqualification of Paul Jones and Baron Von Raschke in the Coliseum.

Jones and Von Raschke won the first fall of the 2-out-of-3 contest. Youngblood and Steamboat rallied, winning the second fall. The disqualification occured in the third fall.

In the Texas street fight, Blackjack Mulligan defeated John Studd.

In other matches, Johnny Weaver and Jim Brunzell defeated Gene Anderson and Steve Muslin; Don Kernodle conquered Doug Sommers; Mr. X No. 1 downed Billy Starr, and Luther Dargan defeated Tony Russo.

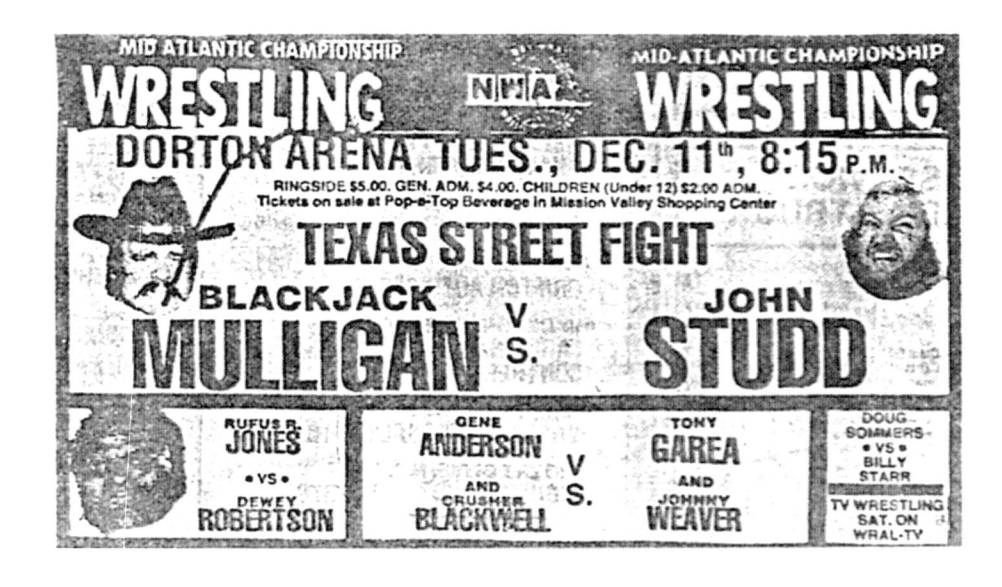

Mulligan wins

Blackjack Mulligan defeated John Studd in a Texas death match, headlining a pro wrestling card at Dorton Arena Tuesday night.

In other matches, Ron Sexton defeated Frank Monte, Billy Starr won a referee's decision over Scott Magee, Rufus R. Jones won by disqualification over Dewey Robertson, and, in a tag team bout, Tony Garea and Johnny Weaver defeated Gene Anderson and Doug Sommers.

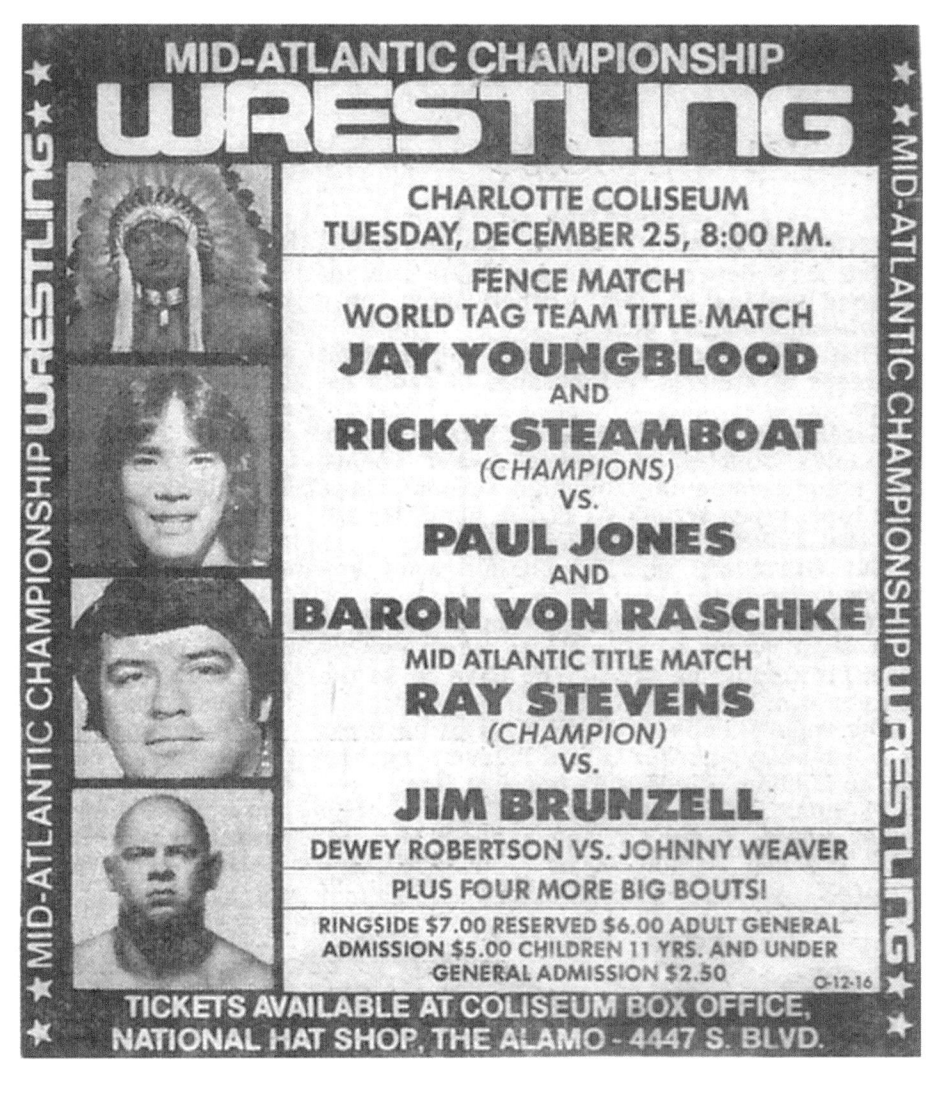

MID-ATLANTIC CHAMPIONSHIP WRESTLING

CHARLOTTE COLISEUM
TUESDAY, DECEMBER 25, 8:00 P.M.

FENCE MATCH
WORLD TAG TEAM TITLE MATCH

JAY YOUNGBLOOD
AND
RICKY STEAMBOAT
(CHAMPIONS)
VS.
PAUL JONES
AND
BARON VON RASCHKE

MID ATLANTIC TITLE MATCH
RAY STEVENS
(CHAMPION)
VS.
JIM BRUNZELL

DEWEY ROBERTSON VS. JOHNNY WEAVER

PLUS FOUR MORE BIG BOUTS!

RINGSIDE $7.00 RESERVED $6.00 ADULT GENERAL ADMISSION $5.00 CHILDREN 11 YRS. AND UNDER GENERAL ADMISSION $2.50

TICKETS AVAILABLE AT COLISEUM BOX OFFICE, NATIONAL HAT SHOP, THE ALAMO - 4447 S. BLVD.

Brunzell Recaptures Mid-Atlantic Crown

Special to The Observer

Jim Brunzell regain the Mid-Atlantic heavyweight title Tuesday night at the Charlotte Coliseum by defeating Ray Stevens before a crowd of 4,500. In the other feature match, Jay Youngblood and Ricky Steamboat retained their tag-team wrestling belts with a victory over Paul Jones and Baron Von Raschke.

In other matches, Johnny Weaver defeated Dewey Robertson by throwing him out of the ring; Special Delivery Jones and Tony Garea beat Frankie Lane and Sgt. Jacques Goulet; Mr. X No. 1 and Doug Summers downed Cocoa Samoa and Abe Jacobs; Luther Dargin stopped Charlie Fulton; Bob Marcus beat Frank Monte.

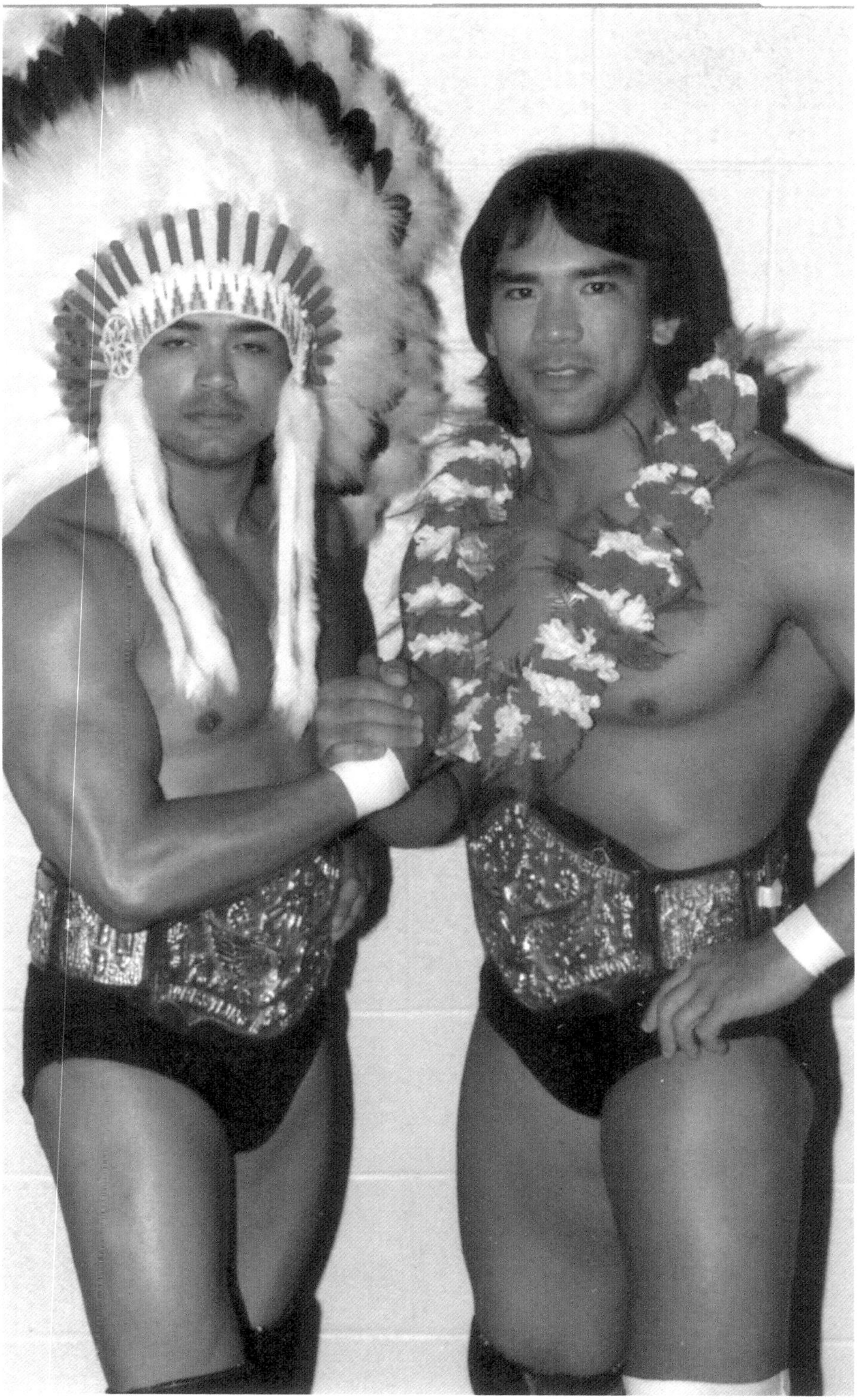

1980

Ads & Results from

Charlotte Coliseum
Dorton Arena
Greensboro Coliseum
Raleigh Civic Center
Winston Salem Memorial Coliseum
Asheville Civic Center
Winston Salem Ernie Shore Field
Gurley Stadium
Scope Coliseum
Cumberland County Memorial Arena
Newton-Conover High School

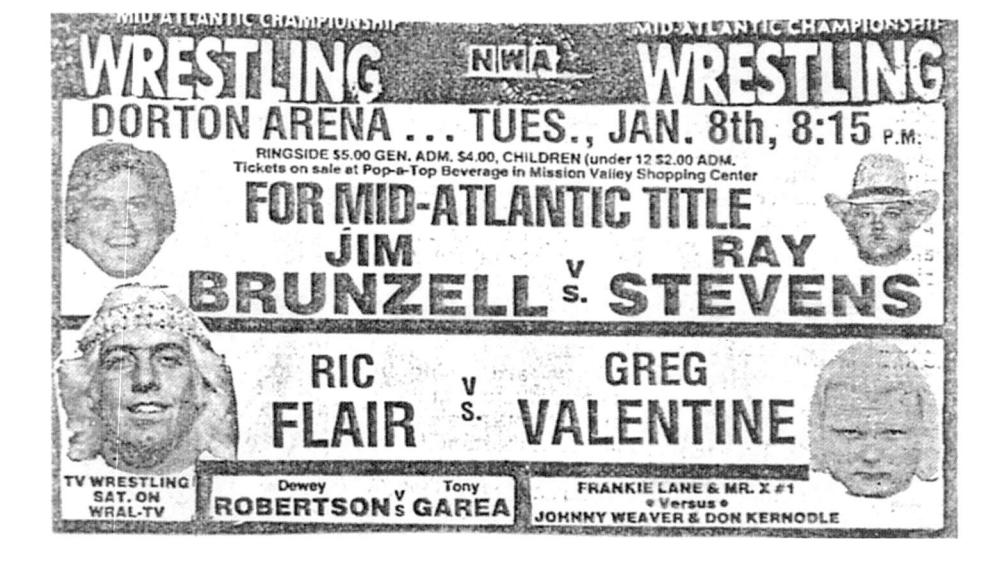

MID-ATLANTIC CHAMPIONSHIP WRESTLING
NWA
MID-ATLANTIC CHAMPIONSHIP WRESTLING

DORTON ARENA ... TUES., JAN. 8th, 8:15 P.M.

RINGSIDE $5.00 GEN. ADM. $4.00, CHILDREN (under 12) $2.00 ADM.
Tickets on sale at Pop-a-Top Beverage in Mission Valley Shopping Center

FOR MID-ATLANTIC TITLE
JIM BRUNZELL vs. RAY STEVENS

RIC FLAIR vs. GREG VALENTINE

TV WRESTLING SAT. ON WRAL-TV

Dewey ROBERTSON vs. Tony GAREA

FRANKIE LANE & MR. X #1
• Versus •
JOHNNY WEAVER & DON KERNODLE

MID-ATLANTIC CHAMPIONSHIP WRESTLING

CHARLOTTE COLISEUM
SUNDAY, JAN. 20, 2:00 P.M.

SUPER BOWL SPECIAL!
3 MAIN EVENTS

U.S. TITLE MATCH
JIMMY SNUKA
VS.
TIM WOODS

MID-ATLANTIC TITLE RETURN
JIM BRUNZELL
VS.
RAY STEVENS

TAG TEAM MATCH
GREG VALENTINE
AND
JOHN STUDD
VS.
RIC FLAIR
AND
BLACKJACK MULLIGAN

PLUS FOUR MORE BIG BOUTS!

RINGSIDE-$7.00 RESERVED-$6.00 ADULT GEN. ADM.
$5.00 CHILDREN 11 YRS. & UNDER GEN. ADM. $2.50

TICKETS AVAILABLE AT COLISEUM BOX OFFICE,
NATIONAL HAT SHOP, THE ALAMO - 4447 S. BLVD.

Pro Wrestling

Jimmy Snuka pinned Tim Woods 24 minutes into their match Sunday and retained his U.S. heavyweight pro wrestling championship. Snuka won in the feature match of a program at the Coliseum.

Jim Brunzell retained his Mid-Atlantic championship when Ray Stevens was disqualified for throwing Brunzell over the top rope.

In tag-team matches, Ric Flair and Blackjack Mulligan defeated John Studd and Greg Valentine, and Rufus R. Jones and Special Delivery Jones beat Doug Sommers and Frankie Lane.

In other matches, Johnny Weaver defeated Bob Marcus, Dewey Robertson beat Tony Garea, and Pedro Morales defeated Mr. X No. 1.

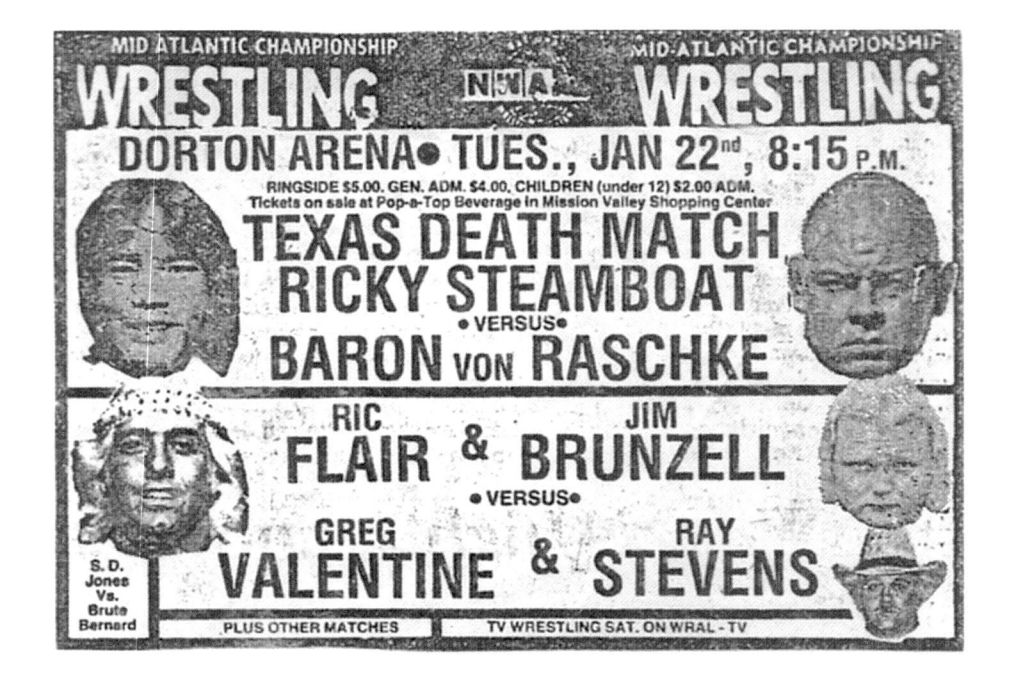

MID-ATLANTIC CHAMPIONSHIP WRESTLING — NWA — **MID-ATLANTIC CHAMPIONSHIP WRESTLING**

DORTON ARENA • TUES., JAN 22nd, 8:15 P.M.

RINGSIDE $5.00, GEN. ADM. $4.00, CHILDREN (under 12) $2.00 ADM.
Tickets on sale at Pop-a-Top Beverage in Mission Valley Shopping Center

TEXAS DEATH MATCH
RICKY STEAMBOAT
• VERSUS •
BARON von RASCHKE

RIC FLAIR & JIM BRUNZELL
• VERSUS •
GREG VALENTINE & RAY STEVENS

S.D. Jones Vs. Brute Bernard

PLUS OTHER MATCHES — TV WRESTLING SAT. ON WRAL-TV

Steamboat wins death match

Ricky Steamboat defeated Baron Van Raschke in a Texas death match and, in a tag-team bout, all four participants were disqualified in a professional wrestling card at Dorton Arena Tuesday night.

Teams of Ric Flair and Jim Brunzel and Ray Stevens and Greg Valentine were involved in the abortive tag-team bout.

In other matches, Coco Somoa defeated Frank Monte, Bob Mercers won over Mr. X No. 1, Frankie Lane defeated Rick McGraw, and Special Delivery Jones won over Brute Bernard.

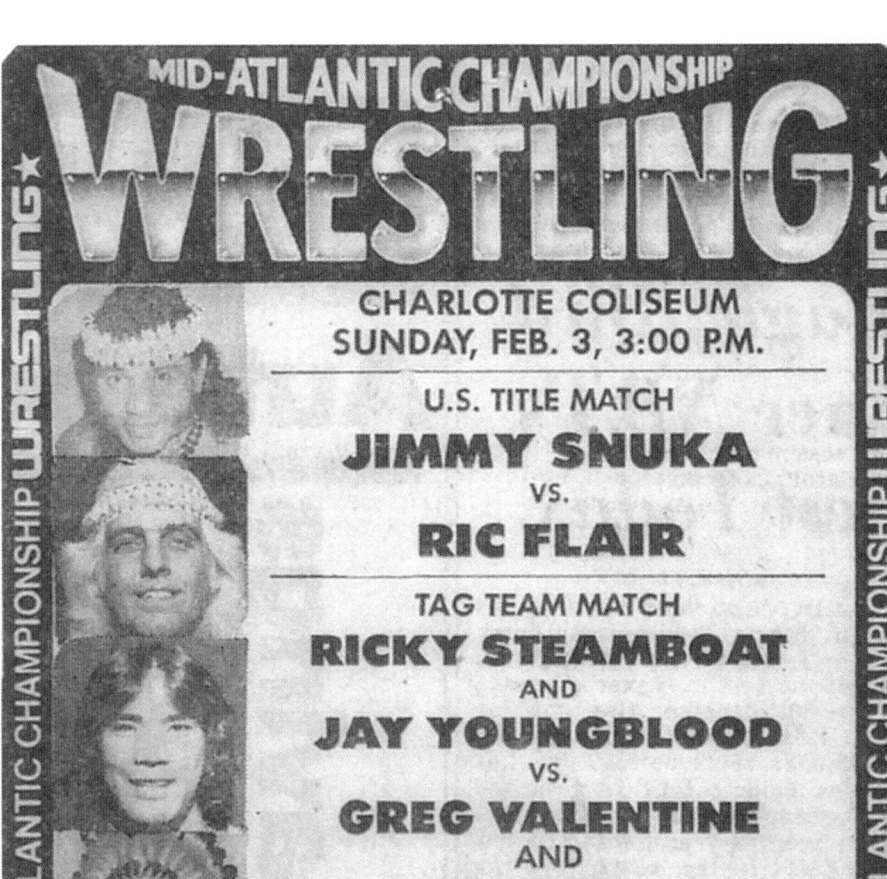

MID-ATLANTIC CHAMPIONSHIP WRESTLING

CHARLOTTE COLISEUM
SUNDAY, FEB. 3, 3:00 P.M.

U.S. TITLE MATCH
JIMMY SNUKA
vs.
RIC FLAIR

TAG TEAM MATCH
RICKY STEAMBOAT
AND
JAY YOUNGBLOOD
vs.
GREG VALENTINE
AND
RAY STEVENS

PLUS 5 OTHER BIG MATCHES

TICKETS AVAILABLE AT COLISEUM BOX OFFICE
NATIONAL HAT SHOP, THE ALAMO - 4447 S. BLVD.

Flair Disqualified

Ric Flair was disqualified Sunday against Jimmy Snuka in a match for the U.S. title in the Charlotte Coliseum. Flair was sanctioned for harassing the referee and the belt does not change hands on a disqualification.

In other action, Greg Valentine and Ray Stevens defeated Ricky Steamboat and Jay Youngblood in a nontitle tag-team match; Rufus R. Jones and Jim Brunzell downed Baron Von Raschke and Paul Jones; Ox Baker conquered Ronnie Saxton; Matt Born battled to a draw with Rick McGraw; and Toney Garea beat the Scorpion.

In an added attraction on the card, the Fabulous Moolah topped Vivian St. John in a women's match.

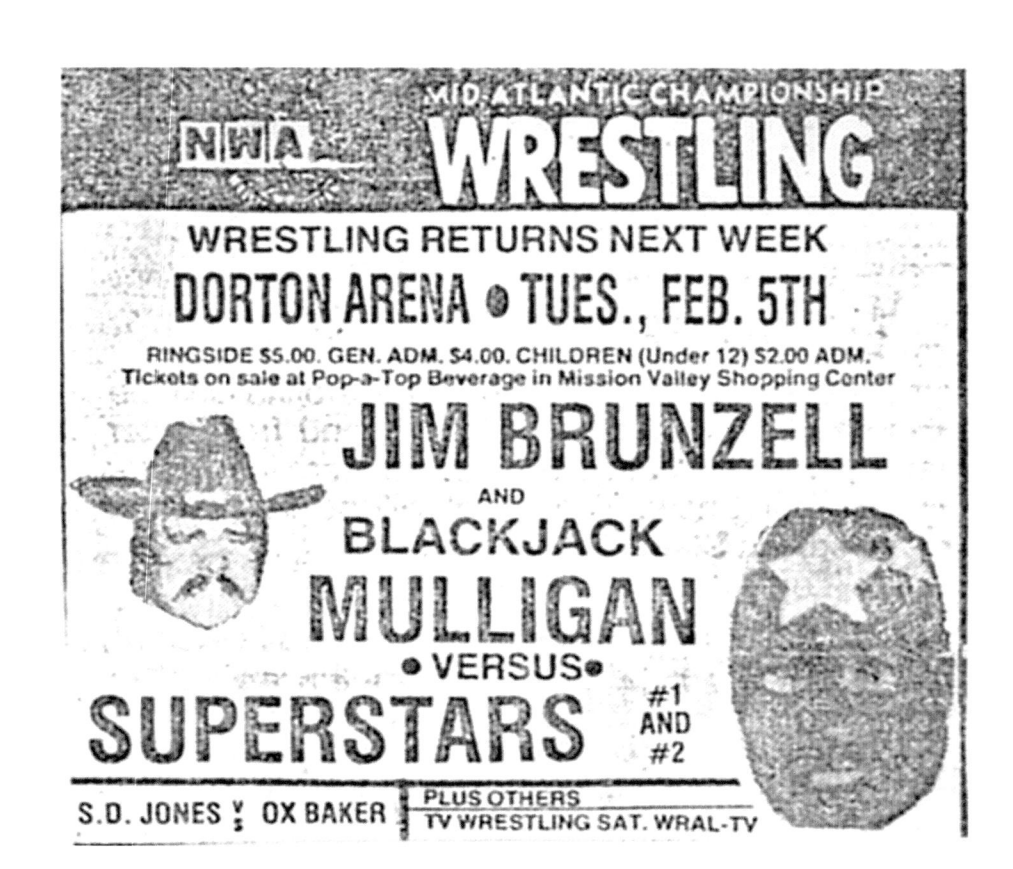

NWA MID ATLANTIC CHAMPIONSHIP WRESTLING

WRESTLING RETURNS NEXT WEEK

DORTON ARENA • TUES., FEB. 5TH

RINGSIDE $5.00. GEN. ADM. $4.00. CHILDREN (Under 12) $2.00 ADM.
Tickets on sale at Pop-a-Top Beverage in Mission Valley Shopping Center

JIM BRUNZELL
AND
BLACKJACK MULLIGAN
• VERSUS •
SUPERSTARS #1 AND #2

S.D. JONES vs. OX BAKER | PLUS OTHERS
TV WRESTLING SAT. WRAL-TV

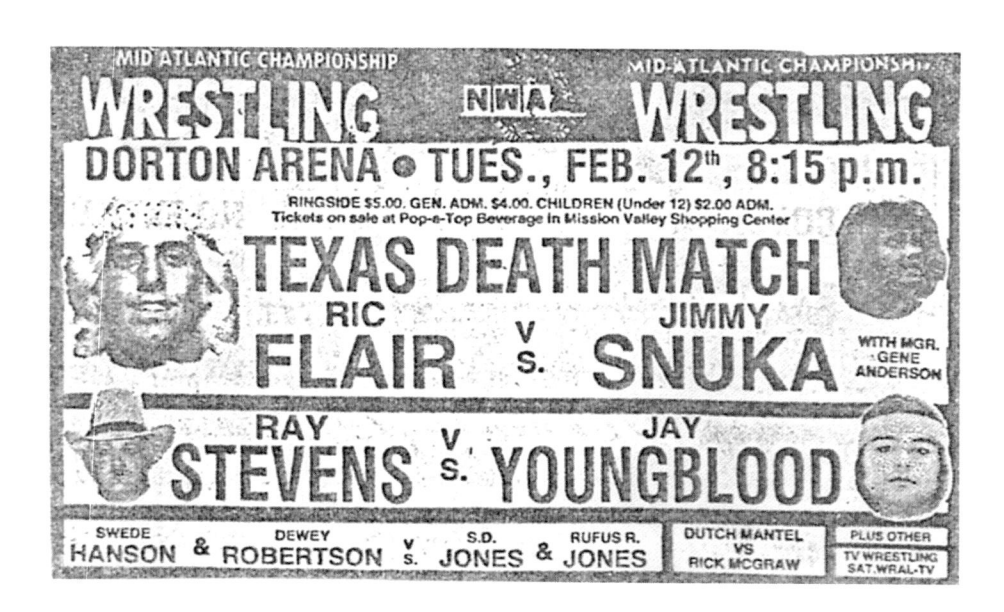

MID ATLANTIC CHAMPIONSHIP WRESTLING — NWA — WRESTLING

DORTON ARENA • TUES., FEB. 12th, 8:15 p.m.

RINGSIDE $5.00. GEN. ADM. $4.00. CHILDREN (Under 12) $2.00 ADM.
Tickets on sale at Pop-a-Top Beverage in Mission Valley Shopping Center

TEXAS DEATH MATCH
RIC FLAIR vs. JIMMY SNUKA
WITH MGR. GENE ANDERSON

RAY STEVENS vs. JAY YOUNGBLOOD

| SWEDE HANSON & DEWEY ROBERTSON vs. S.D. JONES & RUFUS R. JONES | DUTCH MANTEL vs. RICK McGRAW | PLUS OTHER TV WRESTLING SAT. WRAL-TV |

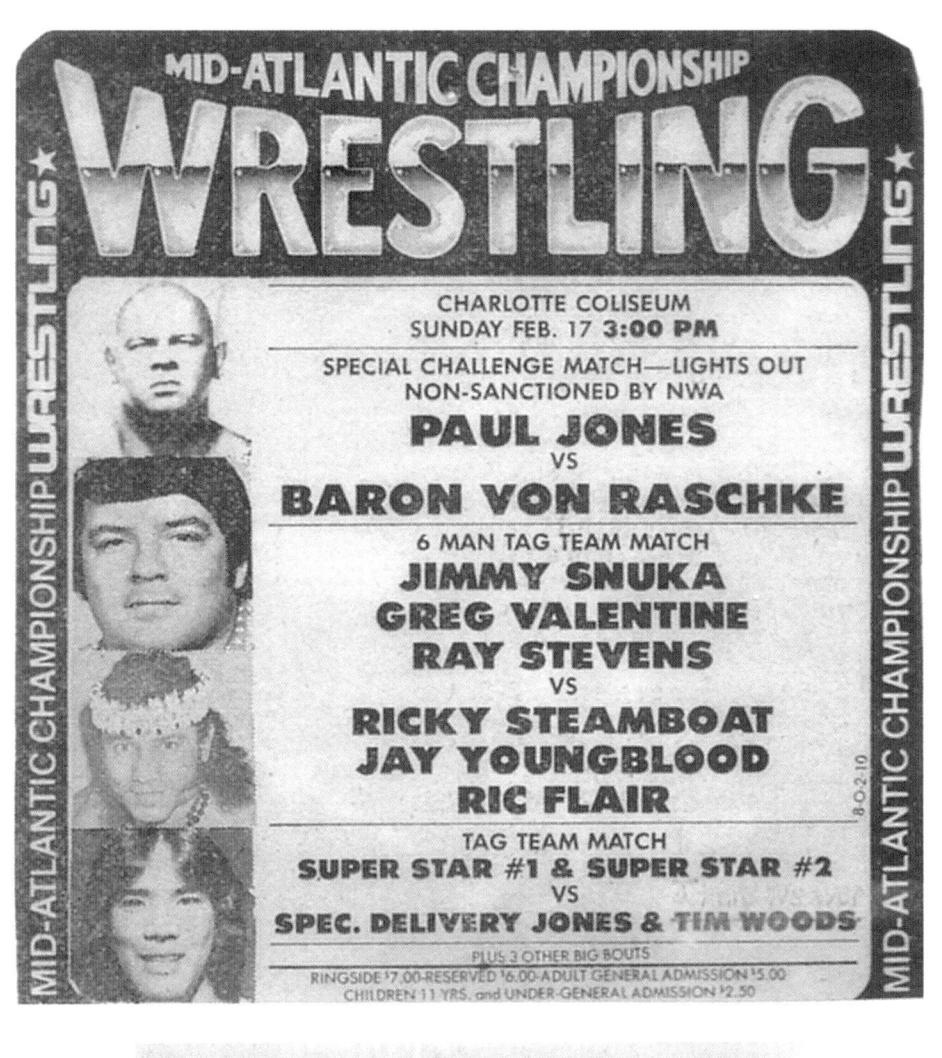

MID-ATLANTIC CHAMPIONSHIP WRESTLING

CHARLOTTE COLISEUM
SUNDAY FEB. 17 3:00 PM

SPECIAL CHALLENGE MATCH—LIGHTS OUT
NON-SANCTIONED BY NWA

PAUL JONES
vs
BARON VON RASCHKE

6 MAN TAG TEAM MATCH

JIMMY SNUKA
GREG VALENTINE
RAY STEVENS
vs
RICKY STEAMBOAT
JAY YOUNGBLOOD
RIC FLAIR

TAG TEAM MATCH
SUPER STAR #1 & SUPER STAR #2
vs
SPEC. DELIVERY JONES & TIM WOODS

PLUS 3 OTHER BIG BOUTS

RINGSIDE $7.00-RESERVED $6.00-ADULT GENERAL ADMISSION $5.00
CHILDREN 11 YRS. and UNDER-GENERAL ADMISSION $2.50

Von Raschke Triumphs

Baron Von Raschke defeated Paul Jones in a lights-out, nonsanctioned bout on the Mid-Atlantic Championship Wrestling card at the Coliseum.

In the other main event, the tag team of Jimmy Snuka, Greg Valentine and Ray Stevens won by disqualification over Ricky Steamboat, Jay Youngblood and Ric Flair.

Superstar No. 1 and Superstar No. 2 stopped Special Delivery Jones and Johnny Weaver in the day's other tag team match.

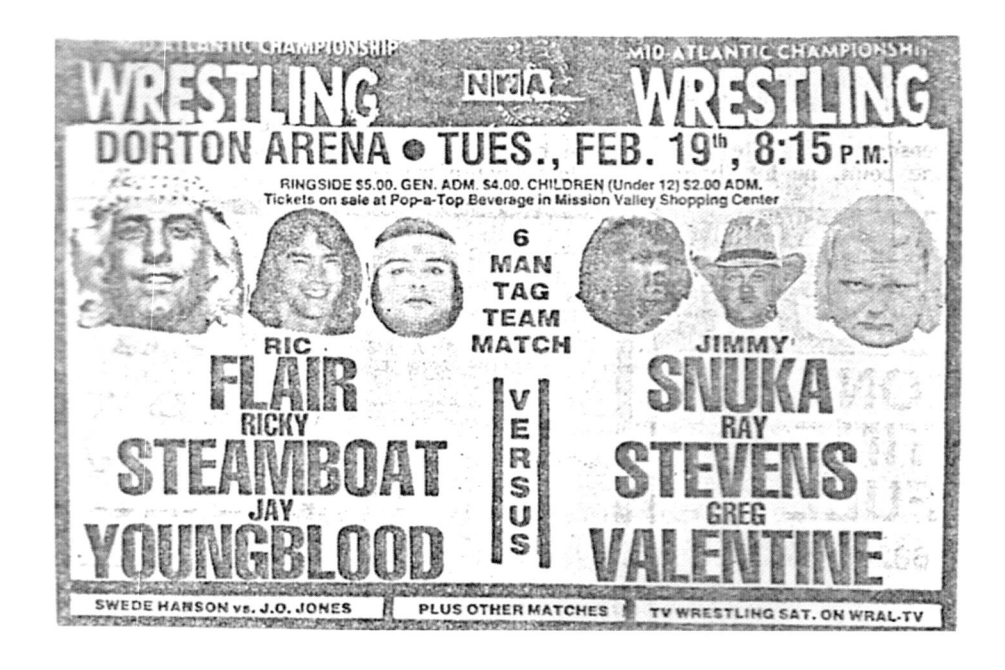

Flair team wins

Ric Flair, Ricky Steamboat and Jay Youngblood defeated Ray Stevens, Greg Valentine and Jimmy Snuka in a six-man tag-team match in the main event on the professional wrestling card Tuesday night at Dorton Arena.

In other matches, Matt Borne defeated Tony Russo, Bob Marcus defeated Billy Starr, Dewey Robertson defeated Ronnie Sexton and S.D. Jones defeated Swede Hanson.

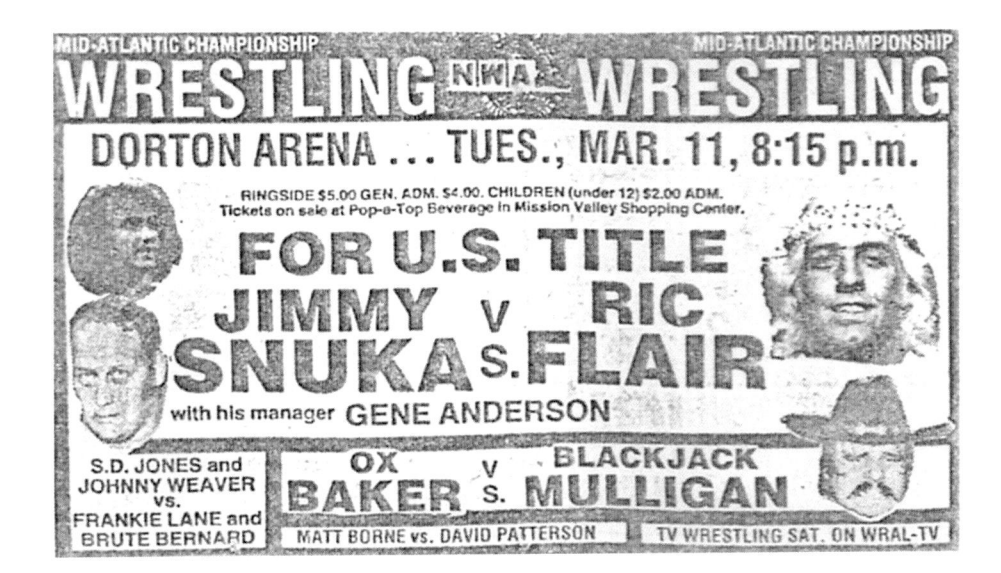

MID-ATLANTIC CHAMPIONSHIP WRESTLING — NWA — WRESTLING

DORTON ARENA ... TUES., MAR. 11, 8:15 p.m.

RINGSIDE $5.00 GEN. ADM. $4.00. CHILDREN (under 12) $2.00 ADM.
Tickets on sale at Pop-a-Top Beverage in Mission Valley Shopping Center.

FOR U.S. TITLE
JIMMY SNUKA vs. **RIC FLAIR**
with his manager GENE ANDERSON

S.D. JONES and JOHNNY WEAVER vs. FRANKIE LANE and BRUTE BERNARD

OX BAKER vs. **BLACKJACK MULLIGAN**

MATT BORNE vs. DAVID PATTERSON

TV WRESTLING SAT. ON WRAL-TV

Snuka keeps title

Jimmy Snuka defeated Rick Flair Tuesday night in Dorton Arena to keep the U.S. wrestling title.

In other matches, Blackjack Mulligan clubbed Ox Baker, Doug Sommers pinned Ron Sexton, Matt Borne bounced David Patterson, and in tag team, S.D. Jones and Johnny Weaver sewed up Brute Bernard and Frankie Lane.

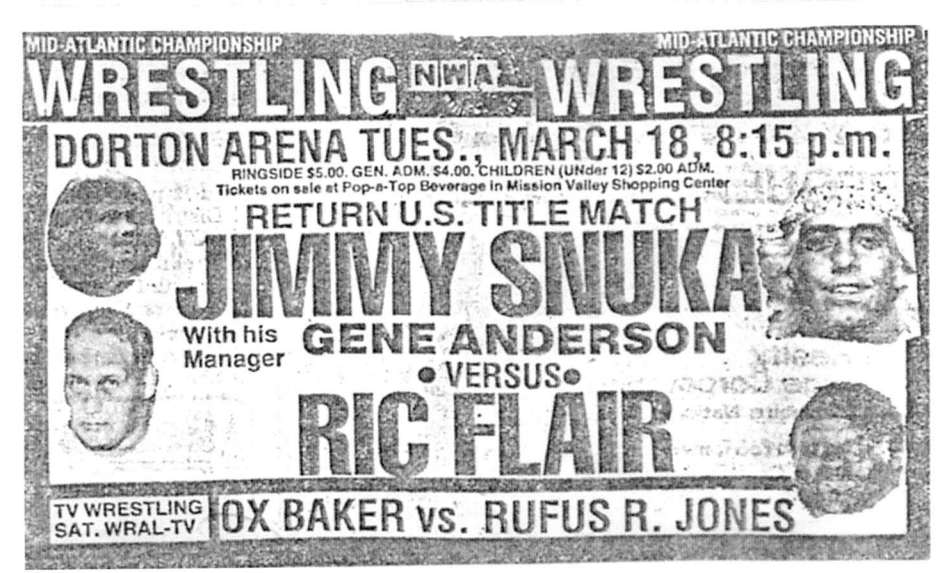

MID-ATLANTIC CHAMPIONSHIP WRESTLING — NWA — WRESTLING

DORTON ARENA TUES., MARCH 18, 8:15 p.m.

RINGSIDE $5.00 GEN. ADM. $4.00. CHILDREN (UNder 12) $2.00 ADM.
Tickets on sale at Pop-a-Top Beverage in Mission Valley Shopping Center

RETURN U.S. TITLE MATCH
JIMMY SNUKA
With his Manager GENE ANDERSON
•VERSUS•
RIC FLAIR

TV WRESTLING SAT. WRAL-TV

OX BAKER vs. RUFUS R. JONES

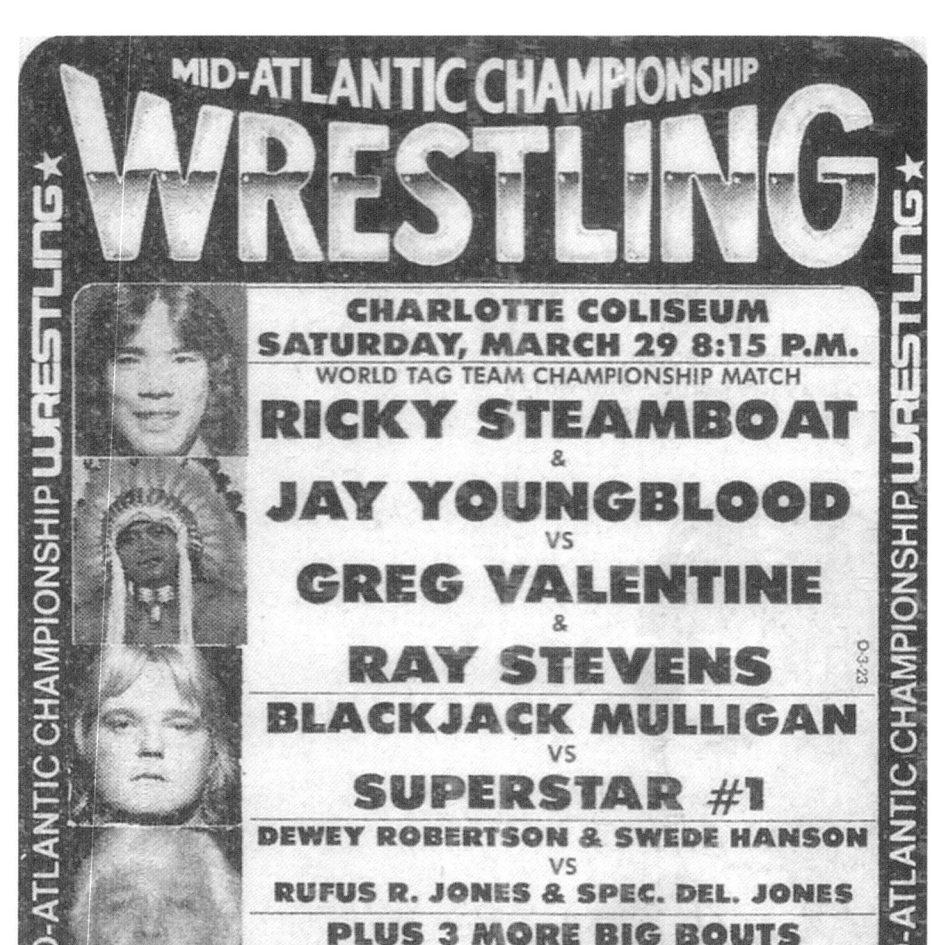

MID-ATLANTIC CHAMPIONSHIP WRESTLING

CHARLOTTE COLISEUM
SATURDAY, MARCH 29 8:15 P.M.

WORLD TAG TEAM CHAMPIONSHIP MATCH

RICKY STEAMBOAT
&
JAY YOUNGBLOOD
vs
GREG VALENTINE
&
RAY STEVENS

BLACKJACK MULLIGAN
vs
SUPERSTAR #1

DEWEY ROBERTSON & SWEDE HANSON
vs
RUFUS R. JONES & SPEC. DEL. JONES

PLUS 3 MORE BIG BOUTS

RINGSIDE: $7.00 — RESERVED: $6.00 — ADULT GENERAL ADMISSION: $5.00
CHILDREN 11 YEARS AND UNDER, GENERAL ADMISSION $2.50

TICKETS AVAILABLE AT COLISEUM BOX OFFICE,
NATIONAL HAT SHOP, THE ALAMO - 4447 S. BLVD.

Valentine, Stevens Win Tag Team Title

Observer Staff Reports

Greg Valentine and Ray Stevens captured the world tag team title with a victory Saturday night over Ricky Steamboat and Jay Youngblood in professional wrestling at the Coliseum.

Superstar No. 1 was disqualified in his battle with Blackjack Mulligan in the second featured event.

In other matches:

Rufus R. Jones and Special Delivery Jones conquered Dewey Robertson and Swede Hanson; Superstar No. 2 beat Johnny Weaver; Matt Borne and Tony Garea drew; and Frankie Lane defeated Ronnie Sexton.

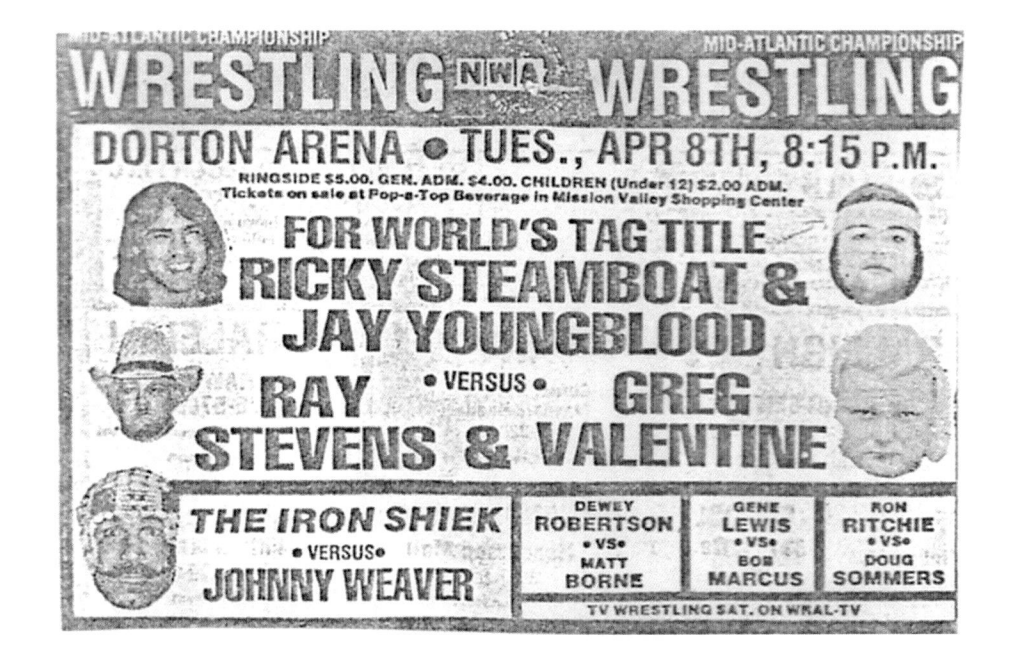

Stevens, Valentine win

In the main event of professional wrestling at Dorton Arena Tuesday night, Ray Stevens and Greg Valentine retained the world's tag-team title by defeating Ricky Steamboat and Jay Youngblood.

Ron Ritchie and Doug Sommers fought to a draw in the opening event, while Gene Lewis defeated Bob Marcus in the second fight. Matt Borne won by disqualification in his match with Dewey Robertson and the Iron Shiek defeated Johnny Weaver.

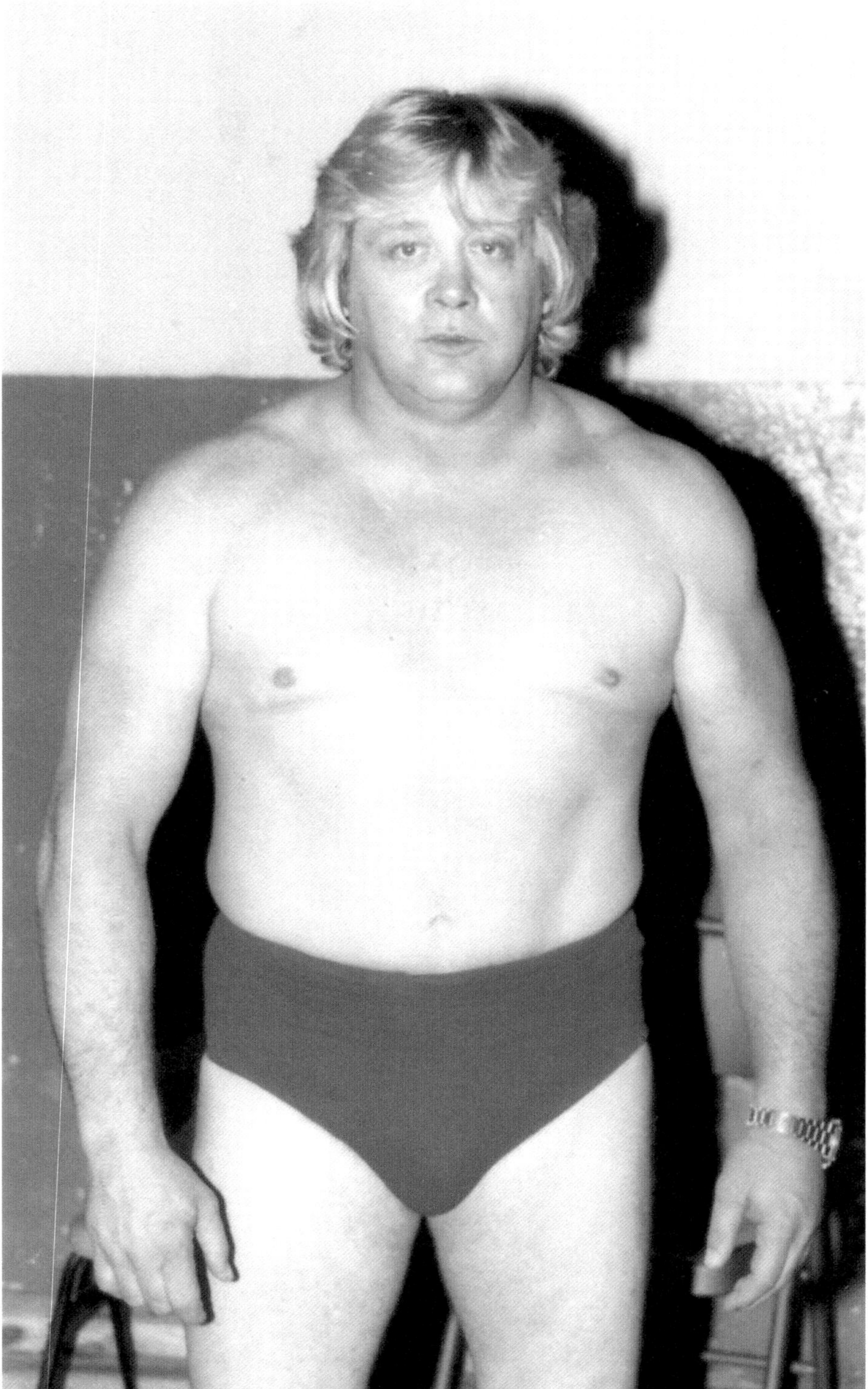

MID-ATLANTIC CHAMPIONSHIP WRESTLING

CHARLOTTE COLISEUM
SUNDAY, APRIL 13   8:00 P.M.

WORLD TAG TEAM TITLE MATCH

RAY STEVENS CHMP.
&
GREG VALENTINE CHMP.
VS
JAY YOUNGBLOOD
&
RICKY STEAMBOAT

TAG TEAM MATCH
SUPERSTAR #1 & SUPERSTAR #2
VS
BLACKJACK MULLIGAN & RICK FLAIR

JIM BRUNZELL
VS
SWEDE HANSON

PLUS 3 MORE BIG BOUTS!

RINGSIDE—$7.00—GEN. ADMISSION $5.50
CHILDREN UNDER 10 YEARS OLD—$2.50 GEN. ADM. ONLY

TICKETS AVAILABLE AT COLISEUM BOX OFFICE,
NATIONAL HAT SHOP, THE ALAMO - 4447 S. BLVD.

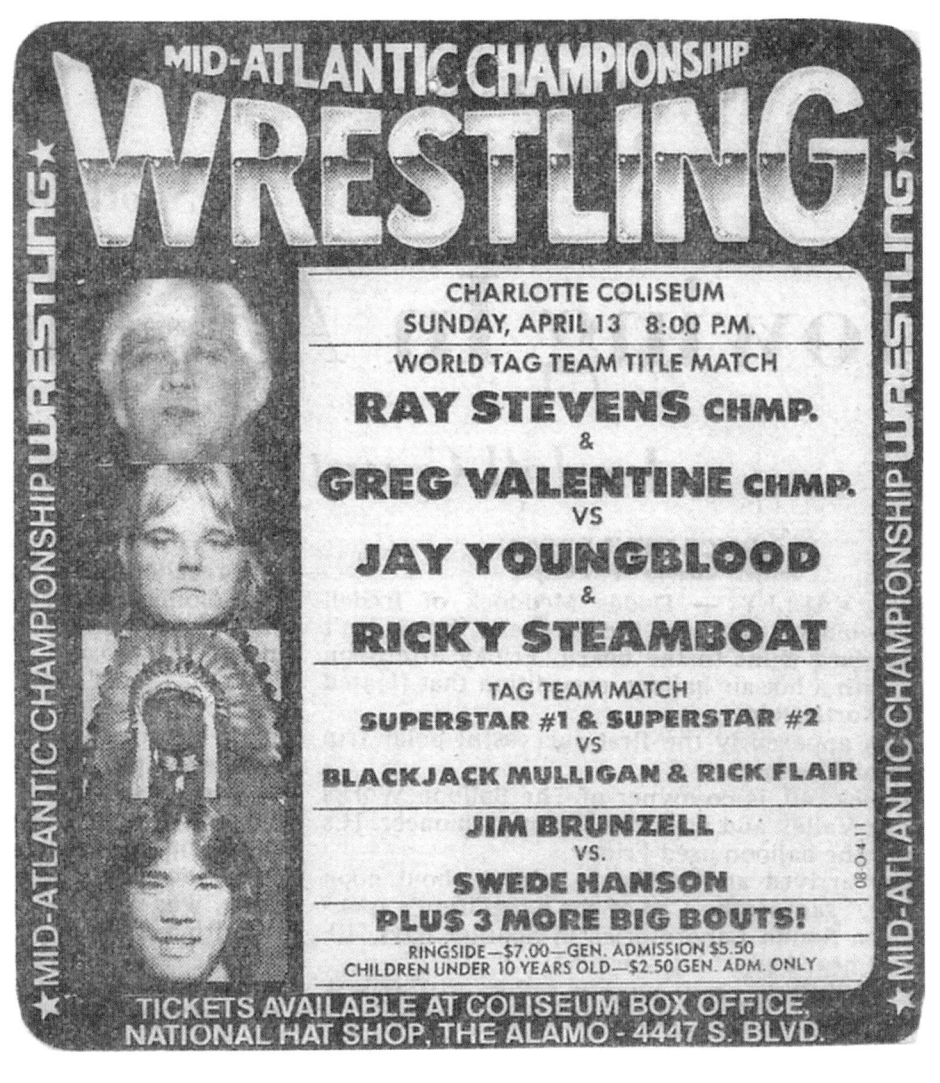

Valentine, Stevens Retain Team Title

Ray Stevens and Greg Valentine retained the world tag team title Sunday with a victory over Ricky Steamboat and Jay Youngblood at the Charlotte Coliseum.

Blackjack Mulligan and Ric Flair defeated Superstars No. 1 and No. 2 in the other main event.

In other matches: Jim Brunzell defeated Swede Hansen; Brute Bernard won over Bob Marcus; Special Delivery Jones defeated Billy Starr; and Buzz Sawyer defeated Coco Samoa.

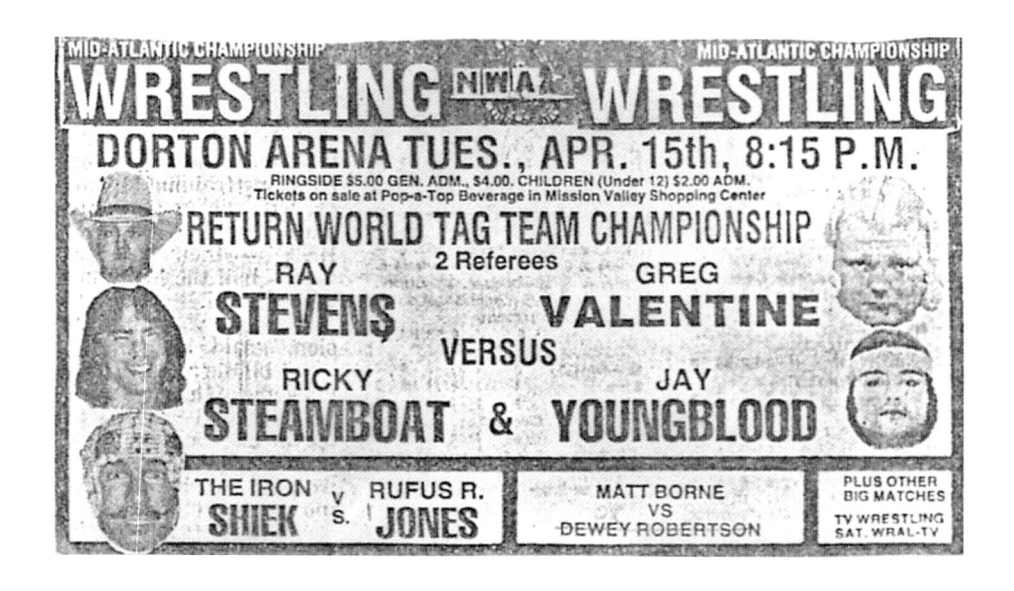

Pro wrestling draw

Ray Stevens and Greg Valentine battled to a one-hour draw with Ricky Steamboat and Jay Youngblood in the main wrestling event at Dorton Arena Tuesday night.

In singles action, Abe Jacobs tamed Tony Russo, Buzz Sawyer conquered Frankie Lane and The Iron Sheik defeated Rufus Jones. Matt Borne won by disqualification over Ox Baker.

MID-ATLANTIC CHAMPIONSHIP WRESTLING

CHARLOTTE COLISEUM
SUNDAY, APRIL 27, 8:00 P.M.

WORLD TAG TEAM TITLE MATCH
TWO REFEREES

GREG VALENTINE
&
RAY STEVENS
vs.
JAY YOUNGBLOOD
&
RICKY STEAMBOAT

BLACKJACK MULLIGAN
vs.
SUPERSTAR #2
(SUPERSTAR #1 IN CAGE)

OX BAKER VS. RUFUS R. JONES

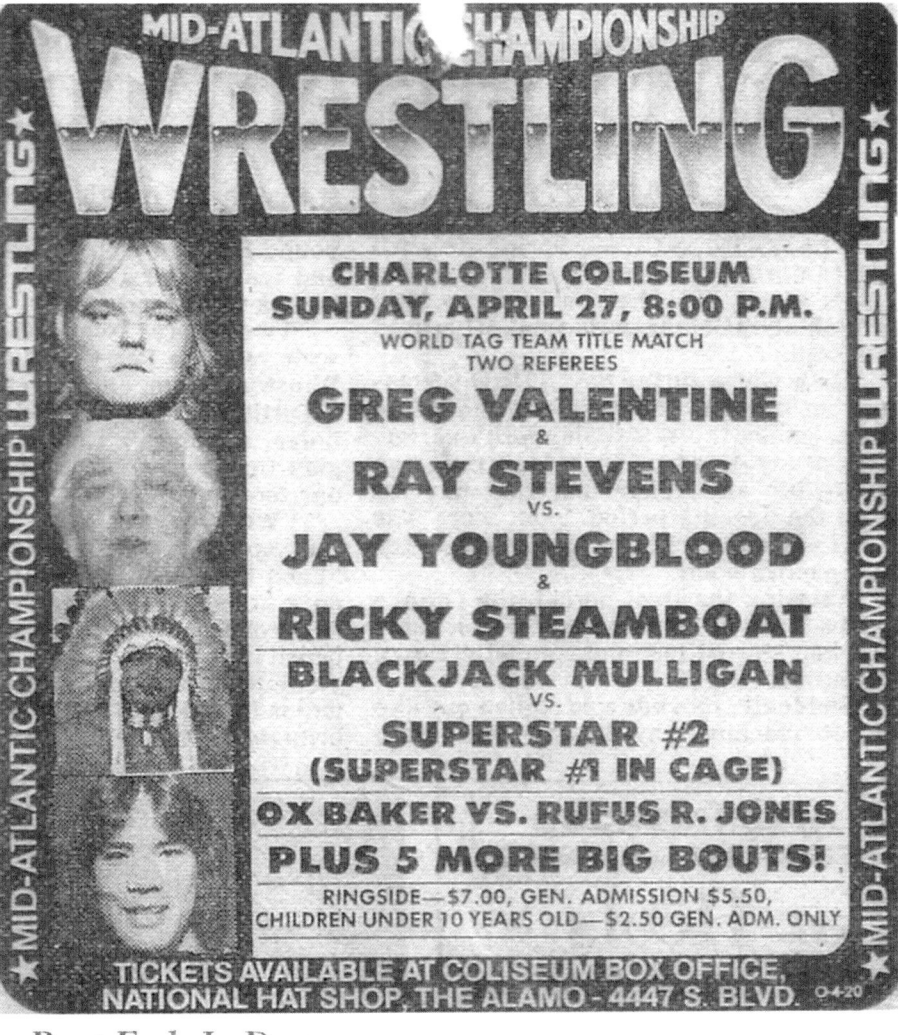

PLUS 5 MORE BIG BOUTS!

RINGSIDE—$7.00, GEN. ADMISSION $5.50,
CHILDREN UNDER 10 YEARS OLD—$2.50 GEN. ADM. ONLY

TICKETS AVAILABLE AT COLISEUM BOX OFFICE,
NATIONAL HAT SHOP, THE ALAMO - 4447 S. BLVD.

Bout Ends In Draw

The world tag team title bout between Greg Valentine and Ray Stevens and the team of Ricky Steamboat and Jay Youngblood ended in an hour draw Sunday at the Charlotte Coliseum.

Blackjack Mulligan defeated Superstar No. 2 and Rufus R. Jones won over Ox Baker.

In other matches: Matt Borne defeated Frankie Lane; Gene Lewis rolled over Abe Jacobs; Buzz Sawyer downed Rick McGraw; Don Kernodle topped Doug Sommers and Ronnie Sexton beat Tony Russo.

Wrestling Mystery

When Blackjack Mulligan unmasked Superstar No. 2 in a hectic pro wrestling clash Sunday at the Coliseum, the crowd buzzed excitedly and then became hushed. They were perplexed because the formerly hooded figure turned out to be a stranger. Who'd they expect: Jimmy Carter? ...

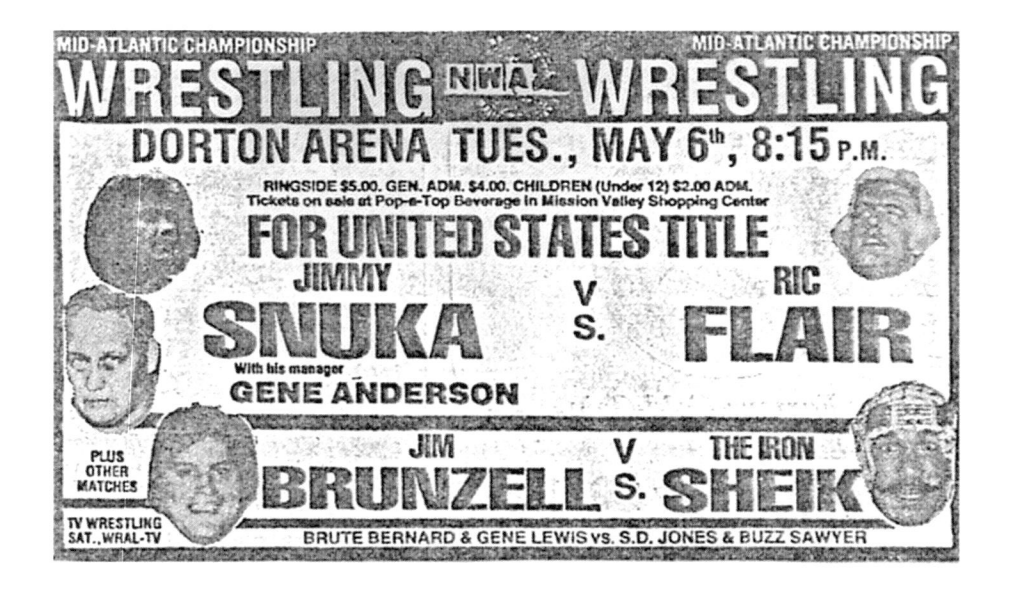

MID-ATLANTIC CHAMPIONSHIP WRESTLING NWA WRESTLING

DORTON ARENA TUES., MAY 6th, 8:15 P.M.

RINGSIDE $5.00. GEN. ADM. $4.00. CHILDREN (Under 12) $2.00 ADM.
Tickets on sale at Pop-a-Top Beverage in Mission Valley Shopping Center

FOR UNITED STATES TITLE

JIMMY SNUKA vs. **RIC FLAIR**

With his manager GENE ANDERSON

JIM BRUNZELL vs. **THE IRON SHEIK**

PLUS OTHER MATCHES

TV WRESTLING SAT., WRAL-TV

BRUTE BERNARD & GENE LEWIS vs. S.D. JONES & BUZZ SAWYER

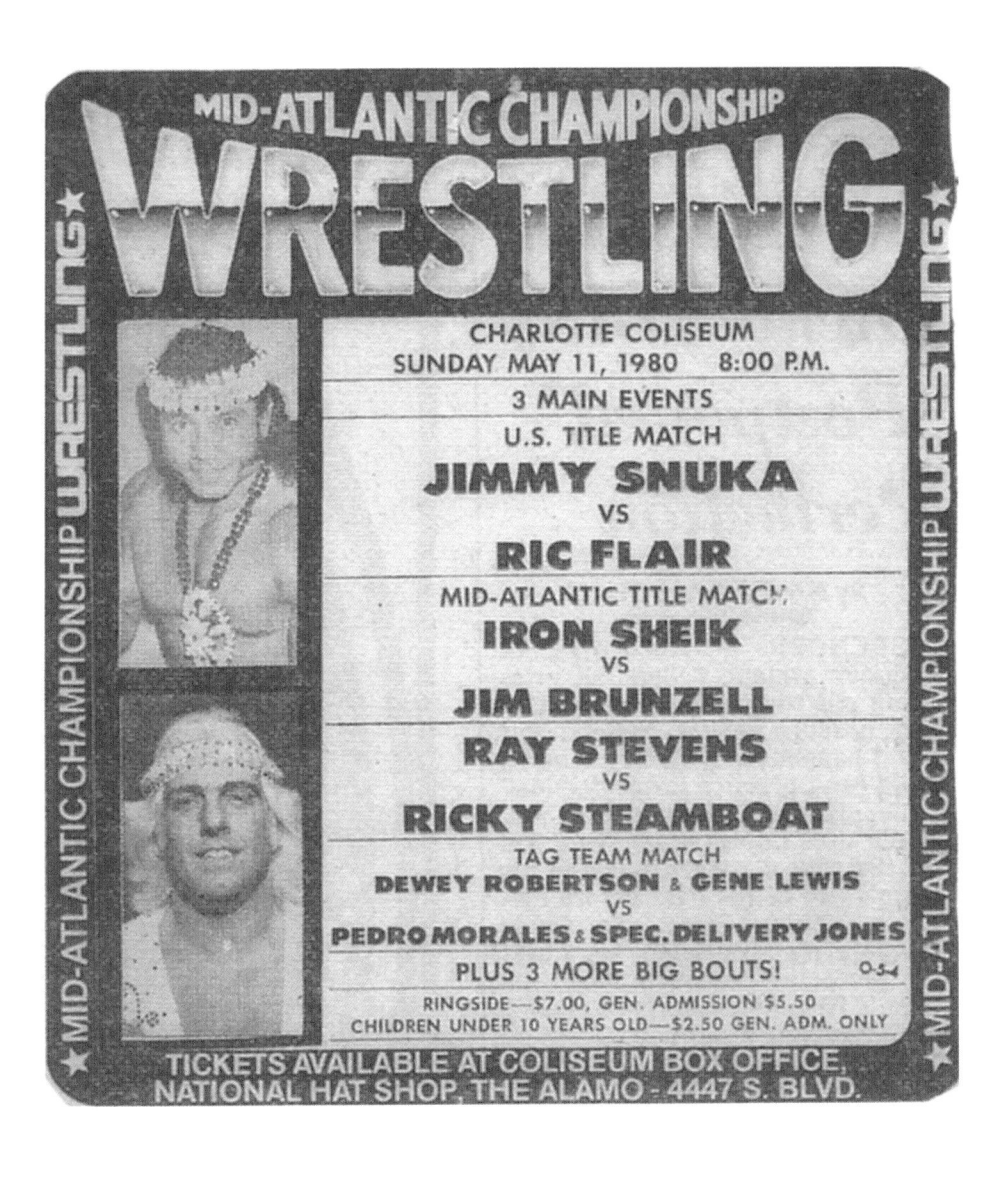

MID-ATLANTIC CHAMPIONSHIP WRESTLING

CHARLOTTE COLISEUM
SUNDAY MAY 11, 1980   8:00 P.M.

3 MAIN EVENTS

U.S. TITLE MATCH
JIMMY SNUKA
VS
RIC FLAIR

MID-ATLANTIC TITLE MATCH
IRON SHEIK
VS
JIM BRUNZELL

RAY STEVENS
VS
RICKY STEAMBOAT

TAG TEAM MATCH
DEWEY ROBERTSON & GENE LEWIS
VS
PEDRO MORALES & SPEC. DELIVERY JONES

PLUS 3 MORE BIG BOUTS!

RINGSIDE—$7.00, GEN. ADMISSION $5.50
CHILDREN UNDER 10 YEARS OLD—$2.50 GEN. ADM. ONLY

TICKETS AVAILABLE AT COLISEUM BOX OFFICE,
NATIONAL HAT SHOP, THE ALAMO - 4447 S. BLVD.

Snuka, Flair Draw

Jimmy Snuka and Ric Flair battled to a draw in their professional wrestling battle for the U.S. heavyweight title Sunday night in the Charlotte Coliseum.

The Iron Sheik took the Mid-Atlantic heavyweight crown from Jim Brunzell and Ricky Steamboat defeated Ray Stevens.

In other action, Lynn Denman and Ron Ritchie drew; Buzz Sawyer and Matt Borne conquered Tank Patton and Doug Sommers; Enforcer Luciano downed Coco Samoa and Dewey Robertson and Gene Lewis beat Pedro Morales and Special Delivery Jones.

MID-ATLANTIC CHAMPIONSHIP WRESTLING — **MID-ATLANTIC CHAMPIONSHIP WRESTLING**

NWA

DORTON ARENA TUES., MAY 13th, 8:15 P.M.

RINGSIDE $5.00, GEN. ADM. $4.00, CHILDREN (Under 12) $2.00 ADM.
Tickets on sale at Pop-a-Top Beverage in Mission Valley Shopping Center

RETURN U.S. TITLE MATCH
No Disqualification

JIMMY SNUKA vs. **RIC FLAIR**
WITH HIS MGR. GENE ANDERSON — CHAMPION

ENFORCER LUCIANO
vs
COCO SOMOA

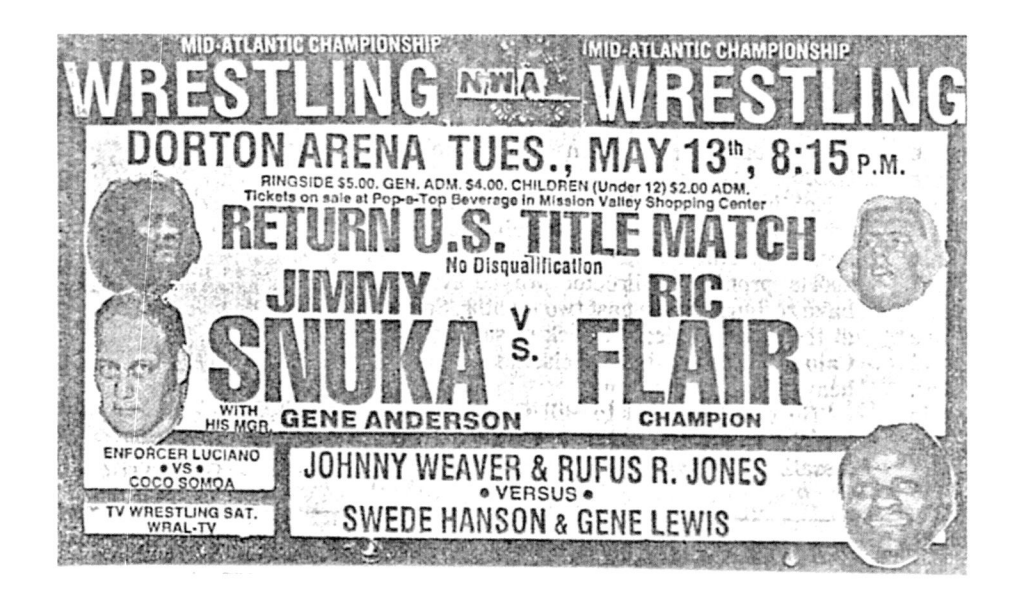

JOHNNY WEAVER & RUFUS R. JONES
• VERSUS •
SWEDE HANSON & GENE LEWIS

TV WRESTLING SAT.
WRAL-TV

Flair wins at Dorton

Ric Flair defeated Jimmy Snuka in the main wrestling event at Dorton Arena in Raleigh Tuesday night.

In other singles matches, Don Kernodle defeated Billy Starr, Len Denton beat Ronnie Sexton, and Enforcer Luciano defeated Coco Somoa.

Rufus Jones and Johnny Weaver beat Swede Hanson and Gene Lewis in a tag-team bout.

MID-ATLANTIC CHAMPIONSHIP WRESTLING NWA

DORTON ARENA • TUES., MAY 22 • 8:15 P.M.

RINGSIDE $5.00, GEN. ADM. $4.00, CHILDREN (Under 12) $2.00 ADM.
Tickets on sale at Pop-a-Top Beverage in Mission Valley Shopping Center

LUMBERJACK MATCH FOR UNITED STATES TITLE

2 REFEREES FOR THIS MATCH

RIC FLAIR (NEW CHAMPION) vs. **JIMMY SNUKA** (GENE ANDERSON)

FOR MID-ATLANTIC TITLE

JIM BRUNZELL vs. **THE IRON SHEIK**

RUFUS JONES & S.D. JONES vs. THE SUPERSTAR #1 & ENFORCER LUCIANO

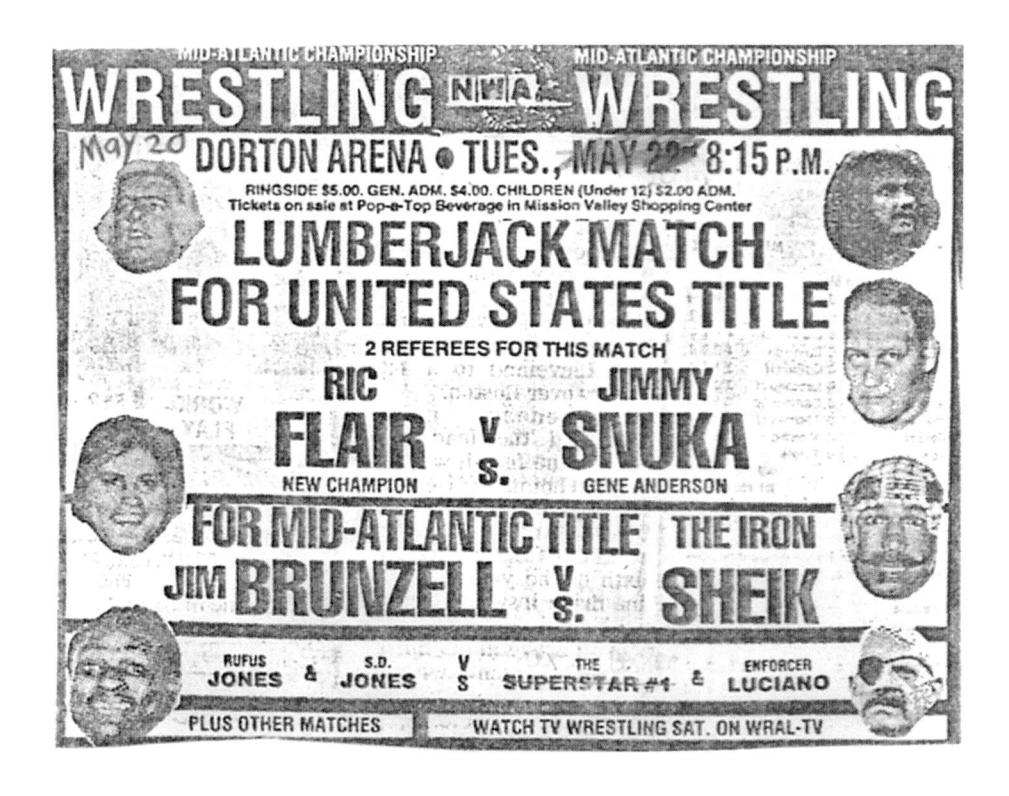

PLUS OTHER MATCHES — WATCH TV WRESTLING SAT. ON WRAL-TV

Flair retains title

Ric Flair defeated Jimmy Snuka to retain his U.S. title and The Iron Sheik downed Jim Brunzell to retain his Mid-Atlantic title in Tuesday night wrestling at Dorton Arena.

In a tag team match, Rufus R. Jones and S.D. Jones defeated Ox Baker and Enforcer Luciano.

Abe Jacobs beat Doug Sommers and Brut Bernard outlasted Ron Ritchie in single matches.

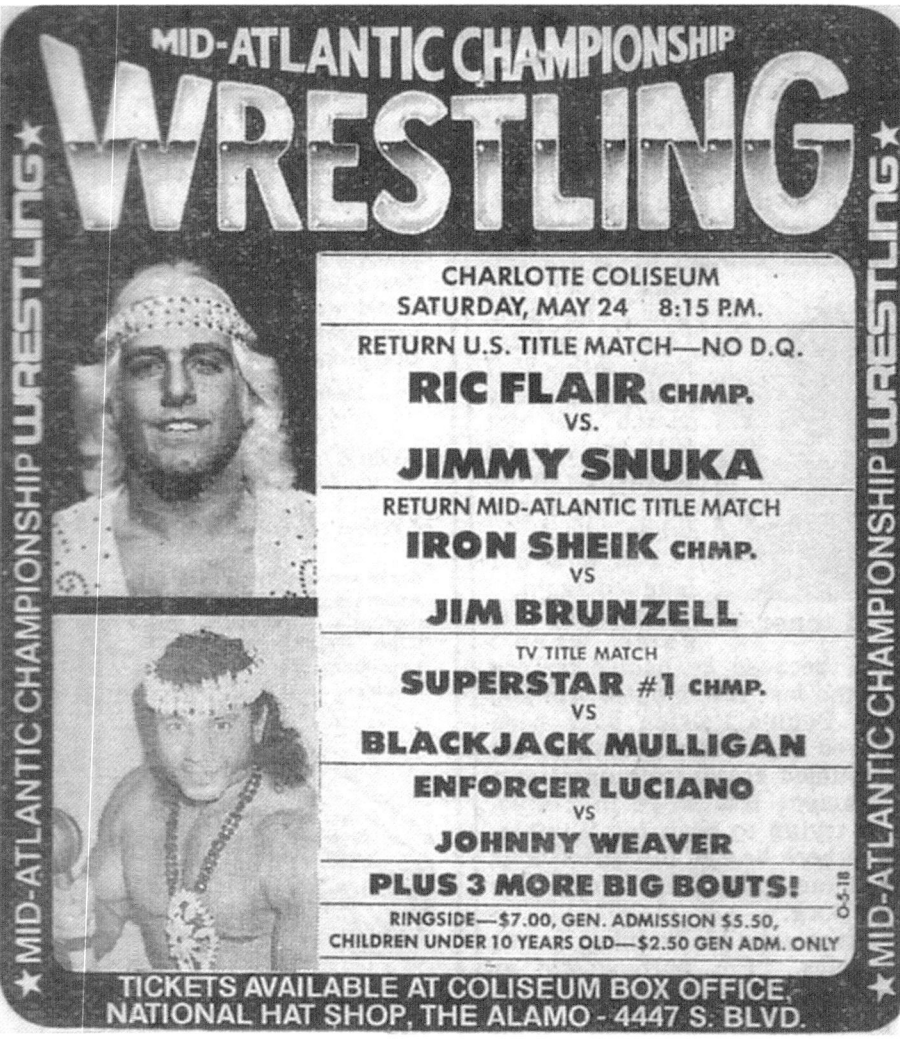

MID-ATLANTIC CHAMPIONSHIP WRESTLING

CHARLOTTE COLISEUM
SATURDAY, MAY 24   8:15 P.M.

RETURN U.S. TITLE MATCH—NO D.Q.
RIC FLAIR CHMP.
VS.
JIMMY SNUKA

RETURN MID-ATLANTIC TITLE MATCH
IRON SHEIK CHMP.
VS
JIM BRUNZELL

TV TITLE MATCH
SUPERSTAR #1 CHMP.
VS
BLACKJACK MULLIGAN

ENFORCER LUCIANO
VS
JOHNNY WEAVER

PLUS 3 MORE BIG BOUTS!

RINGSIDE—$7.00, GEN. ADMISSION $5.50,
CHILDREN UNDER 10 YEARS OLD—$2.50 GEN ADM. ONLY

TICKETS AVAILABLE AT COLISEUM BOX OFFICE,
NATIONAL HAT SHOP, THE ALAMO - 4447 S. BLVD.

Pro Wrestling Card

Ric Flair successfully defended his U.S. heavyweight title, defeating Jimmy Snuka in the feature event on a Coliseum pro wrestling card.

In a Mid-Atlantic title match, Jim Brunzell defeated champion Iron Sheik, but on a disqualification, meaning the title did not change hands. The same was the case in the TV title match, when Blackjack Mulligan beat champion Superstar No. 1.

Other results:
Enforcer Luciano defeated Johnny Weaver, Matt Bourne and Buzz Sawyer beat Dewey Robertson and Gene Lewis, Tony Gerea beat Brute Bernard, and Don Kernodle defeated The Scorpion.

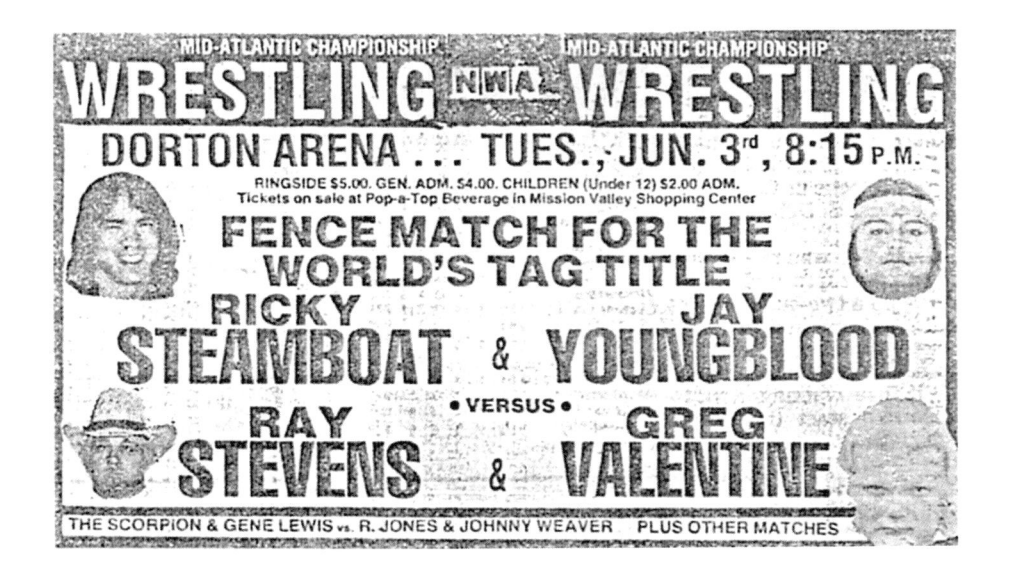

MID-ATLANTIC CHAMPIONSHIP WRESTLING — NWA

DORTON ARENA ... TUES., JUN. 3rd, 8:15 P.M.

RINGSIDE $5.00, GEN. ADM. $4.00, CHILDREN (Under 12) $2.00 ADM.
Tickets on sale at Pop-a-Top Beverage in Mission Valley Shopping Center

FENCE MATCH FOR THE WORLD'S TAG TITLE

RICKY STEAMBOAT & JAY YOUNGBLOOD

• VERSUS •

RAY STEVENS & GREG VALENTINE

THE SCORPION & GENE LEWIS vs. R. JONES & JOHNNY WEAVER   PLUS OTHER MATCHES

Steamboat-Youngblood wins

Ricky Steamboat and Jay Youngblood retained their world tag-team title by defeating Ray Stevens and Greg Valentine in a fence match in the main event at Dorton Arena Tuesday night.

In other matches, Tony Russo wrestled to a draw with CoCo Somoa, Abe Jacobs won by disqualification over Billy Starr, and Rufus R. Jones and Johnny Weaver defeated Gene Lewis and The Scorpion in a tag

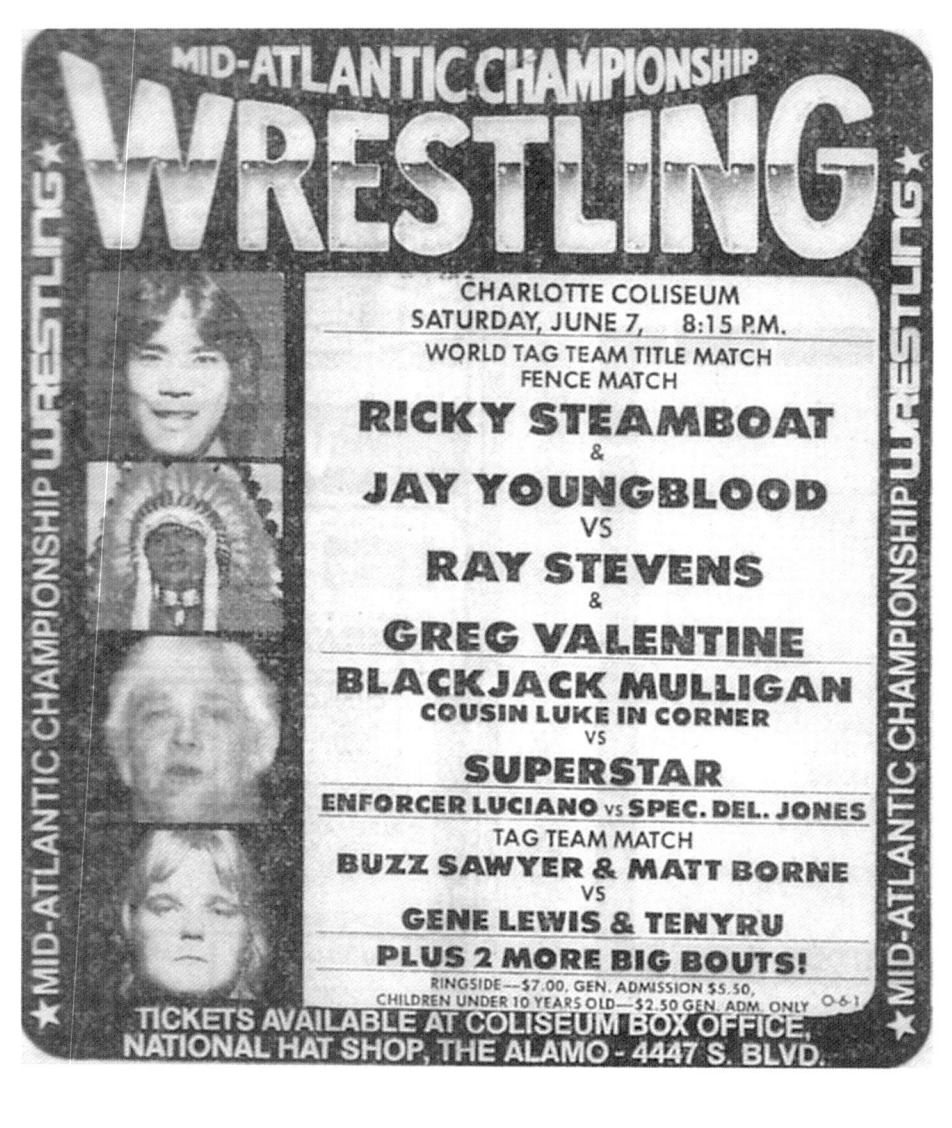

MID-ATLANTIC CHAMPIONSHIP WRESTLING

CHARLOTTE COLISEUM
SATURDAY, JUNE 7, 8:15 P.M.

WORLD TAG TEAM TITLE MATCH
FENCE MATCH

RICKY STEAMBOAT
&
JAY YOUNGBLOOD
VS
RAY STEVENS
&
GREG VALENTINE

BLACKJACK MULLIGAN
COUSIN LUKE IN CORNER
VS
SUPERSTAR

ENFORCER LUCIANO vs SPEC. DEL. JONES

TAG TEAM MATCH
BUZZ SAWYER & MATT BORNE
VS
GENE LEWIS & TENYRU

PLUS 2 MORE BIG BOUTS!

RINGSIDE—$7.00, GEN. ADMISSION $5.50,
CHILDREN UNDER 10 YEARS OLD—$2.50 GEN. ADM. ONLY

TICKETS AVAILABLE AT COLISEUM BOX OFFICE,
NATIONAL HAT SHOP, THE ALAMO - 4447 S. BLVD.

Pro Wrestling Card

Ricky Steamboat pinned Ray Stevens in the featured fence match, and Steamboat and Jay Youngblood retained their world tag team pro wrestling championship at the Coliseum. Stevens's partner was Greg Valentine.

In other top matches, Blackjack Mulligan defeated the Superstar on a disqualification, and Enforcer Luciano pinned Special Delivery Jones.

Other results:
Buzz Sawyer and Matt Borne defeated Gene Lewis and Tenyru; Pedro Morales beat Doug Sommers on a disqualification; and Don Kernodle and Abe Jacobs defeated the Scorpion and Billy Starr.

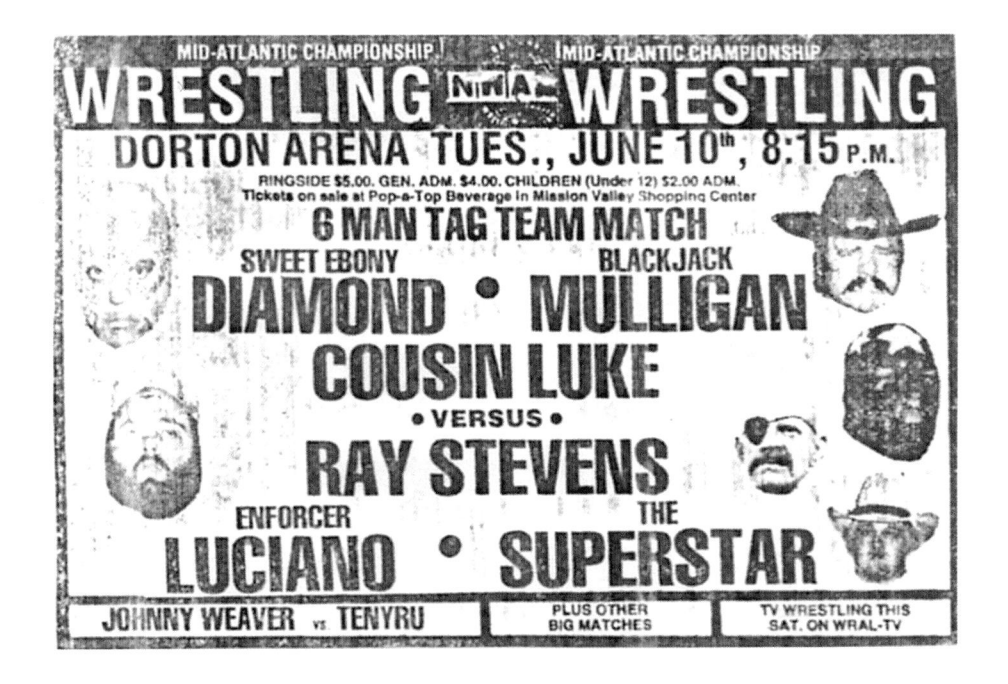

MID-ATLANTIC CHAMPIONSHIP WRESTLING — NWA — MID-ATLANTIC CHAMPIONSHIP WRESTLING

DORTON ARENA TUES., JUNE 10th, 8:15 P.M.

RINGSIDE $5.00. GEN. ADM. $4.00. CHILDREN (Under 12) $2.00 ADM.
Tickets on sale at Pop-a-Top Beverage in Mission Valley Shopping Center

6 MAN TAG TEAM MATCH

SWEET EBONY DIAMOND • BLACKJACK MULLIGAN • COUSIN LUKE

• VERSUS •

RAY STEVENS • ENFORCER LUCIANO • THE SUPERSTAR

JOHNNY WEAVER vs. TENYRU | PLUS OTHER BIG MATCHES | TV WRESTLING THIS SAT. ON WRAL-TV

Superstar team wins

Ray Stevens, Enforcer Luciano and The Superstar won by disqualification over Sweet Ebony Diamond, Blackjack Mulligan and Cousin Luke in a six-man tag team match for the main event on Tuesday night's professional wrestling card at Dorton Arena.

In other matches, Ron Ritchie defeated Billy Starr, S.D. Jones defeated Len Denton and Johnny Weaver defeated Tenyru.

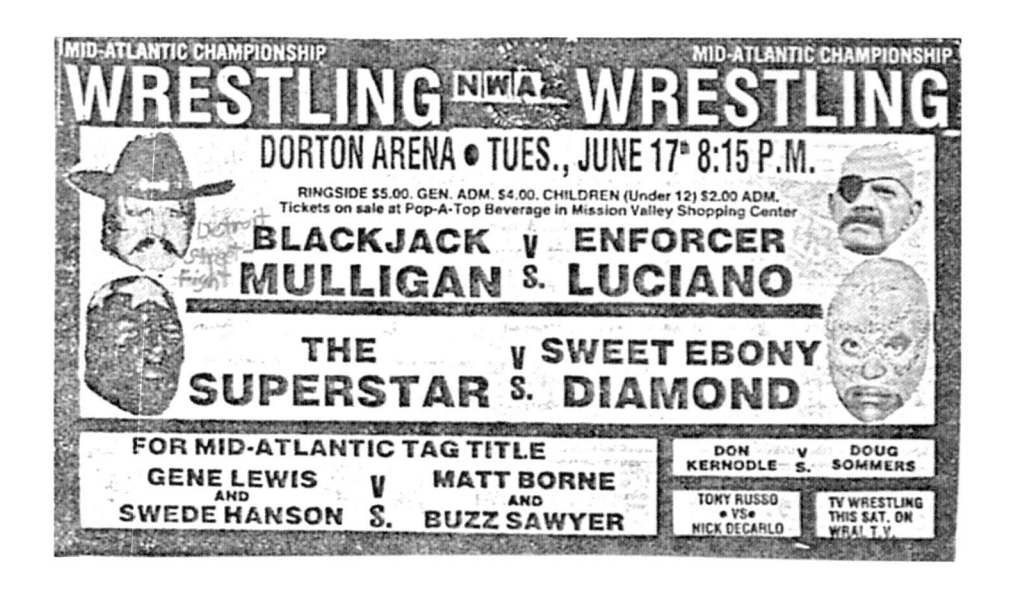

MID-ATLANTIC CHAMPIONSHIP WRESTLING — NWA

DORTON ARENA • TUES., JUNE 17th 8:15 P.M.

RINGSIDE $5.00, GEN. ADM. $4.00, CHILDREN (Under 12) $2.00 ADM.
Tickets on sale at Pop-A-Top Beverage in Mission Valley Shopping Center

BLACKJACK MULLIGAN v.s. **ENFORCER LUCIANO**

THE SUPERSTAR v.s. **SWEET EBONY DIAMOND**

FOR MID-ATLANTIC TAG TITLE
GENE LEWIS AND SWEDE HANSON v.s. **MATT BORNE AND BUZZ SAWYER**

DON KERNODLE v.s. DOUG SOMMERS

TONY RUSSO • VS • NICK DECARLO

TV WRESTLING THIS SAT. ON WRAL T.V.

Duo retains tag title

Matt Borne and Buzz Sawyer retained their Mid-Atlantic tag-team title Tuesday night, defeating Swede Hanson and Gene Lewis in a feature bout at Dorton Arena.

In other matches, Sweet Ebony Diamond won by disqualification over The Superstar, Enforcer Luciano defeated Black Jack Mulligan in a Detroit Streetfight, Nick DeCarlo defeated Tony Russo, and Don Kernodle beat Doug Sommers.

MID-ATLANTIC CHAMPIONSHIP WRESTLING

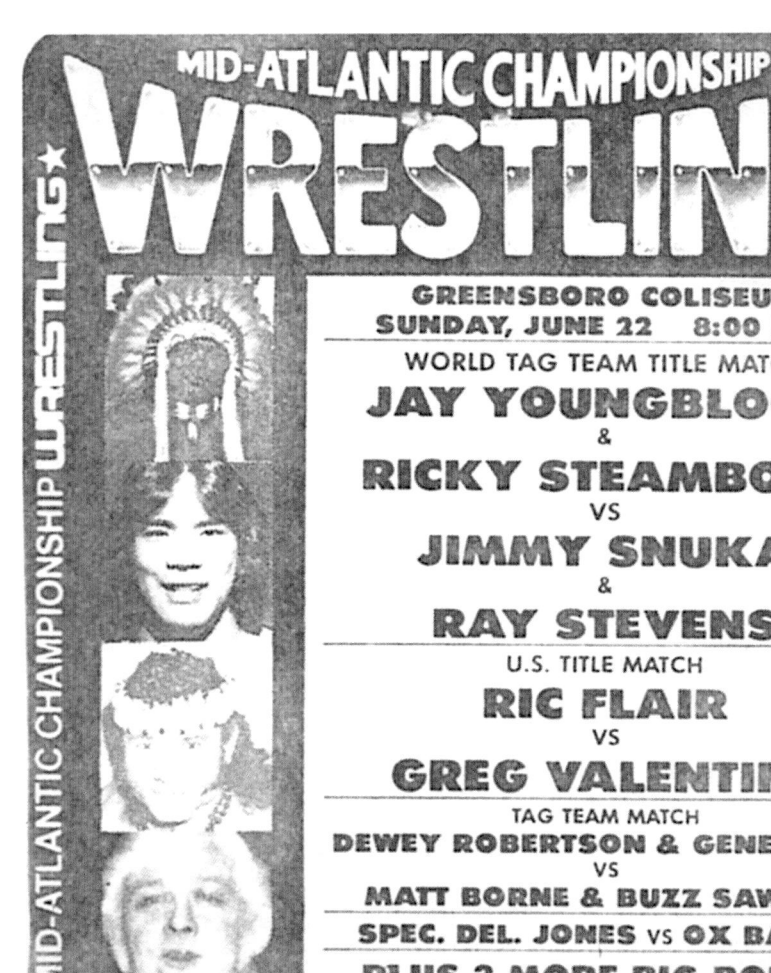

GREENSBORO COLISEUM
SUNDAY, JUNE 22   8:00 P.M.

WORLD TAG TEAM TITLE MATCH
JAY YOUNGBLOOD
&
RICKY STEAMBOAT
VS
JIMMY SNUKA
&
RAY STEVENS

U.S. TITLE MATCH
RIC FLAIR
VS
GREG VALENTINE

TAG TEAM MATCH
DEWEY ROBERTSON & GENE LEWIS
VS
MATT BORNE & BUZZ SAWYER

SPEC. DEL. JONES VS **OX BAKER**

PLUS 3 MORE BIG BOUTS!

Snuka takes title

Jimmy Snuka, using a suplex hold, downed Jay Youngblood to boost Snuka and partner Ray Stevens to the World Tag Team Title in Mid-Atlantic Championship Wrestling action last night at the Coliseum. Youngblood and Ricky Steamboat were the former holders of the title.

In another title event, both Ric Flair and Greg Valentine were disqualified when the bout was declared uncontrollable by the referee.

Also before last night's crowd of 5,319, Matt Borne and Buzzz Sawyer captured a tag team match over Dewey Robertson and Gene Lewis, while Special Delivery Jones knocked off Ox Baker. John Kernodle beat The Scorpian, Abe Jacobs downed Billy Star and Nick DeCarlo triumphed over Tony Russo.

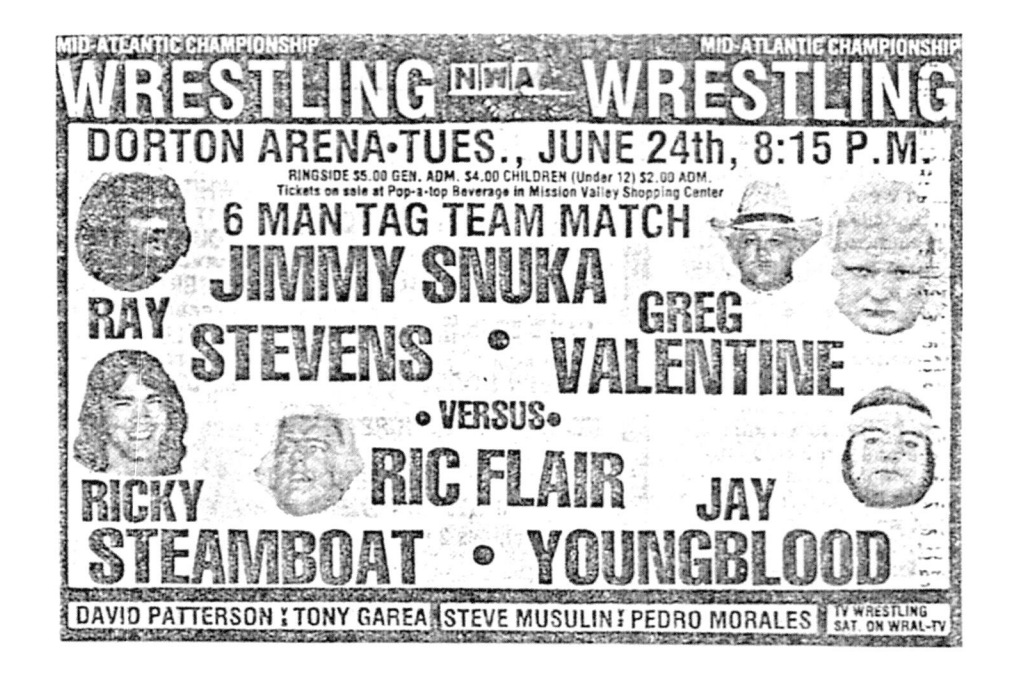

MID-ATLANTIC CHAMPIONSHIP WRESTLING — NWA — MID-ATLANTIC CHAMPIONSHIP WRESTLING

DORTON ARENA • TUES., JUNE 24th, 8:15 P.M.

RINGSIDE $5.00 GEN. ADM. $4.00 CHILDREN (Under 12) $2.00 ADM.
Tickets on sale at Pop-a-top Beverage in Mission Valley Shopping Center

6 MAN TAG TEAM MATCH

JIMMY SNUKA • RAY STEVENS • GREG VALENTINE

• VERSUS •

RIC FLAIR • RICKY STEAMBOAT • JAY YOUNGBLOOD

DAVID PATTERSON vs TONY GAREA | STEVE MUSULIN vs PEDRO MORALES | TV WRESTLING SAT. ON WRAL-TV

Flair team wins match

Ric Flair, Ricky Steamboat and Jay Youngblood defeated Jimmy Snuka, Ray Stevens and Greg Valentine in the six-man, tag-team main event Tuesday on the pro wrestling card at Dorton Arena.

In other matches Ben Alexander wrestled to a draw against Nick DeCarlo, Tony Garea defeated David Patterson and Steve Musulin beat Pedro Morales.

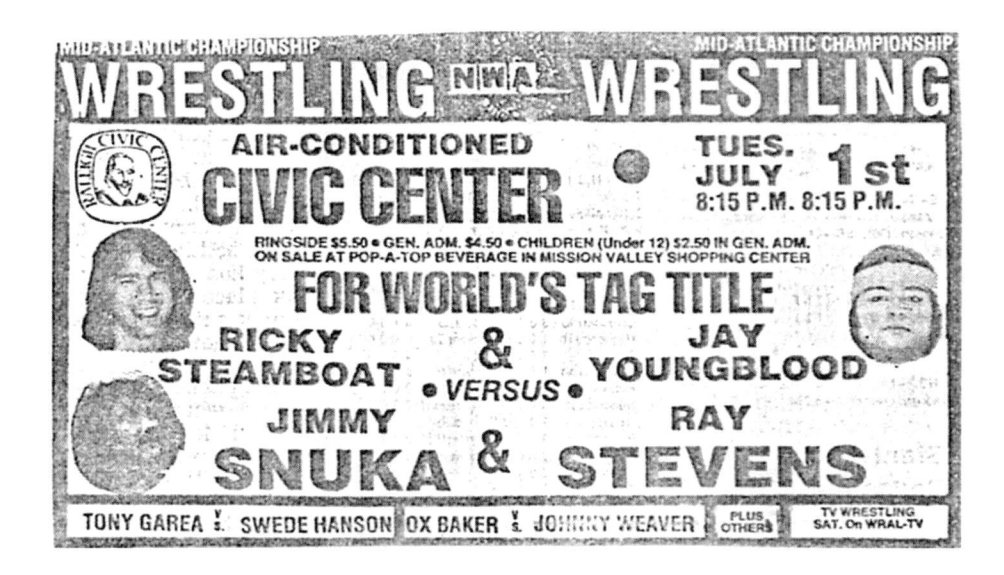

MID-ATLANTIC CHAMPIONSHIP WRESTLING NWA WRESTLING

AIR-CONDITIONED CIVIC CENTER

TUES. JULY 1st 8:15 P.M. 8:15 P.M.

RINGSIDE $5.50 • GEN. ADM. $4.50 • CHILDREN (Under 12) $2.50 IN GEN. ADM.
ON SALE AT POP-A-TOP BEVERAGE IN MISSION VALLEY SHOPPING CENTER

FOR WORLD'S TAG TITLE

RICKY STEAMBOAT & JAY YOUNGBLOOD
• VERSUS •
JIMMY SNUKA & RAY STEVENS

TONY GAREA vs. SWEDE HANSON | OX BAKER vs. JOHNNY WEAVER | PLUS OTHERS | TV WRESTLING SAT. On WRAL-TV

Stevens, Snuka win

Ray Stevens and Jimmy Snuka retained their world tag-team title Tuesday night, defeating Ricky Steamboat and Jay Youngblood by disqualification in a featured professional wrestling match at the Raleigh Civic Center.

In other bouts, Don Kernodle was a double winner, defeating Ricky Ferrara and Ox Baker, Ron Ritchie won over David Patterson on a referee's decision and Swede Hanson beat Tony Garea.

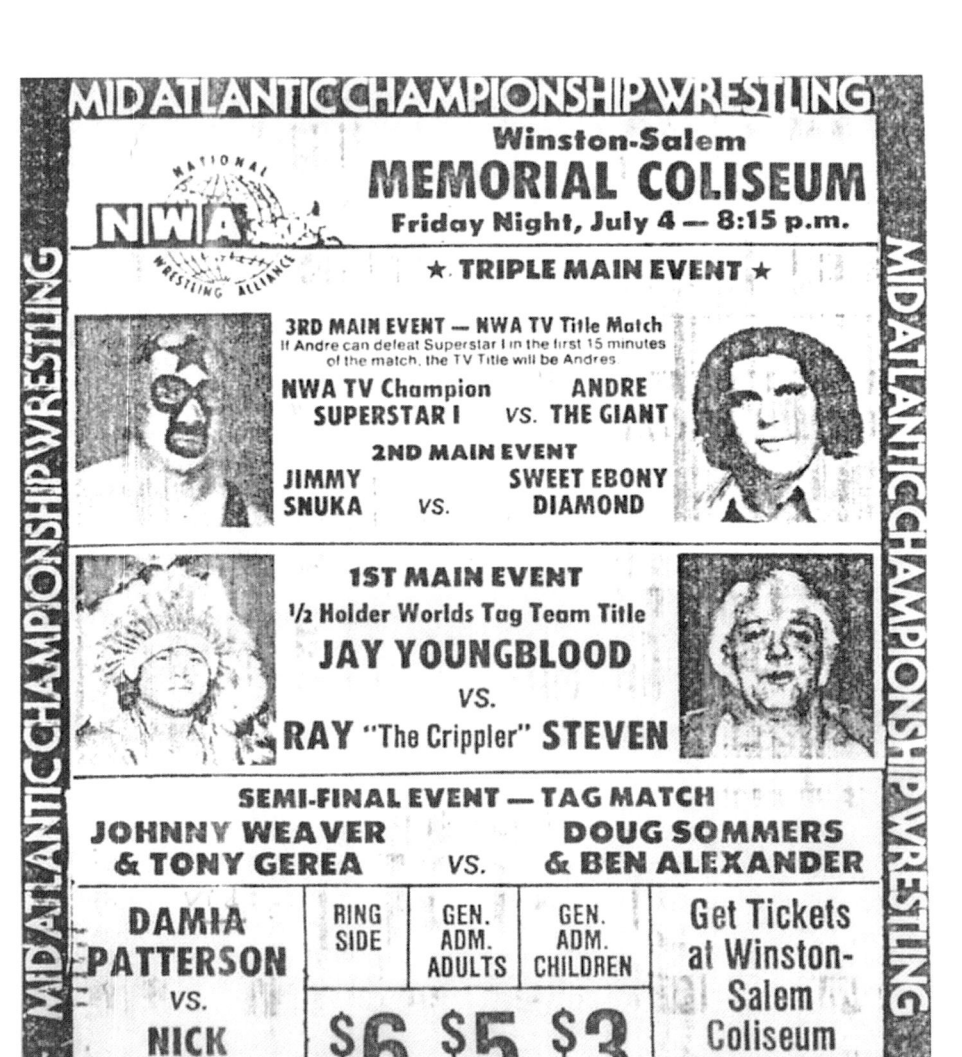

MID ATLANTIC CHAMPIONSHIP WRESTLING

Winston-Salem MEMORIAL COLISEUM
Friday Night, July 4 — 8:15 p.m.

NWA

★ **TRIPLE MAIN EVENT** ★

3RD MAIN EVENT — NWA TV Title Match
If Andre can defeat Superstar I in the first 15 minutes of the match, the TV Title will be Andres

NWA TV Champion SUPERSTAR I vs. **ANDRE THE GIANT**

2ND MAIN EVENT
JIMMY SNUKA vs. **SWEET EBONY DIAMOND**

1ST MAIN EVENT
½ Holder Worlds Tag Team Title
JAY YOUNGBLOOD vs. **RAY "The Crippler" STEVEN**

SEMI-FINAL EVENT — TAG MATCH
JOHNNY WEAVER & TONY GEREA vs. **DOUG SOMMERS & BEN ALEXANDER**

DAMIA PATTERSON vs. **NICK DECARLO**

RING SIDE	GEN. ADM. ADULTS	GEN. ADM. CHILDREN
$6	$5	$3

Get Tickets at Winston-Salem Coliseum Box Office.

WIDE WORLD WRESTLING

TOMORROW JULY 6 3:00 P.M.

HOLIDAY WRESTLING CARD

WORLD TAG TEAM TITLE MATCH

(WORLD TAG CHAMPS)

(THE CRIPPLER) **RAY STEVENS**
&
(MGR. GENE ANDERSON) **JIMMY SNUKA**

-VS-

RICKY STEAMBOAT
&
JAY YOUNGBLOOD

PLUS **FOUR SINGLE MATCHES**

SWEET EBONY DIAMOND	VS	GENE LEWIS
STEVE MUSULIN	VS	TONY GAREA
DAVID PATTERSON	VS	RON RITCHIE
RICKY FARRARA	VS	COCO SOMOA

BOX OFFICE — 255-5771 • RINGSIDE - $6.00
General Admission $5.00 • Children Under 10 $3.00
Box Office Open Mon.-Fri. 10:00-5:30; Sat. 11:00-4:00; Day of Match 1:00 P.M.
NO CHECKS OR CREDIT CARDS DAY OF MATCH

Mid-Atlantic Wrestling

Asheville Civic Center
Ray Stevens and Jimmy Snuka vs. Ricky Steamboat and Jay Youngblood, double throw-out; Sweet Ebony Diamond def. Gene Lewis; Steve Musulin vs. Tony Garea, draw; David Patterson def. Ron Ritchie; Ricky Farrara def. Coco Somoa.

MID-ATLANTIC CHAMPIONSHIP WRESTLING — NWA — WRESTLING

AIR-CONDITIONED CIVIC CENTER
TUES. 8th JULY 8:15 P.M.

RINGSIDE $5.50. GEN. ADM. $4.50. CHILDREN (Under 12) $2.50 ADM.
Tickets on sale at Pop-e-Top Beverage In Mission Valley Shopping Center
AND AT THE CIVIC CENTER BOX OFFICE

JIM BRUNZELL & THE IRON SHEIK • VERSUS • **RIC FLAIR & GREG VALENTINE**

SPECIAL DELIVERY JONES • VS • DEWEY ROBERTSON

SWEDE HANSON vs. SWEET EBONY DIAMOND

PLUS OTHER MATCHES

TV WRESTLING THIS SATURDAY ON WRAL-TV

Brunzell, Flair triumph

Jim Brunzell and Rik Flair defeated Greg Valentine and The Iron Sheik in the main wrestling event Tuesday night at the Raleigh Civic Center.

Don Kernodle tamed Tony Russo, Sweet Ebony Diamond stopped Swede Hanson and Special Delivery Jones won by disqualification over Dewey Robertson in singles matches. Doug Sommers and Abe Jacobs battled to a draw.

MID-ATLANTIC CHAMPIONSHIP WRESTLING — NWA

AIR CONDITIONED RALEIGH CIVIC CENTER
TUES. JULY 15TH — 8:15 P.M.

RINGSIDE $5.50, GEN. ADM. $4.50, CHILDREN (Under 12) $2.50 in GEN. ADM.
Tickets on sale at Pop-e-Top Beverage in Mission Valley Shopping Center AND THE CIVIC CENTER BOX OFFICE

FOR UNITED STATES CHAMPIONSHIP
RIC FLAIR vs. GREG VALENTINE

THE SUPERSTAR versus SWEET EBONY DIAMOND

GENE LEWIS & DEWEY ROBERTSON vs. MATT BORNE & BUZZ SAWYER

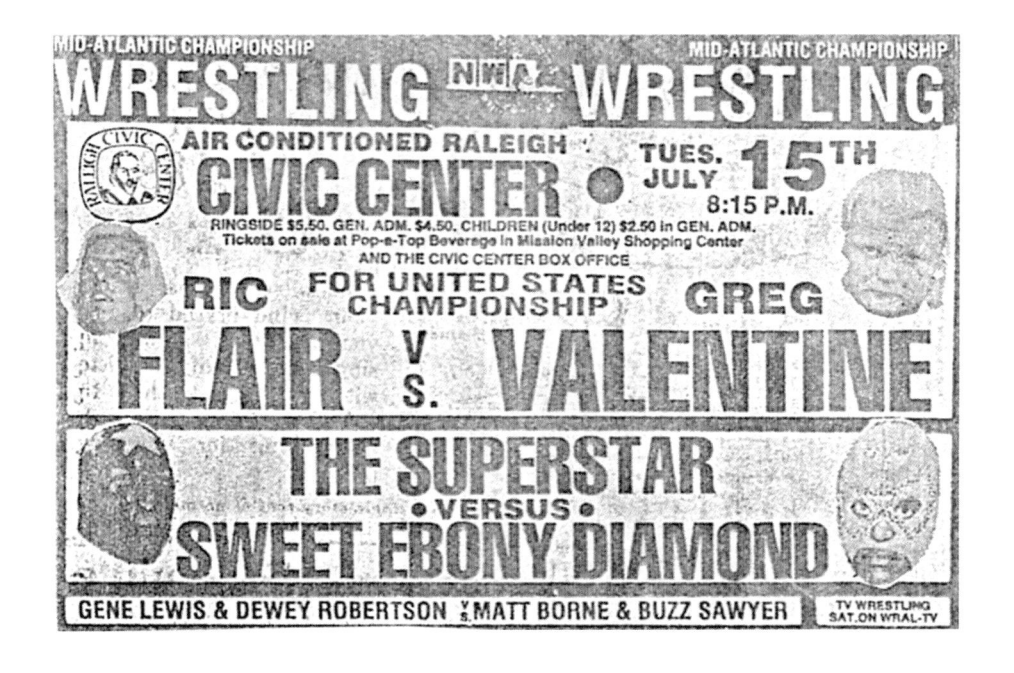

TV WRESTLING SAT. ON WRAL-TV

Flair retains crown

Ric Flair defeated Greg Valentine Tuesday night at the Raleigh Civic Center to retain his U.S. wrestling title.

In other matches, Sweet Ebony Diamond won by disqualification over The Superstar, Ron Ritchie defeated Ricky Ferrara, Steve Musulin defeated Ox Baker, and Gene Lewis and Dewey Robertson defeated Matt Borne and Buzz Sawyer.

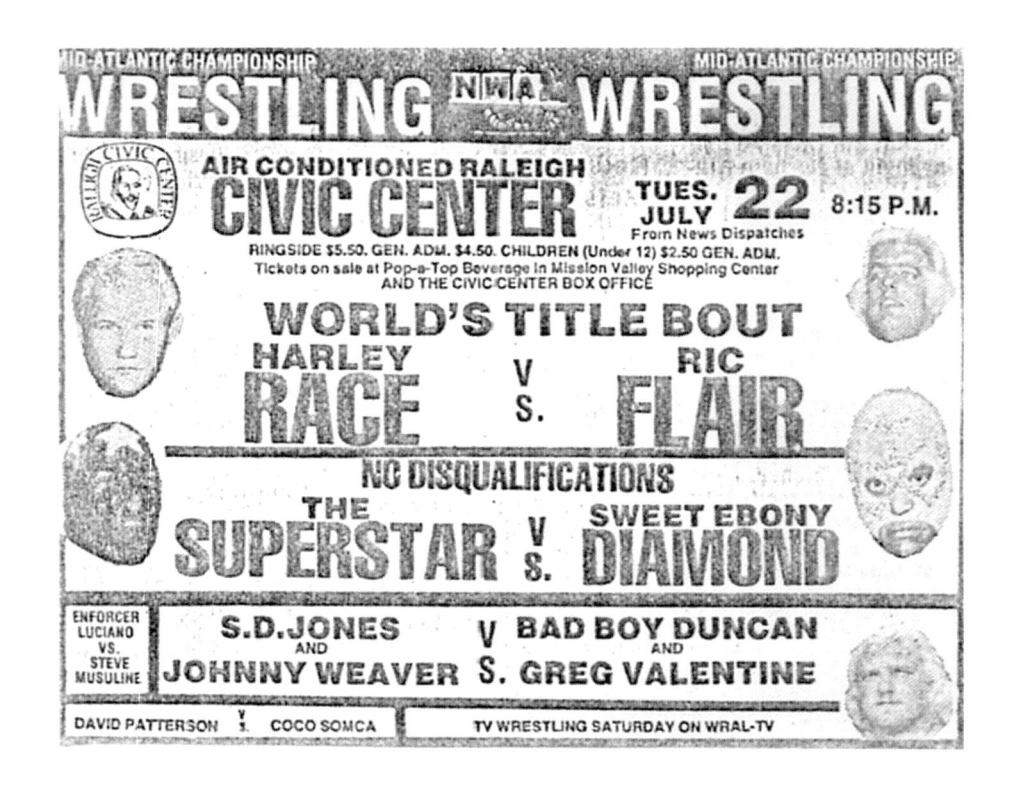

Race retains title

Harley Race retained his world's title Tuesday night when Ric Flair was counted out of the ring in the main event on the professional wrestling card at the Civic Center.

In another main event, Sweet Ebony Diamond defeated The Superstar. In other matches, David Patterson defeated Coco Somoa, Enforcer Luciano defeated Steve Musulin, Bad Boy Duncum and Greg Valetine defeated S.D. Jones and Johnny Weaver.

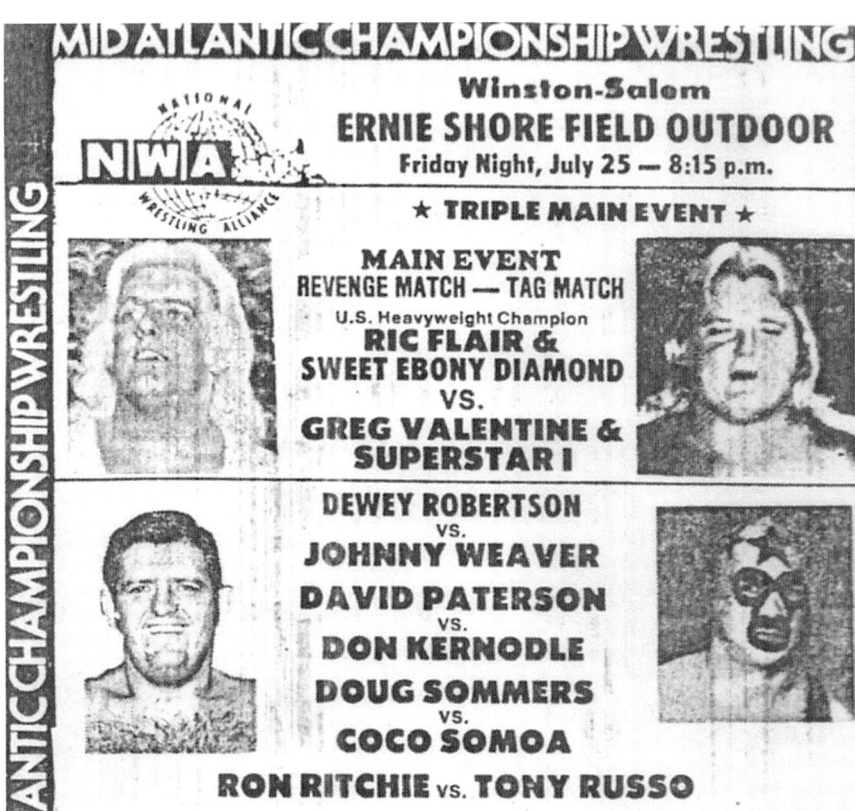

MID ATLANTIC CHAMPIONSHIP WRESTLING

Winston-Salem
ERNIE SHORE FIELD OUTDOOR
Friday Night, July 25 — 8:15 p.m.

NWA — National Wrestling Alliance

★ **TRIPLE MAIN EVENT** ★

MAIN EVENT
REVENGE MATCH — TAG MATCH
U.S. Heavyweight Champion
RIC FLAIR & SWEET EBONY DIAMOND
vs.
GREG VALENTINE & SUPERSTAR I

DEWEY ROBERTSON
vs.
JOHNNY WEAVER

DAVID PATERSON
vs.
DON KERNODLE

DOUG SOMMERS
vs.
COCO SOMOA

RON RITCHIE vs. TONY RUSSO

WIDE WORLD WRESTLING

TODAY JULY 27 3:00 P.M.

SIX MAN TAG TEAM MATCH

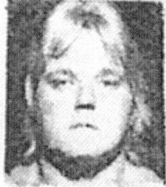

**MAIN EVENT
SIX MAN
TAG TEAM MATCH**

(U.S. CHAMP)
RIC FLAIR
&
RICK STEAMBOAT
&
JAY YOUNGBLOOD
- VS. -
GREG VALENTINE
&
(WORLD TAG CHAMPS)
RAY STEVENS
&
JIMMY SNUKA
(WITH MGR. GENE ANDERSON)

PLUS 3 SINGLE MATCHES

BOX OFFICE — 255-5771 • RINGSIDE - $6.00
General Admission $5.00 • Children Under 10 $3.00
Box Office Open Mon.-Fri. 10:00-5:30; Sat. 11:00-4:00; Day of Match 1:00 P.M.
NO CHECKS OR CREDIT CARDS DAY OF MATCH

SEE NWA WORLD WIDE WRESTLING SATURDAY
ON WLOS-TV CHANNEL 13 11:30 PM-12:30 AM

Asheville Civic Center

WRESTLING

CIVIC CENTER WRESTLING
Six-Man Tag Team: Ric Flair, Ricky Steamboat and Jay Youngblood d. Greg Valentine, Ray Stevens and Jimmy Snuka; Johnny Weaver d. Bad Boy Duncum by disqualification; Swede Hanson d. Ritchie; Ben Alexander d. Steve Musulin.

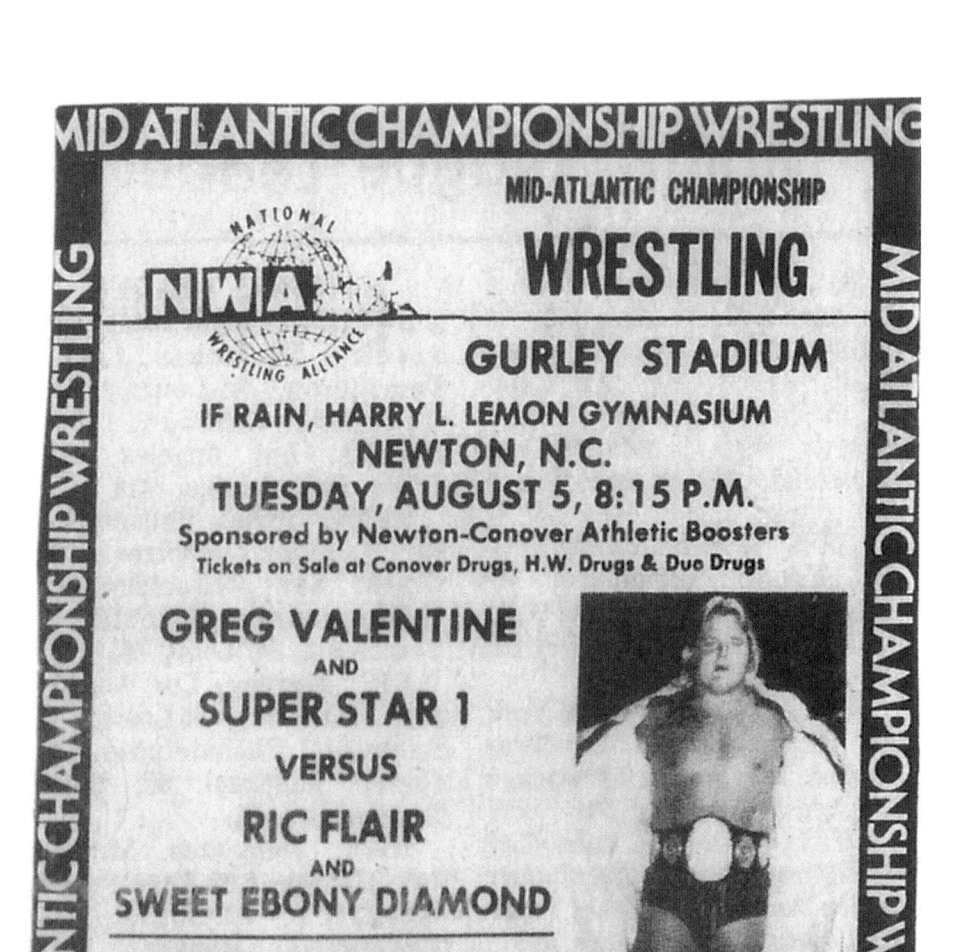

MID-ATLANTIC CHAMPIONSHIP WRESTLING

NWA - National Wrestling Alliance

GURLEY STADIUM

IF RAIN, HARRY L. LEMON GYMNASIUM
NEWTON, N.C.
TUESDAY, AUGUST 5, 8:15 P.M.

Sponsored by Newton-Conover Athletic Boosters
Tickets on Sale at Conover Drugs, H.W. Drugs & Duo Drugs

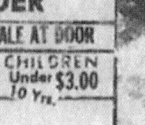

GREG VALENTINE
AND
SUPER STAR 1
VERSUS
RIC FLAIR
AND
SWEET EBONY DIAMOND

TENYRU vs. STEVE MUSULIN

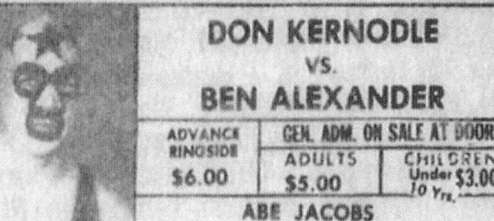

DON KERNODLE vs. BEN ALEXANDER

ADVANCE RINGSIDE	GEN. ADM. ON SALE AT DOOR	
$6.00	ADULTS $5.00	CHILDREN Under 10 Yrs. $3.00

ABE JACOBS vs. RICK FERRARA

NWA MID-ATLANTIC CHAMPIONSHIP WRESTLING

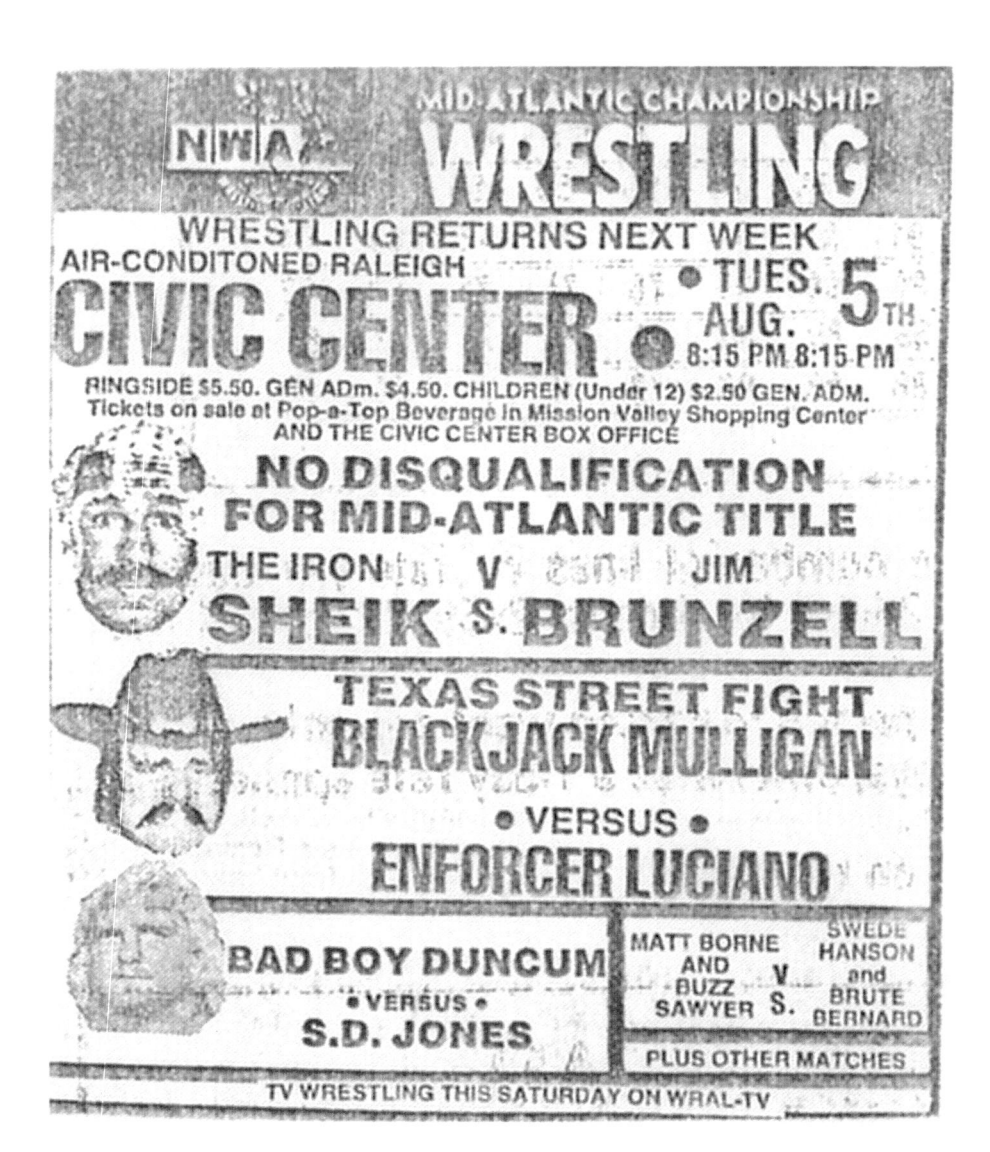

WRESTLING RETURNS NEXT WEEK

AIR-CONDITIONED RALEIGH **CIVIC CENTER** • TUES. AUG. 5TH 8:15 PM 8:15 PM

RINGSIDE $5.50. GEN ADm. $4.50. CHILDREN (Under 12) $2.50 GEN. ADM.
Tickets on sale at Pop-a-Top Beverage in Mission Valley Shopping Center
AND THE CIVIC CENTER BOX OFFICE

NO DISQUALIFICATION FOR MID-ATLANTIC TITLE
THE IRON **SHEIK** V.S. JIM **BRUNZELL**

TEXAS STREET FIGHT
BLACKJACK MULLIGAN
• VERSUS •
ENFORCER LUCIANO

BAD BOY DUNCUM • VERSUS • **S.D. JONES**

MATT BORNE AND BUZZ SAWYER V.S. SWEDE HANSON and BRUTE BERNARD

PLUS OTHER MATCHES

TV WRESTLING THIS SATURDAY ON WRAL-TV

Sheik retains title

The Iron Sheik retained his Mid-Atlantic heavyweight title, defeating Jim Brunzell, Tuesday night in the main event of a pro wrestling card at the Raleigh Civic Center.

In another main event, Black Jack Milligan defeated Enforcer Luciano in Texas street-fight.

In other matches, Cocoa Somoa won on a referee's decision over Billy Starr, Matt Borne and Buzz Sawyer beat Brute Bernard and Swede Hansen in a tag-team bout, and Bad Boy Duncan defeated S.E. Jones.

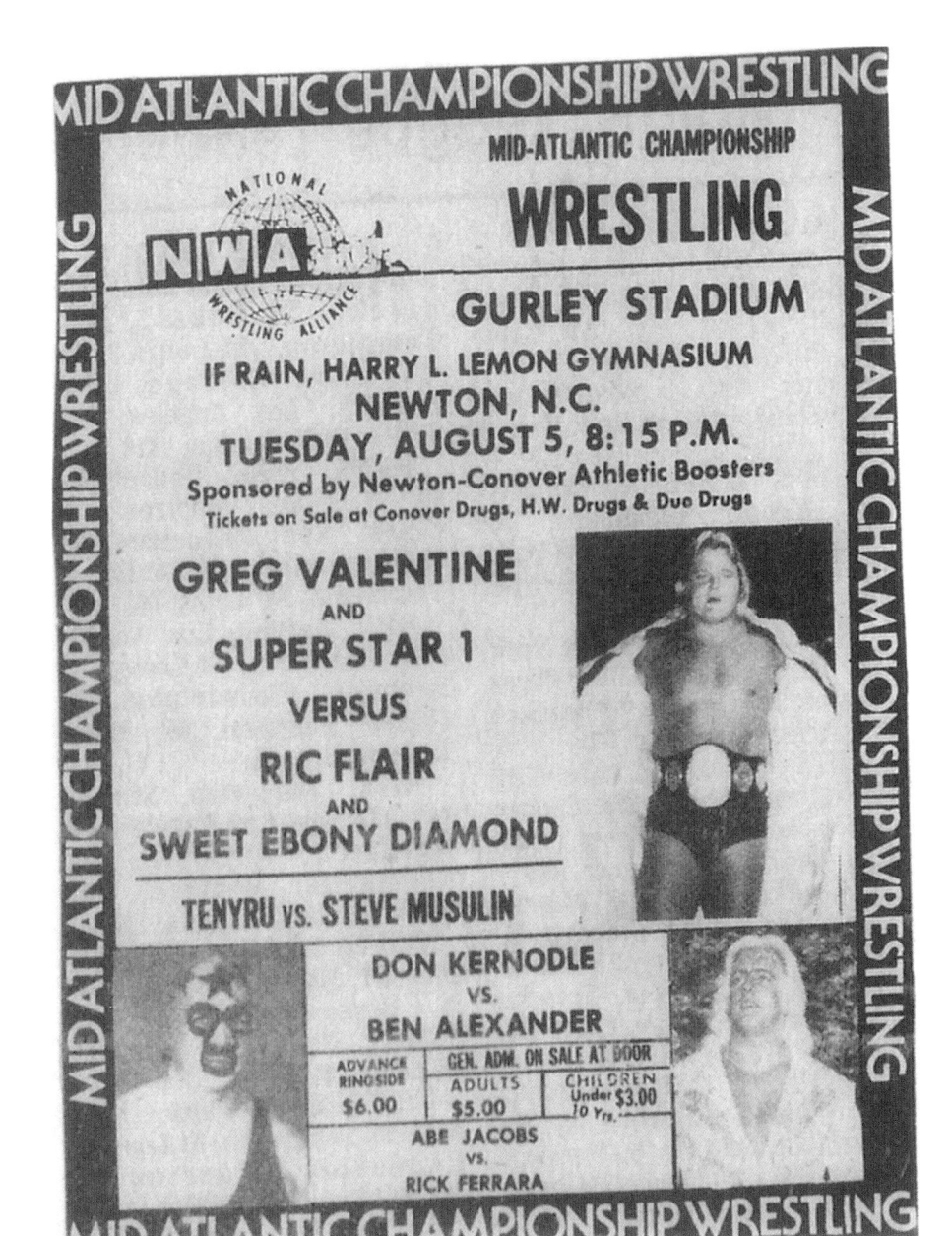

MID ATLANTIC CHAMPIONSHIP WRESTLING

NWA — National Wrestling Alliance

MID-ATLANTIC CHAMPIONSHIP WRESTLING

GURLEY STADIUM

IF RAIN, HARRY L. LEMON GYMNASIUM
NEWTON, N.C.
TUESDAY, AUGUST 5, 8:15 P.M.

Sponsored by Newton-Conover Athletic Boosters
Tickets on Sale at Conover Drugs, H.W. Drugs & Duo Drugs

GREG VALENTINE
AND
SUPER STAR 1
VERSUS
RIC FLAIR
AND
SWEET EBONY DIAMOND

TENYRU vs. STEVE MUSULIN

DON KERNODLE vs. BEN ALEXANDER

ADVANCE RINGSIDE	GEN. ADM. ON SALE AT DOOR	
$6.00	ADULTS $5.00	CHILDREN Under 10 Yrs. $3.00

ABE JACOBS vs. RICK FERRARA

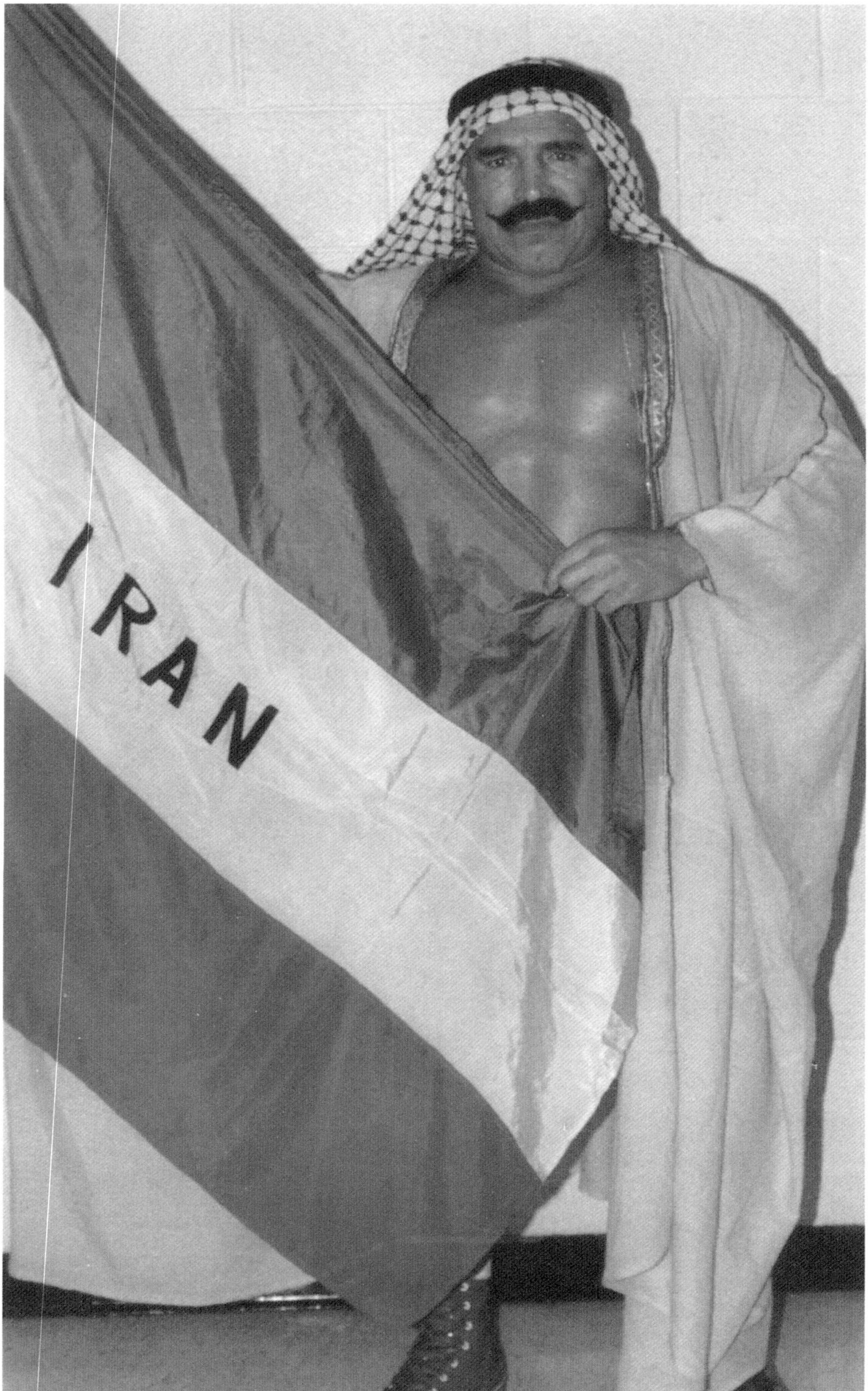
IRAN

NWA MID-ATLANTIC CHAMPIONSHIP WRESTLING

WRESTLING RETURNS NEXT WEEK

AIR-CONDITONED RALEIGH **CIVIC CENTER** • TUES. AUG. 5TH 8:15 PM

RINGSIDE $5.50. GEN ADm. $4.50. CHILDREN (Under 12) $2.50 GEN. ADM.
Tickets on sale at Pop-a-Top Beverage in Mission Valley Shopping Center
AND THE CIVIC CENTER BOX OFFICE

NO DISQUALIFICATION FOR MID-ATLANTIC TITLE
THE IRON SHEIK vs. JIM BRUNZELL

TEXAS STREET FIGHT
BLACKJACK MULLIGAN • VERSUS • ENFORCER LUCIANO

BAD BOY DUNCUM • VERSUS • S.D. JONES

MATT BORNE AND BUZZ SAWYER vs. SWEDE HANSON and BRUTE BERNARD

PLUS OTHER MATCHES

TV WRESTLING THIS SATURDAY ON WRAL-TV

Sheik retains title

The Iron Sheik retained his Mid-Atlantic heavyweight title, defeating Jim Brunzell, Tuesday night in the main event of a pro wrestling card at the Raleigh Civic Center.

In another main event, Black Jack Millugan defeated Enforcer Luciano in Texas street-fight.

In other matches, Cocoa Somoa won on a referee's decision over Billy Starr, Matt Borne and Buzz Sawyer beat Brute Bernard and Swede Hansen in a tag-team bout, and Bad Boy Duncan defeated S.E. Jones.

WIDE WORLD WRESTLING

TOMORROW AUGUST 10 3:00 P.M.

TRIPLE MAIN EVENT

T.V. TITLE MATCH

(T.V. CHAMP)
MASKED SUPERSTAR
-VS-
WRESTLING NO. 2

SUPER STAR | JIM

(½ WORLD TAG CHAMPS)
JIMMY SNUKA
-VS-
JAY YOUNGBLOOD

JIM BRUNZELL
-VS-
BAD BOY DUNCUM

JIMMY | JAY

TAG TEAM MATCH

COWBOY FRANKIE LANE & JAPAN'S TENYRU
-VS-
(MID ATL. TAG CHAMPS)
MATT BORNE & BUZ SAWYER

PRO WRESTLING

ASHEVILLE CIVIC CENTER
Jay Youngblood over Jimmy Snuka; Mr. Wrestling over Masked Superstar; Bad Boy Dungum over Jim Brunzell; Don Kernodle over Coco Somoa; Matt Borne and Buz Sawyer over Frankie Lane and Tenyru.

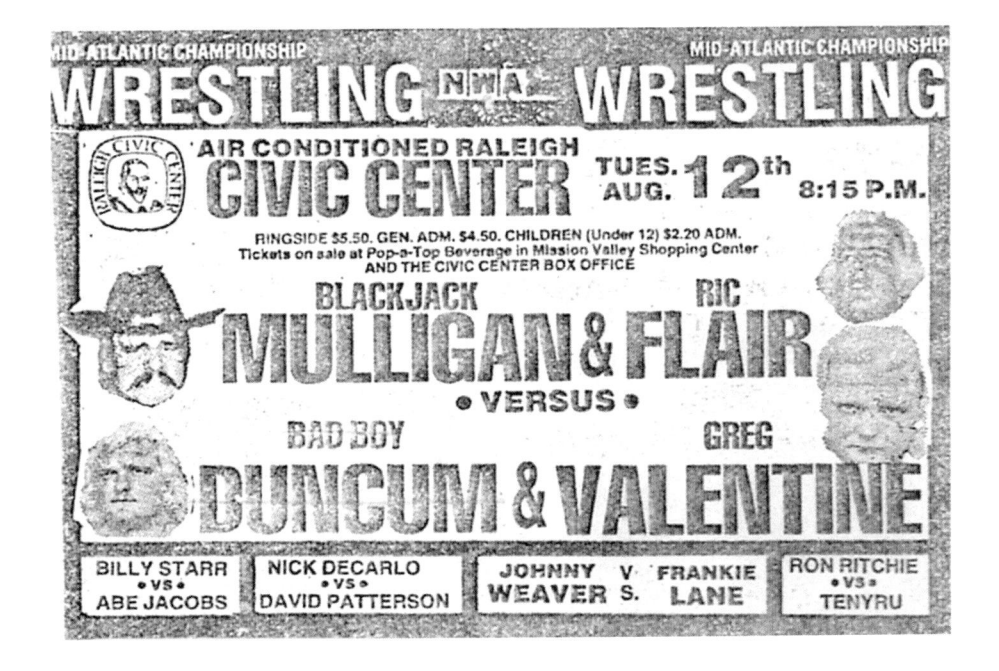

Flair-Mulligan team wins

Ric Flair and Blackjack Mulligan defeated Greg Valentine and the Superstar in the main event Tuesday night at Dorton arena.

In the preliminary matches, Abe Jacobs defeated Billy Starr, David Patterson wrestled to a draw with Nick DeCarlo, Tenyru defeated Ron Ritchie and Johnny Weaver triumphed over Frankie Lane.

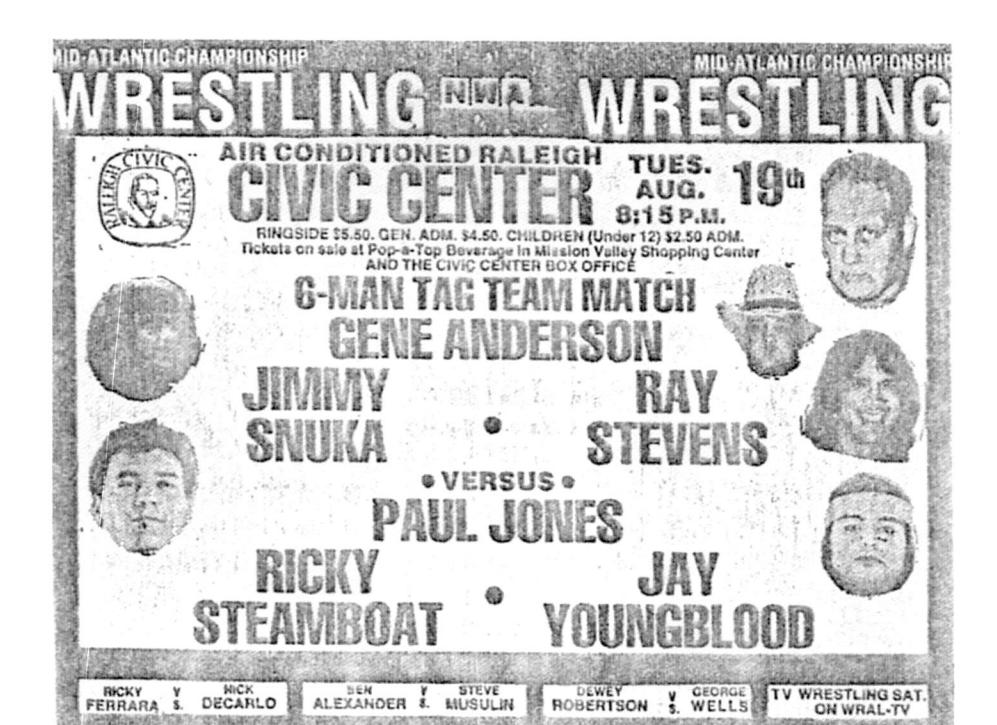

MID-ATLANTIC CHAMPIONSHIP WRESTLING NWA WRESTLING

AIR CONDITIONED RALEIGH CIVIC CENTER
TUES. AUG. 19th 8:15 P.M.

RINGSIDE $5.50. GEN. ADM. $4.50. CHILDREN (Under 12) $2.50 ADM.
Tickets on sale at Pop-a-Top Beverage in Mission Valley Shopping Center AND THE CIVIC CENTER BOX OFFICE

6-MAN TAG TEAM MATCH

GENE ANDERSON
JIMMY SNUKA • **RAY STEVENS**

• VERSUS •

PAUL JONES
RICKY STEAMBOAT • **JAY YOUNGBLOOD**

| RICKY FERRARA | v s. | RICK DECARLO | BEN ALEXANDER | v s. | STEVE MUSULIN | DEWEY ROBERTSON | v s. | GEORGE WELLS | TV WRESTLING SAT. ON WRAL-TV |

Race retains mat crown

Harley Race retained his world's title Tuesday night at the Raleigh Civic Center as he wrestled to a one-hour draw against Rick Flair.

Don Kernodle defeated Billy Star, Tenyru and Steve Musulin battled to a draw, and The Super Star conquered Johnny Weaver in other singles duels.

WIDE WORLD WRESTLING

SUNDAY AUGUST 31 3:00 P.M.

DOUBLE MAIN EVENT

U.S. TITLE MATCH
(U.S. CHAMP) **GREG VALENTINE**
-VS-
(#1) **PAUL JONES**

MAIN EVENT
(NATURE BOY) **RIC FLAIR**
-VS-
BAD BOY DUNCUM

SIX MAN TAG TEAM MATCH

(MID ATL. CHAMPS)
MATT BORNE & BUZ SAWYER & JOHNNY WEAVER
-VS-
GENE LEWIS & BRUTE BERNARD & JAPAN'S TENYRU

PLUS 2 SINGLE MATCHES

BOX OFFICE — 255-5771 • RINGSIDE - $6.00
General Admission $5.00 • Children Under 10 $3.00
Box Office Open Mon.-Fri. 10:00-5:30; Sat. 11:00-4:00; Day of Match 1:00 P.M.
NO CHECKS OR CREDIT CARDS DAY OF MATCH

SEE NWA WORLD WIDE WRESTLING SATURDAY
ON WLOS-TV CHANNEL 13 11:30 PM-12:30 AM

Asheville Civic Center

CIVIC CENTER WRESTLING
Greg Valentine d. Paul Jones; Ric Flair d. Bad Boy Duncam; Matt Borne, Buz Sawyer and Johnny Weaver d. Gene Lewis, Brute Bernard and Tenyru; Ben Alexander and Nick DeCarlo: draw; Abe Jacobs d. Tony 3Russo.

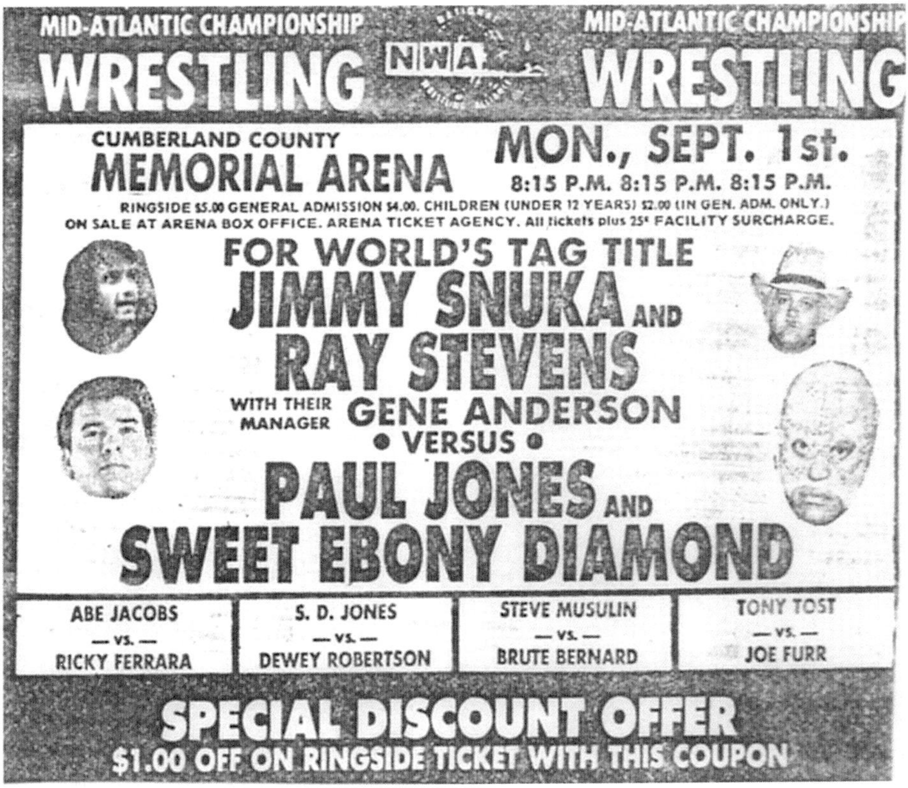

MID-ATLANTIC CHAMPIONSHIP WRESTLING
NWA
MID-ATLANTIC CHAMPIONSHIP WRESTLING

CUMBERLAND COUNTY MEMORIAL ARENA

MON., SEPT. 1st.
8:15 P.M. 8:15 P.M. 8:15 P.M.

RINGSIDE $5.00 GENERAL ADMISSION $4.00. CHILDREN (UNDER 12 YEARS) $2.00 (IN GEN. ADM. ONLY.)
ON SALE AT ARENA BOX OFFICE. ARENA TICKET AGENCY. All tickets plus 25¢ FACILITY SURCHARGE.

FOR WORLD'S TAG TITLE
JIMMY SNUKA AND RAY STEVENS
WITH THEIR MANAGER **GENE ANDERSON**
• VERSUS •
PAUL JONES AND SWEET EBONY DIAMOND

ABE JACOBS	S. D. JONES	STEVE MUSULIN	TONY TOST
— vs. —	— vs. —	— vs. —	— vs. —
RICKY FERRARA	DEWEY ROBERTSON	BRUTE BERNARD	JOE FURR

SPECIAL DISCOUNT OFFER
$1.00 OFF ON RINGSIDE TICKET WITH THIS COUPON

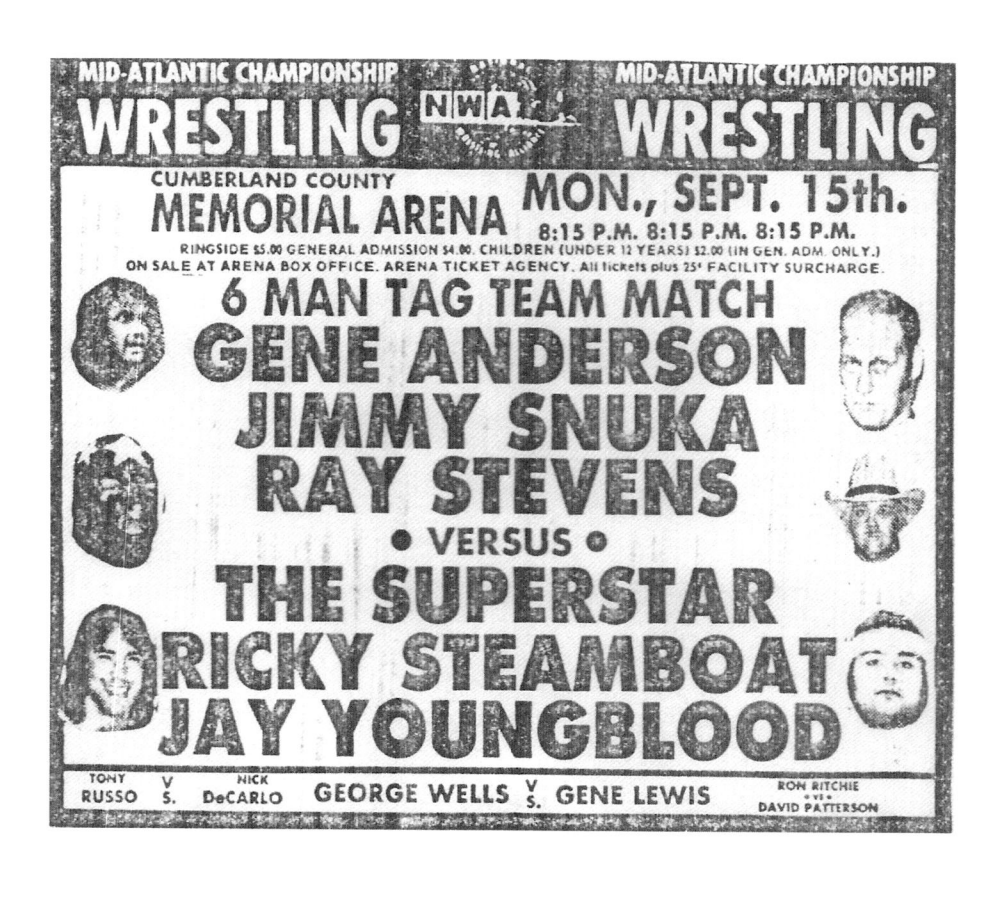

MID-ATLANTIC CHAMPIONSHIP WRESTLING
MID-ATLANTIC CHAMPIONSHIP WRESTLING

NWA

CUMBERLAND COUNTY MEMORIAL ARENA

MON., SEPT. 15th.

8:15 P.M. 8:15 P.M. 8:15 P.M.

RINGSIDE $5.00 GENERAL ADMISSION $4.00. CHILDREN (UNDER 12 YEARS) $2.00 (IN GEN. ADM. ONLY.)
ON SALE AT ARENA BOX OFFICE, ARENA TICKET AGENCY. All tickets plus 25¢ FACILITY SURCHARGE.

6 MAN TAG TEAM MATCH

GENE ANDERSON
JIMMY SNUKA
RAY STEVENS

• VERSUS •

THE SUPERSTAR
RICKY STEAMBOAT
JAY YOUNGBLOOD

TONY RUSSO vs. NICK DeCARLO   GEORGE WELLS vs. GENE LEWIS   RON RITCHIE vs. DAVID PATTERSON

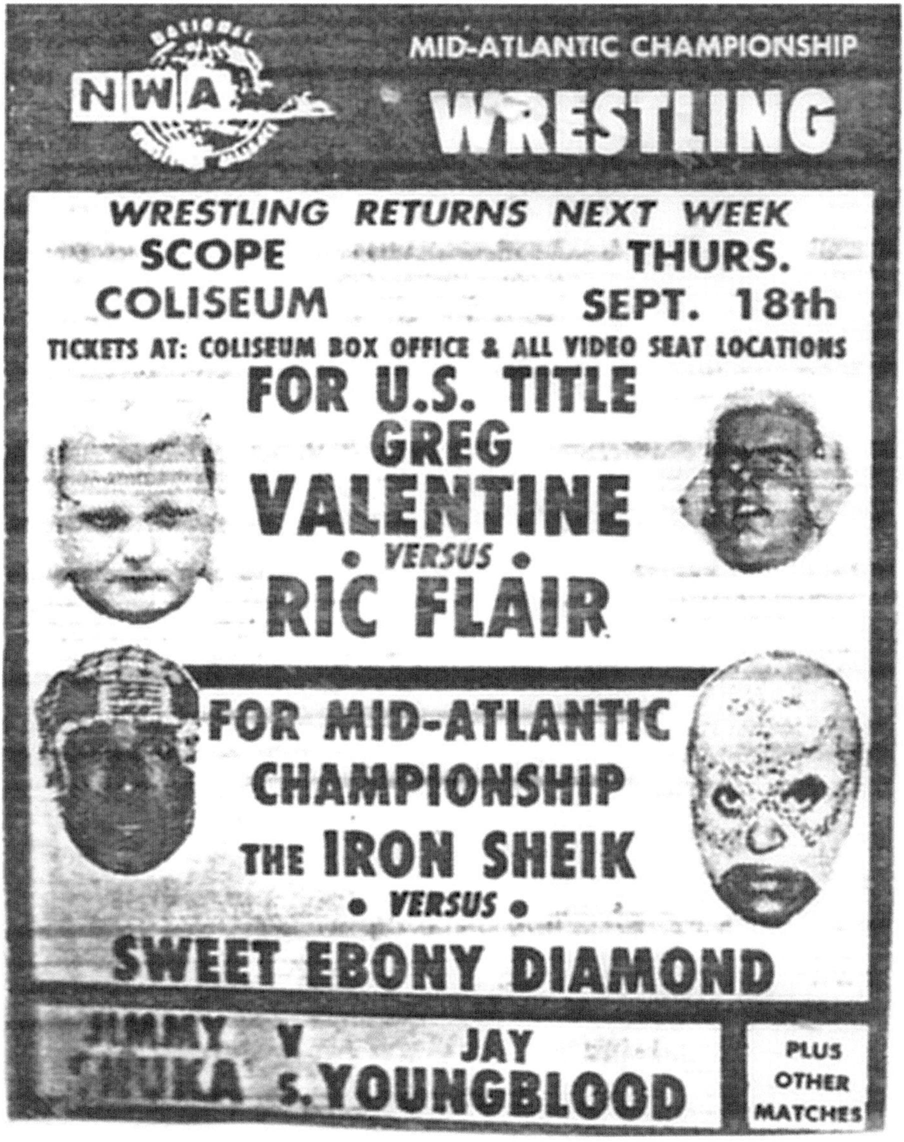

Valentine Mat Victor

NORFOLK—Greg Valentine conquered Ric Flair in the feature of the pro wrestling program Thursday night at Scope.

In other bouts: Sweet Ebony Diamond topped the Iron Sheik; Jimmy Snuka stopped Jay Youngblood; the team of George Wells-Matt Borne-Buzz Sawyer defeated Dewey Robertson and the Sheepherders; Steve Musulin won on disqualification over Tenyru; Ron Ritchie beat Ricky Ferrara; and Abe Jacobs won on a referee's decision over David Patterson.

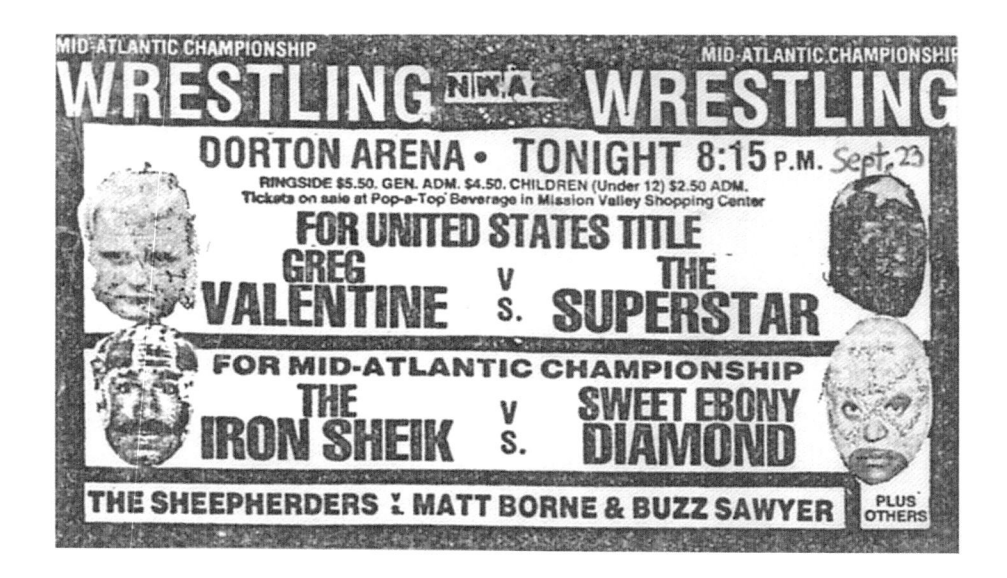

MID-ATLANTIC CHAMPIONSHIP WRESTLING NWA **WRESTLING**

DORTON ARENA • TONIGHT 8:15 P.M. Sept. 23

RINGSIDE $5.50. GEN. ADM. $4.50. CHILDREN (Under 12) $2.50 ADM.
Tickets on sale at Pop-a-Top Beverage in Mission Valley Shopping Center

FOR UNITED STATES TITLE
GREG VALENTINE vs. **THE SUPERSTAR**

FOR MID-ATLANTIC CHAMPIONSHIP
THE IRON SHEIK vs. **SWEET EBONY DIAMOND**

THE SHEEPHERDERS vs. MATT BORNE & BUZZ SAWYER — PLUS OTHERS

Iron Shiek defeats Diamond

In wrestling action Tuesday night at the Dorton Arena, the Iron Sheik defeated Sweet Ebony Diamond and The Superstar was declared a winner over Greg Valentine when Valentine was counted out of the ring.

In other matches, Steve Muslin defeated Tony Russo, Dan Kernodle defeated David Patterson, and the tag team of Matt Borne and Buzz Sawyer defeated the Sheepherders.

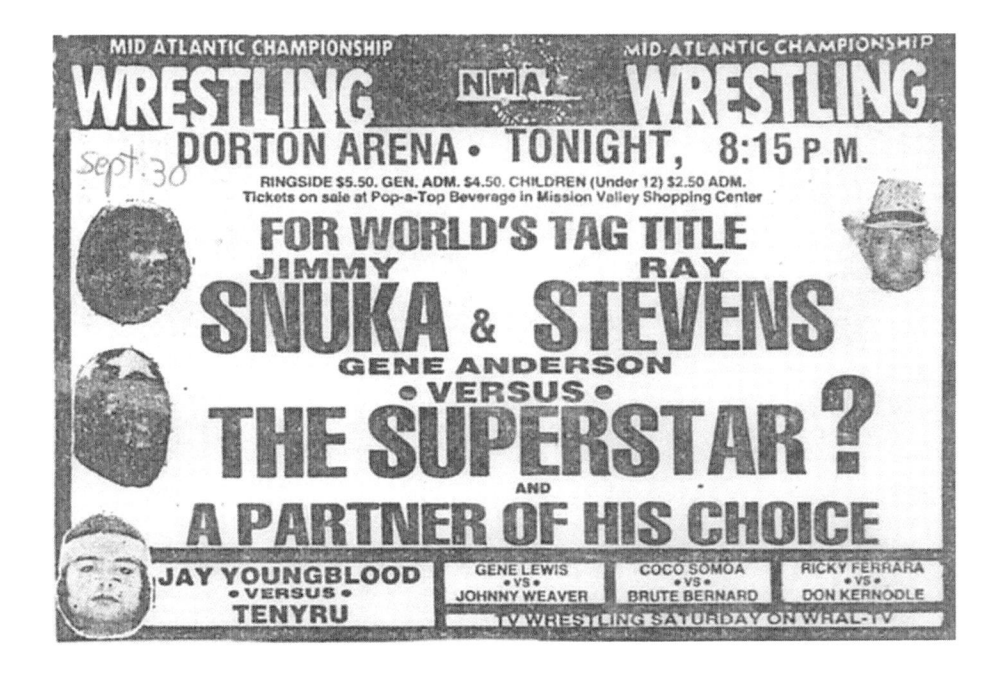

MID-ATLANTIC CHAMPIONSHIP WRESTLING — NWA — **MID-ATLANTIC CHAMPIONSHIP WRESTLING**

DORTON ARENA • TONIGHT, 8:15 P.M.

Sept. 30

RINGSIDE $5.50, GEN. ADM. $4.50, CHILDREN (Under 12) $2.50 ADM.
Tickets on sale at Pop-a-Top Beverage in Mission Valley Shopping Center

FOR WORLD'S TAG TITLE
JIMMY SNUKA & RAY STEVENS
GENE ANDERSON
• VERSUS •
THE SUPERSTAR?
AND
A PARTNER OF HIS CHOICE

| JAY YOUNGBLOOD • VERSUS • TENYRU | GENE LEWIS • VS • JOHNNY WEAVER | COCO SOMOA • VS • BRUTE BERNARD | RICKY FERRARA • VS • DON KERNODLE |

TV WRESTLING SATURDAY ON WRAL-TV

Jones-Superstar win match

The tag team of Paul Jones and The Superstar defeated Jimmy Snuka and Ray Stevens by disqualification Tuesday night, headlining the wrestling card at the Dorton Arena.

In other matches, Jay Youngblood defeated Tenyru, Johnny Weaver was a winner over Gene Lewis, Brute Bernard stopped Coco Somoa and Don Kernodle defeated Ricky Ferrara.

MID-ATLANTIC CHAMPIONSHIP WRESTLING

NWA

DORTON ARENA • TUES., OCT. 7th, 8:15 P.M.

RINGSIDE $5.50. GEN. ADM. $4.50. CHILDREN (Under 12) $2.50 ADM.
Tickets on sale at Pop-a-Top Beverage in Mission Valley Shopping Center

RETURN WORLD TAG TEAM CHAMPIONSHIP

JIMMY SNUKA & RAY STEVENS

• VERSUS •

THE SUPERSTAR & PAUL JONES

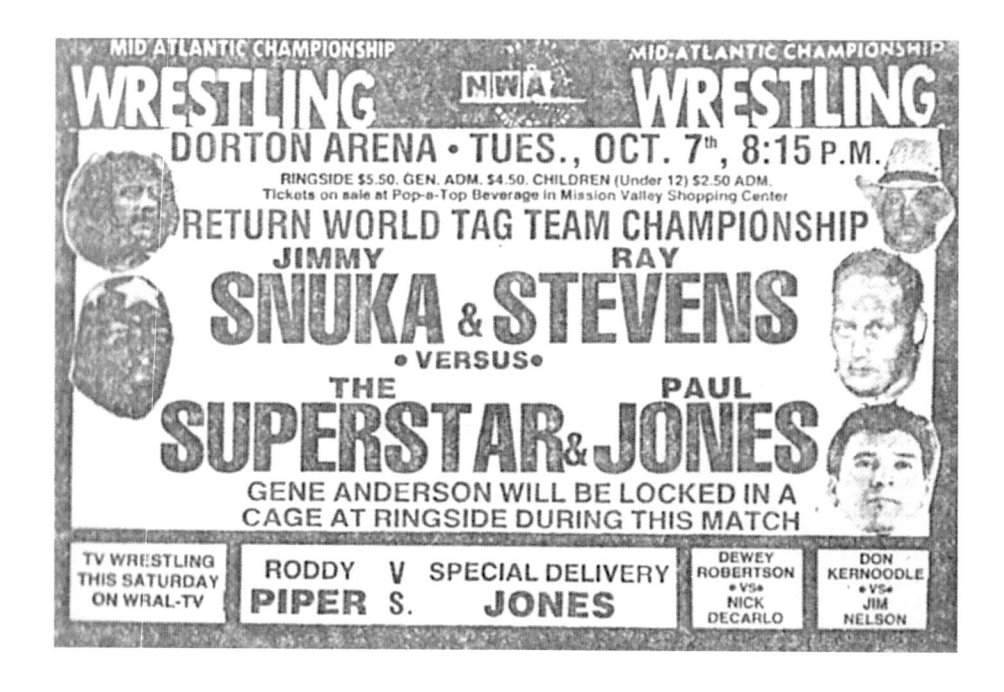

GENE ANDERSON WILL BE LOCKED IN A CAGE AT RINGSIDE DURING THIS MATCH

| TV WRESTLING THIS SATURDAY ON WRAL-TV | RODDY PIPER V S. SPECIAL DELIVERY JONES | DEWEY ROBERTSON • VS • NICK DECARLO | DON KERNOODLE • VS • JIM NELSON |

Jones-Superstar wins match

Paul Jones and the Superstar were declared the winners of the main event at Dorton Arena Tuesday night when Jimmy Snuka and Ray Stevens were counted out of the ring in a pro wrestling tag-team match.

In other bouts, Tenyru defeated Ron Ritchie, Don Kernogle defeated Jim Nelson, Dewey Robertson defeated Nick DeCarlo and Roddey Piper defeated S.D. Jones.

WIDE WORLD WRESTLING

SATURDAY OCTOBER 11 8:15 P.M.

DOUBLE MAIN EVENT

FEATURE MAIN EVENT
MID-ATLANTIC TITLE MATCH

(MID-ATL. CHAMP)
IRON SHIEK
-VS-
#1
PAUL JONES

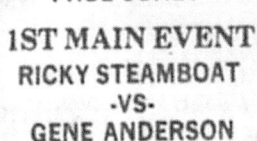

IRON SHIEK — PAUL

1ST MAIN EVENT
RICKY STEAMBOAT
-VS-
GENE ANDERSON

GENE ANDERSON — RICK

TAG TEAM MATCH

(MID-ATL. TAG CHAMPS)
MATT BORNE & BUZ SAWYER
-VS-
GENE LEWIS & JAPAN'S TENYRU

PLUS 2 SINGLE MATCHES

BOX OFFICE — 255-5771 • RINGSIDE - $6.00
General Admission $5.00 • Children Under 10 $3.00
Box Office Open Mon.-Fri. 10:00-5:30; Sat. 11:00-4:00; Day of Match 1:00 P.M.
NO CHECKS OR CREDIT CARDS DAY OF MATCH

SEE NWA WORLD WIDE WRESTLING SATURDAY ON WLOS-TV CHANNEL 13 11:30 PM-12:30 AM

Asheville Civic Center

CIVIC CENTER WRESTLING

The Iron Shiek d. Paul Jones; Ricky Steamboat d. Gene Anderson; Gene Lewis and Tenyru d. Matt Borne and Buz Sawyer; Roddy Piper d. Ron Ritvhie; Abe Jacobs d. Jim Nelson.

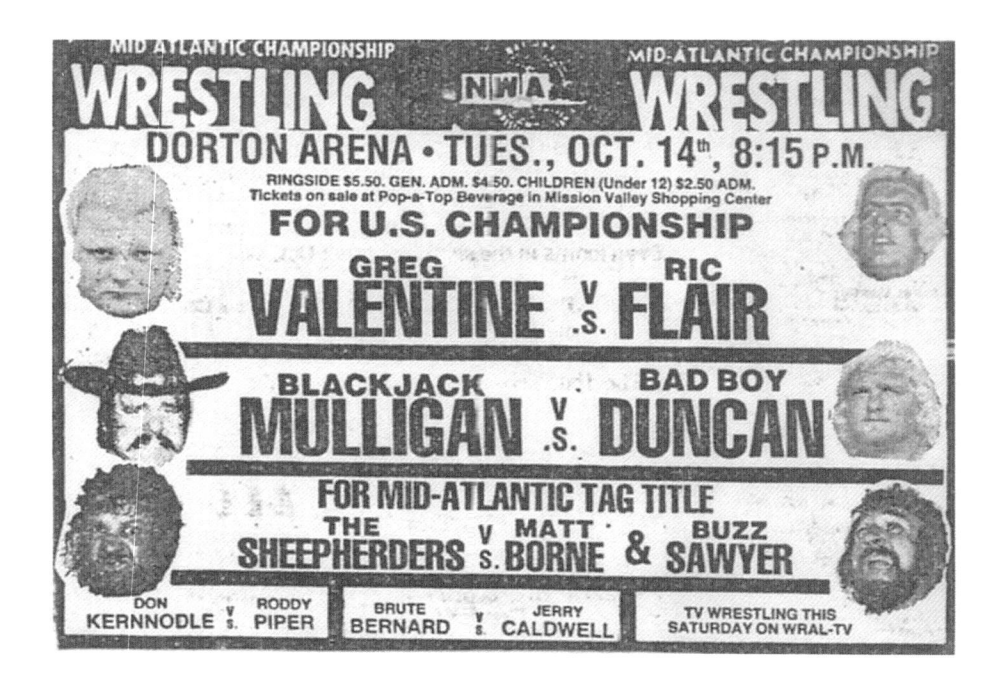

Valentine retains title

Greg Valentine retained his U.S. heavyweight championship, wrestling to a one-hour draw with Ric Flair in the pro headliner at Dorton Arena Tuesday night.

In other matches, the Sheepherders retained their Mid-Atlantic title, defeating Matt Borne and Buzz Sawyer, and Blackjack Mulligan won by disqualification over Bad Boy Duncum. Also, Brute Bernard defeated Jerry Caldwell, and Roddy Piper defeated Don Kernodle.

NWA MID-ATLANTIC CHAMPIONSHIP WRESTLING

SCOPE COLISEUM • THURS. OCT. 16th

TICKETS AT: COLISEUM BOX OFFICE & ALL VIDEO SEAT LOCATIONS

FOR U.S. TITLE
2 REFEREES
GREG VALENTINE v.s. RIC FLAIR

FOR WORLD'S TITLE
RAY STEVENS & JIMMY SNUKA
GENE ANDERSON
• VERSUS •
THE SUPERSTAR
AND A PARTNER OF HIS CHOICE

| THE SHEEPHERDERS V.S. MATT BORNE | & | BUZZ SAWYER | ROONEY PIPER V.S. GEORGE WELLS |

Snuka-Anderson Win

Jimmy Snuka and Gene Anderson won the professional wrestling feature Thursday night at Scope when the referee disqualified Paul Jones and Superstar.

In other bouts: Ric Flair and Greg Valentine fought to a draw; Rodney Piper topped George Wells; Dewey Robertson stopped Nick DeCarlo; Ben Alexander-Swede Hanson conquered Jerry Caldwell-Ron Richie; and The Sheepherders defeated Matt Borne-Steve Musulin.

WIDE WORLD WRESTLING

TODAY OCT. 26 3 P.M.

DOUBLE MAIN EVENT

FEATURE MAIN EVENT
RICKY STEAMBOAT
-VS-
(½ World Tag Champs)
JIMMY SNUKA

JIMMY — *RICK*

1ST MAIN EVENT
MASKED SUPER STAR
-VS-
IRON SHIEK
(MGR. GENE ANDERSON)

RODDY PIPER
-VS-
MATT BORNE

IRON SHIEK — *SUPER STAR*

TAG TEAM MATCH

JOHNNY WEAVER
&
SPC. DELIVERY JONES
-VS-
JAPAN'S TENYRU
&
DEWEY ROBERTSON

PLUS 1 SINGLE MATCH

BOX OFFICE — 255-5771 • RINGSIDE - $6.00
General Admission $5.00 • Children Under 10 $3.00
Box Office Open Mon.-Fri. 10:00-5:30; Sat. 11:00-4:00; Day of Match 1:00 P.M.
NO CHECKS OR CREDIT CARDS DAY OF MATCH

SEE NWA WORLD WIDE WRESTLING SATURDAY
ON WLOS-TV CHANNEL 13 11:30 PM-12:30 AM

Asheville Civic Center

MID ATLANTIC WRESTLING
Main Events — Ricky Steamboat d. Jimmy Snuka; Masked Superstar d. Iron Shiek; Roddy Piper d. Matt Borne; **Tag Team** — Johnny Weaver-Special Delivery Jones d. Japan's Tenyru-Dewey Robertson; Jim Nelson and Waynes Rogers wrestled to draw.

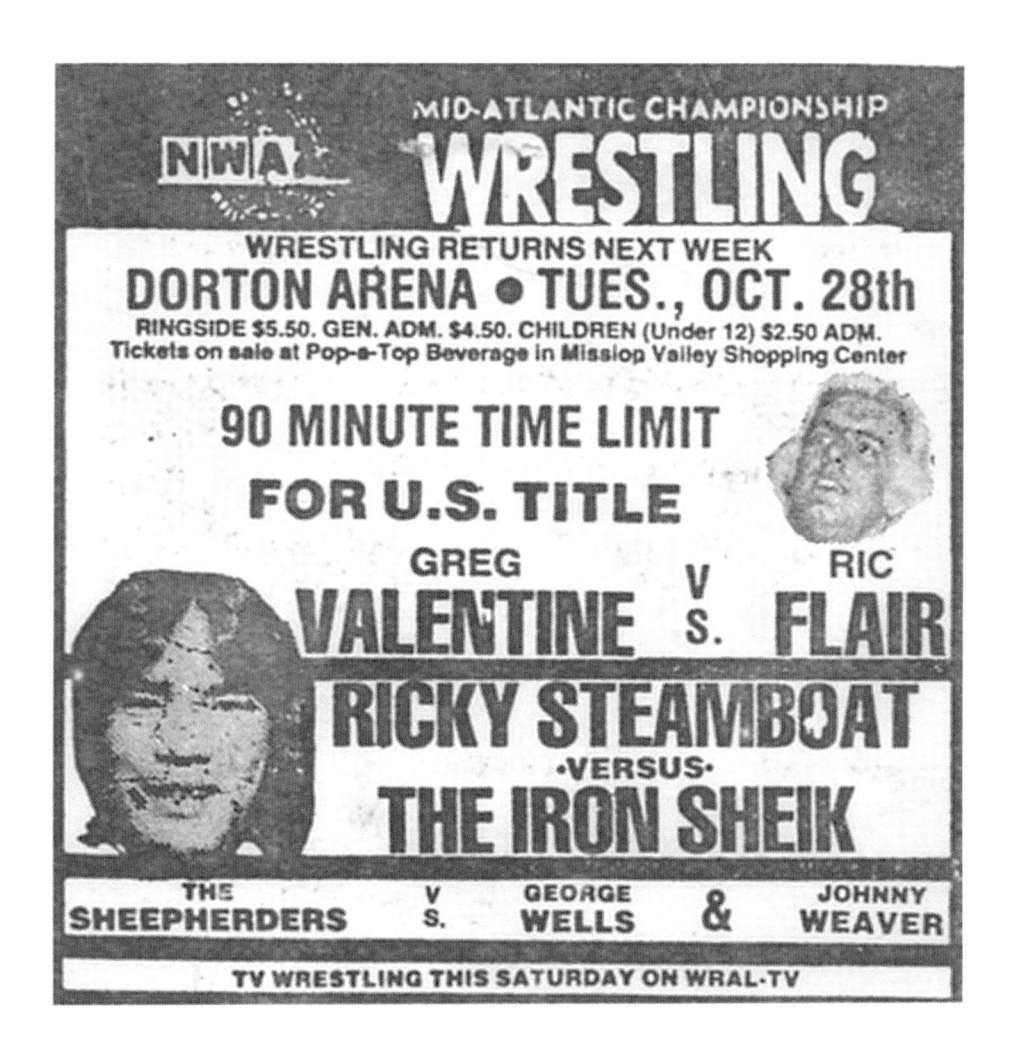

MID-ATLANTIC CHAMPIONSHIP NWA WRESTLING

WRESTLING RETURNS NEXT WEEK
DORTON ARENA • TUES., OCT. 28th

RINGSIDE $5.50. GEN. ADM. $4.50. CHILDREN (Under 12) $2.50 ADM.
Tickets on sale at Pop-a-Top Beverage in Mission Valley Shopping Center

90 MINUTE TIME LIMIT FOR U.S. TITLE
GREG VALENTINE vs. RIC FLAIR

RICKY STEAMBOAT VERSUS THE IRON SHEIK

THE SHEEPHERDERS vs. GEORGE WELLS & JOHNNY WEAVER

TV WRESTLING THIS SATURDAY ON WRAL-TV

Steamboat defeats Sheik

Ricky Steamboat defeated the Iron Sheik Tuesday night at Dorton Arena in one of two pro wrestling main events.

In the other, Ric Flair and Greg Valentine ended their match in a draw with both wrestlers being counted out of the ring.

Tony Tosi defeated Jim Nelson. Ben Alexander drew with Abe Jacobs. In a tag match, George Wells and Johnny Weaver won by disqualification over the Sheepherders.

GREENSBORO COLISEUM

MID-ATLANTIC CHAMPIONSHIP WRESTLING

SUN., NOV. 2nd 8:00 PM

MAIN EVENT: TEXAS DEATH MATCH

BLACKJACK MULLIGAN vs. BAD BOY DUNCUM

PLUS

19 MAN TWO RING BATTLE ROYAL
7 BIG MATCHES — $10,000 TO WINNER

Ricky Steamboat	Ole Anderson	Butch Miller	Sweet Ebony Diamond	Greg Valentine
Luke Williams	Johnny Weaver	Ivan Koloff	Tenyru	Special Delivery Jones
Terry Funk	Brute Bernard	Don Kernodle	Matt Borne	ALREADY
Swede Hanson	Angelo Mosca	Steve Musulin	Nick DeCarlo	ENTERED
Terry Taylor				

Mulligan Tops Duncum

Blackjack Mulligan won over Bad Boy Duncum at 27:40 of their match Sunday evening in the featured match of pro wrestling action at the Greensboro Coliseum before 4,126 spectators.

Ricky Steamboat took the battle royal with Ole Anderson the other wrestler left in the ring.

In a tag team match, the team of Butch Miller-Luke Williams defeated Special Delivery Jones and Nick DeCarlo.

In other matches, Angelo Mosca defeated Swede Hanson, George Wells toppled Gene Lewis and Matt Warren and Tenyru fought to a draw in the curtain raiser.

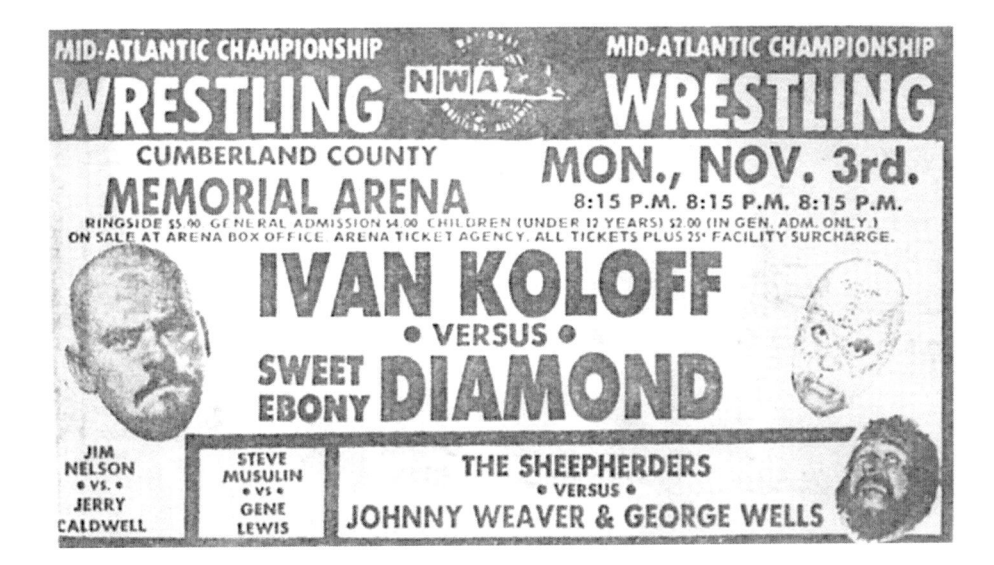

MID-ATLANTIC CHAMPIONSHIP WRESTLING

NWA

CUMBERLAND COUNTY MEMORIAL ARENA

MON., NOV. 3rd.
8:15 P.M. 8:15 P.M. 8:15 P.M.

RINGSIDE $5.00 GENERAL ADMISSION $4.00 CHILDREN (UNDER 12 YEARS) $2.00 (IN GEN. ADM. ONLY.)
ON SALE AT ARENA BOX OFFICE, ARENA TICKET AGENCY. ALL TICKETS PLUS 25¢ FACILITY SURCHARGE.

IVAN KOLOFF
• VERSUS •
SWEET EBONY DIAMOND

JIM NELSON vs. JERRY CALDWELL

STEVE MUSULIN vs. GENE LEWIS

THE SHEEPHERDERS
• VERSUS •
JOHNNY WEAVER & GEORGE WELLS

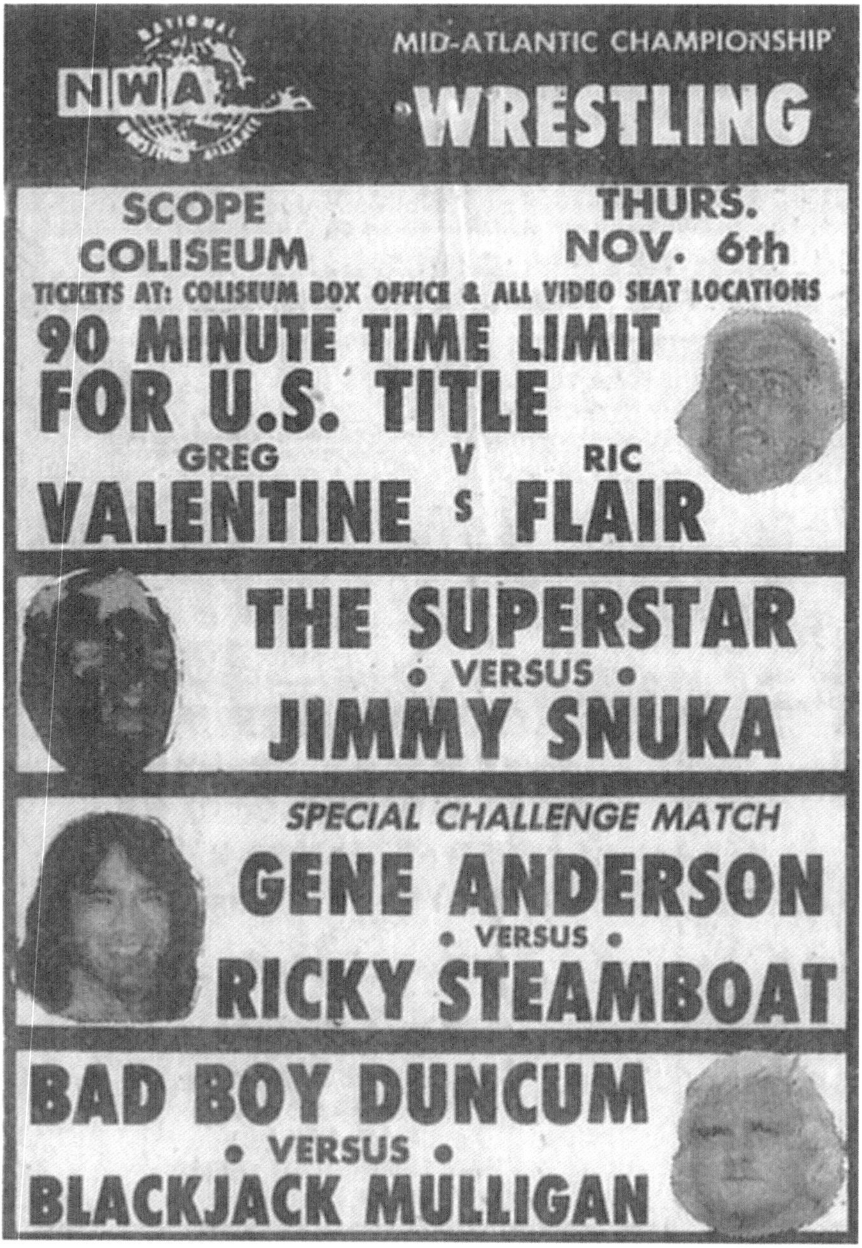

NWA MID-ATLANTIC CHAMPIONSHIP WRESTLING

SCOPE COLISEUM — THURS. NOV. 6th

TICKETS AT: COLISEUM BOX OFFICE & ALL VIDEO SEAT LOCATIONS

90 MINUTE TIME LIMIT FOR U.S. TITLE
GREG VALENTINE vs RIC FLAIR

THE SUPERSTAR VERSUS JIMMY SNUKA

SPECIAL CHALLENGE MATCH
GENE ANDERSON VERSUS RICKY STEAMBOAT

BAD BOY DUNCUM VERSUS BLACKJACK MULLIGAN

Ric Flair Wins

Ric Flair conquered Greg Valentine when Valentine left the ring and was counted out in the feature of the pro wrestling card at Scope Thursday night.

In other bouts, Superstar topped Jimmy Snuka; Ricky Steamboat defeated Gene Anderson; Blackjack Mulligan downed Bad Boy Duncum; Special Delivery Jones-George Wells defeated The Sheepherders; Roddy Piper stopped Matt Borne; Nick DeCarlo-Ron Ritchie beat Ben Alexander-Gene Lewis.

MID ATLANTIC CHAMPIONSHIP WRESTLING

NWA — National Wrestling Alliance

Newton-Conover High School
Harry L. Lemon Gymnasium

November 8, 1980 — 8:15 P.M.

Ricky Steamboat
vs.
Ray Stevens

Sheephearders vs. Johnny Weaver & Matt Barn

Black Jack Mulligan
vs.
Bad Boy Duncum

Sponsored by the Newton-Conover High School Athletic Boosters Club

Roddy Piper vs. **Steve Musulin**

Wayne Rogers vs. **Brute Bernard**

Reserved Ringside	Adult Gen. Adm.	Children Gen. Adm.
$6.00	$5.00	$3.00

Advanced Reserve Tickets On Sale at:
- Conover Drugs, Conover, N.C.
- H&W Drugs, Newton, N.C.
- City Pharmacy, Newton, N.C.
- Bowman Drugs, Conover, N.C.

MID ATLANTIC CHAMPIONSHIP WRESTLING

WIDE WORLD WRESTLING

SUNDAY NOV. 9 3: P.M.

TRIPLE MAIN EVENT

FEATURE MAIN EVENT
U.S. TITLE MATCH

GREG VALENTINE
-VS-
NATURE BOY RIC FLAIR

GREG | RIC

BLACK JACK MULLIGAN
-VS-
BAD BOY BOBBY DUNCAN

RODDY PIPER
-VS-
#1 PAUL JONES

BOB | BLACKJACK

TAG TEAM MATCH

Mid Atl. Tag Champs
"The Sheepherders"
LUKE WILLIAMS & BUTCH MILLER
-VS-
SPC DELIVERY JONES & JOHNNY WEAVER

PLUS 2 SINGLE MATCHES

BOX OFFICE — 255-6771 • RINGSIDE - $6.00
General Admission $5.00 • Children Under 10 $3.00
Box Office Open Mon.-Fri. 10:00-5:30; Sat. 11:00-4:00; Day of Match 1:00 P.M.
NO CHECKS OR CREDIT CARDS DAY OF MATCH

SEE NWA WORLD WIDE WRESTLING SATURDAY
ON WLOS-TV CHANNEL 13 11:30 PM-12:30 AM

Asheville Civic Center

MID ATLANTIC CHAMPIONSHIP WRESTLING

Nature Boy Ric Flair d. Greg Valentine; Blackjack Mulligan d. Bad Boy Duncan; Roddy Piper d. Paul Jones; Japan's Tenyru vs. Dewey Robertson—both were disqualified; Steve Musulin d. Jim Nelson

Tag Teams — Luke Williams-Butch Miller d. Special Delivery Jones-Johnny Weaver

Diamond defeats Koloff

Sweet Ebony Diamond defeated Ivan Koloff and Ricky Steamboat won by disqualification over Roddy Piper in wrestling action Tuesday night at Dorton Arena.

In a tag team match, the Sheepherders beat Matt Borne and S.D. Jones. Steve Muslin whipped Ricky Ferrara and Kim Duk defeated Abe Jacobs in other matches.

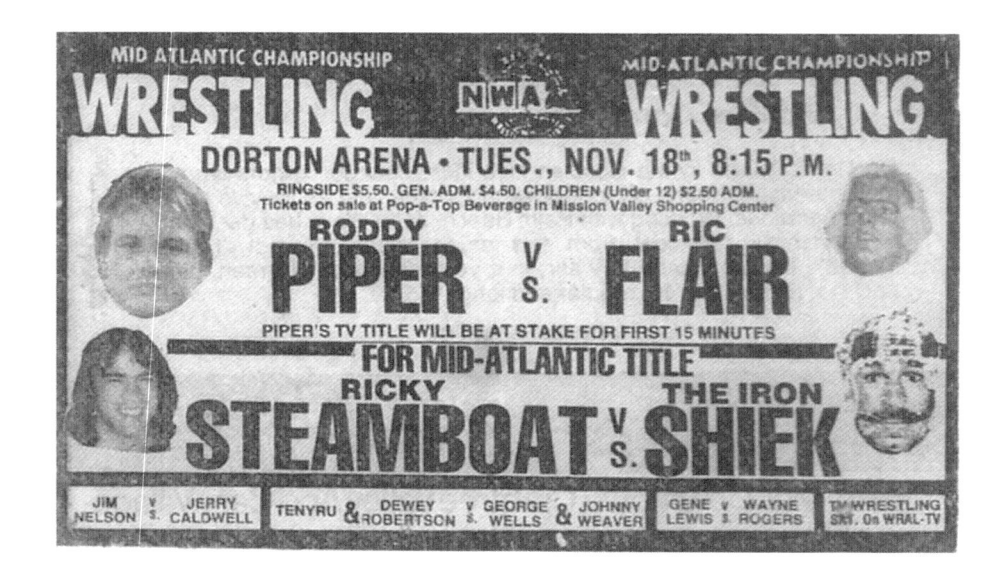

Steamboat, Piper win

Ricky Steamboat retained his Mid-Atlantic title by conquering the Iron Sheik and Roddy Piper defeated Rik Flair in the main wrestling events at Dorton Arena Tuesday night.

Jim Nelson whipped Jerry Caldwell and Gene Lewis tamed Wayne Rogers in singles events. In a tag-team match, Johnny Weaver and George Wells beat Dewey Robertson and Tenyru.

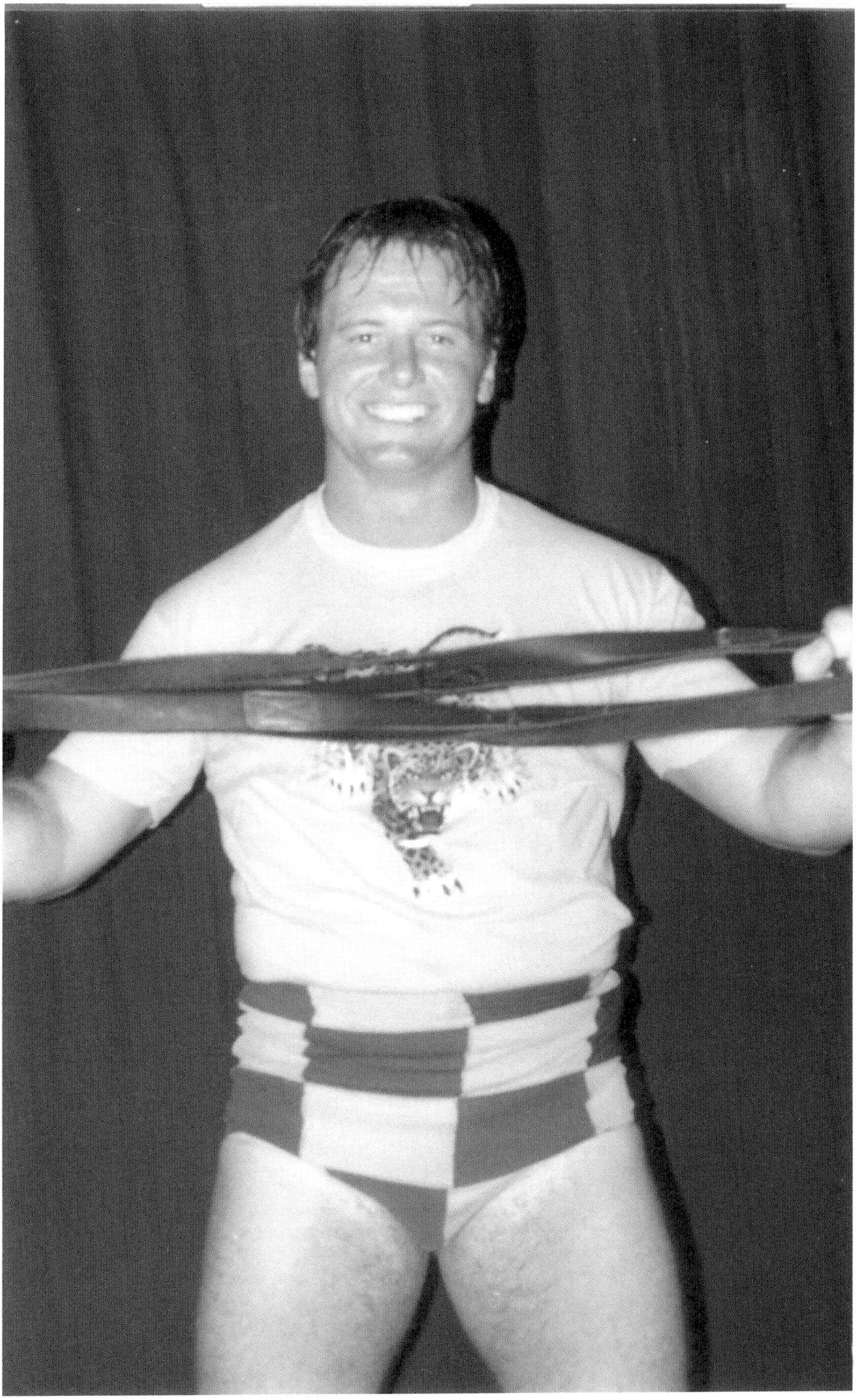

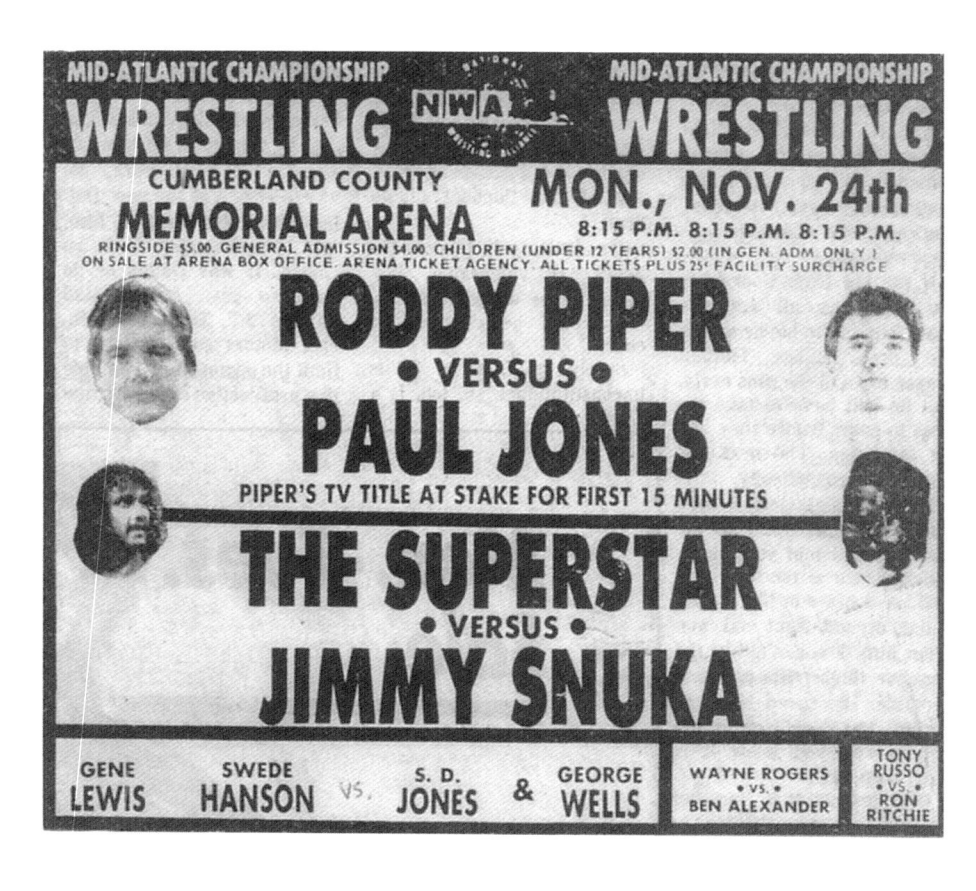

MID-ATLANTIC CHAMPIONSHIP WRESTLING

MID-ATLANTIC CHAMPIONSHIP WRESTLING

NWA

CUMBERLAND COUNTY MEMORIAL ARENA

MON., NOV. 24th
8:15 P.M. 8:15 P.M. 8:15 P.M.

RINGSIDE $5.00. GENERAL ADMISSION $4.00. CHILDREN (UNDER 12 YEARS) $2.00 (IN GEN. ADM. ONLY.)
ON SALE AT ARENA BOX OFFICE. ARENA TICKET AGENCY. ALL TICKETS PLUS 25¢ FACILITY SURCHARGE

RODDY PIPER
• VERSUS •
PAUL JONES

PIPER'S TV TITLE AT STAKE FOR FIRST 15 MINUTES

THE SUPERSTAR
• VERSUS •
JIMMY SNUKA

| GENE LEWIS | SWEDE HANSON | VS. | S. D. JONES | & | GEORGE WELLS | WAYNE ROGERS • VS. • BEN ALEXANDER | TONY RUSSO • VS. • RON RITCHIE |

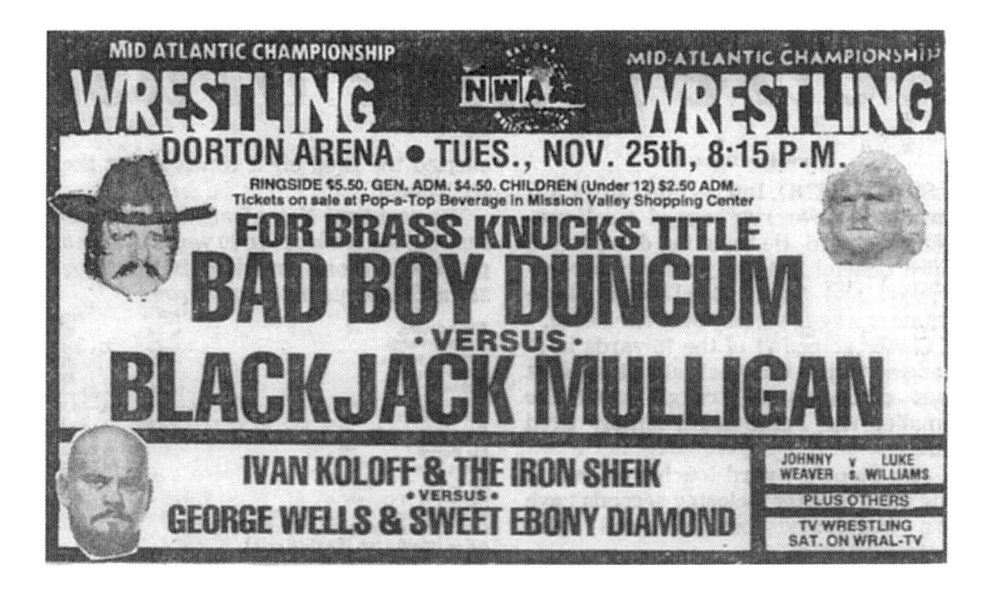

MID ATLANTIC CHAMPIONSHIP WRESTLING

NWA

DORTON ARENA • TUES., NOV. 25th, 8:15 P.M.

RINGSIDE $5.50. GEN. ADM. $4.50. CHILDREN (Under 12) $2.50 ADM.
Tickets on sale at Pop-a-Top Beverage in Mission Valley Shopping Center

FOR BRASS KNUCKS TITLE
BAD BOY DUNCUM
· VERSUS ·
BLACKJACK MULLIGAN

IVAN KOLOFF & THE IRON SHEIK
· VERSUS ·
GEORGE WELLS & SWEET EBONY DIAMOND

JOHNNY WEAVER v LUKE S. WILLIAMS

PLUS OTHERS

TV WRESTLING SAT. ON WRAL-TV

Duncam retains title

Bad Boy Duncam retained his Brass Knucks title Tuesday night when he defeated Black Jack Mulligan in the main event on the championship wrestling card at Dorton Arena.

In a tag-team match, George Wells and Sweet Ebony Diamond won by disqualification over Ivan Koloff and The Iron Sheik. In othe matches, Tenyru defeated Wayne Rogers, Steve Musulin was declared the winner on referee's decision over Butch Miller and Johnny Weaver defeated **Luke Williams**.

TONITE

THANKSGIVING NIGHT SPECTACULAR AT THE GREENSBORO COLISEUM FEATURING THE BIGGEST NIGHT OF MID-ATLANTIC CHAMPIONSHIP WRESTLING EVER...

GREENSBORO COLISEUM · THURSDAY, NOVEMBER 27, 1980 · 8:15 P.M.

4 SUPER CHAMPIONSHIP MATCHES

WORLD'S TAG TEAM CHAMPIONSHIP MATCH INSIDE A 10 FOOT STEEL LINK CAGE

JIMMY SNUKA AND RAY STEVENS VS PAUL JONES AND SUPERSTAR

IF JONES AND THE SUPERSTAR DO NOT WIN THEY WILL HAND OUT 1000 ONE DOLLAR BILLS TO THE FANS AND THE SUPERSTAR WILL UNMASK IN THE RING WIN OR LOSE.

UNITED STATES HEAVYWEIGHT CHAMPIONSHIP MATCH INSIDE A 10 FOOT STEEL LINK CAGE...

GREG VALENTINE VS RIC FLAIR

MID-ATLANTIC TAG TEAM CHAMPIONSHIP MATCH	Plus	N.W.A. TV TITLE MATCH
THE SHEEPHERDERS VERSUS DEWEY ROBERTSON AND MATT BORNE	**3 more big bouts**	**RODDY PIPER VERSUS JOHNNY WEAVER**

All seats reserved. $10.00 ringside, all others $7.00 and $5.00. Children 10 & under—$3.50 & $2.50. Phone Coliseum Box Office for reservations. 919-294-2870

11-26R

Jones And Superstar Gain Tag Team Title

Paul Jones and Superstar defeated Jimmy Snuka and Ray Stevens for the World Tag Team Championship Thursday night at the Coliseum.

A crowd of almost 12,000 attended the Thanksgiving Day matches, which saw Ric Flair win the U.S. Heavyweight crown over Greg Valentine. In the NWA-TV title match, Roddy Piper successfully defended against Johnny Weaver, while the Sheepherders ripped through Dewey Robertson and Matt Borne in the Mid-Atlantic Tag Team championship.

In other matches, Candy Malloy beat Wendy Richer, "Special Delivery" Jones defeated Ben Alexander, and Ricky Ferrara and Abe Jacobs battled to a 15-minutes draw.

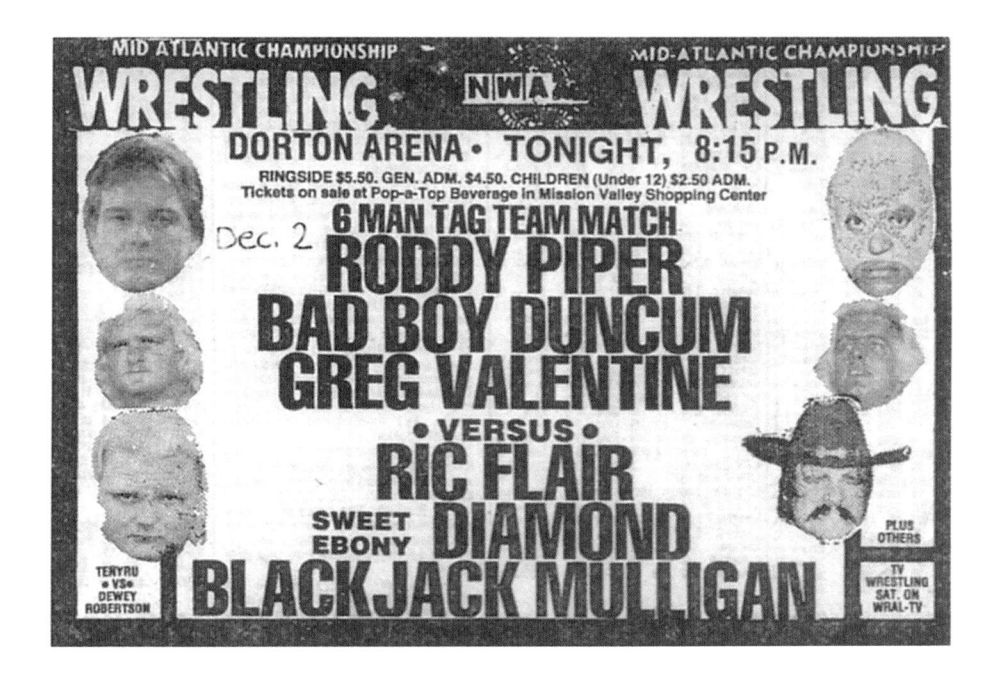

MID ATLANTIC CHAMPIONSHIP WRESTLING
NWA
MID-ATLANTIC CHAMPIONSHIP WRESTLING

DORTON ARENA • TONIGHT, 8:15 P.M.
RINGSIDE $5.50. GEN. ADM. $4.50. CHILDREN (Under 12) $2.50 ADM.
Tickets on sale at Pop-a-Top Beverage in Mission Valley Shopping Center

Dec. 2

6 MAN TAG TEAM MATCH
RODDY PIPER
BAD BOY DUNCUM
GREG VALENTINE

• VERSUS •

RIC FLAIR
SWEET EBONY DIAMOND
BLACKJACK MULLIGAN

PLUS OTHERS

TENYRU • VS • DEWEY ROBERTSON

TV WRESTLING SAT. ON WRAL-TV

Flair team loses

Robby Piper, Bad Boy Duncam and Greg Valentine defeated Ric Flair, Sweet Ebony Diamond and Black Jack Mulligan in a six-man tag team match Tuesday night in championship wrestling at Dorton Arena.

In other matches, Steve Musulin wrestled to a draw against Jim Nelson, Swede Hanson defeated S.D. Jones and Dewey Robertson won over Tenyru.

WIDE WORLD WRESTLING

SUNDAY DEC. 7 3:00 P.M.

DOUBLE MAIN EVENT

FEATURE MAIN EVENT
T.V. TITLE MATCH

(T.V. CHAMP) **RODDY PIPER**
-VS-
(U.S. CHAMP) **RIC FLAIR**

GREG VALENTINE
-VS-
SWEET EBONY DIAMOND

NO DQ NO COUNT OUT
JAPAN'S TENYURU
-VS-
DEWEY ROBERTSON

TAG TEAM MATCH
KIM DUK & SWEDE HANSON
-VS-
DON KERNODLE & MATT BORNE

PLUS 1 SINGLE MATCH

BOX OFFICE—255-5771 • RINGSIDE - $6.00
General Admission $5.00 • Children Under 10 $3.00
Box Office Open Mon.-Fri. 10:00-5:30; Sat. 11:00-4:00; Day of Match 1:00 P.M.
NO CHECKS OR CREDIT CARDS DAY OF MATCH

SEE NWA WORLD WIDE WRESTLING SATURDAY
ON WLOS-TV CHANNEL 13 1:30 PM-12:30 AM

Asheville Civic Center

WRESTLING
CIVIC CENTER WRESTLING
Roddy Piper d. Ric Flair; Greg Valentine d. Sweet Ebony Diamond; Dewey Robertson d. Japan's Tenyru; Kim Duk and Swede Hanson d. Don Kernodle and Matt Borne; Nick DeCarlo d. Ben Alexander.

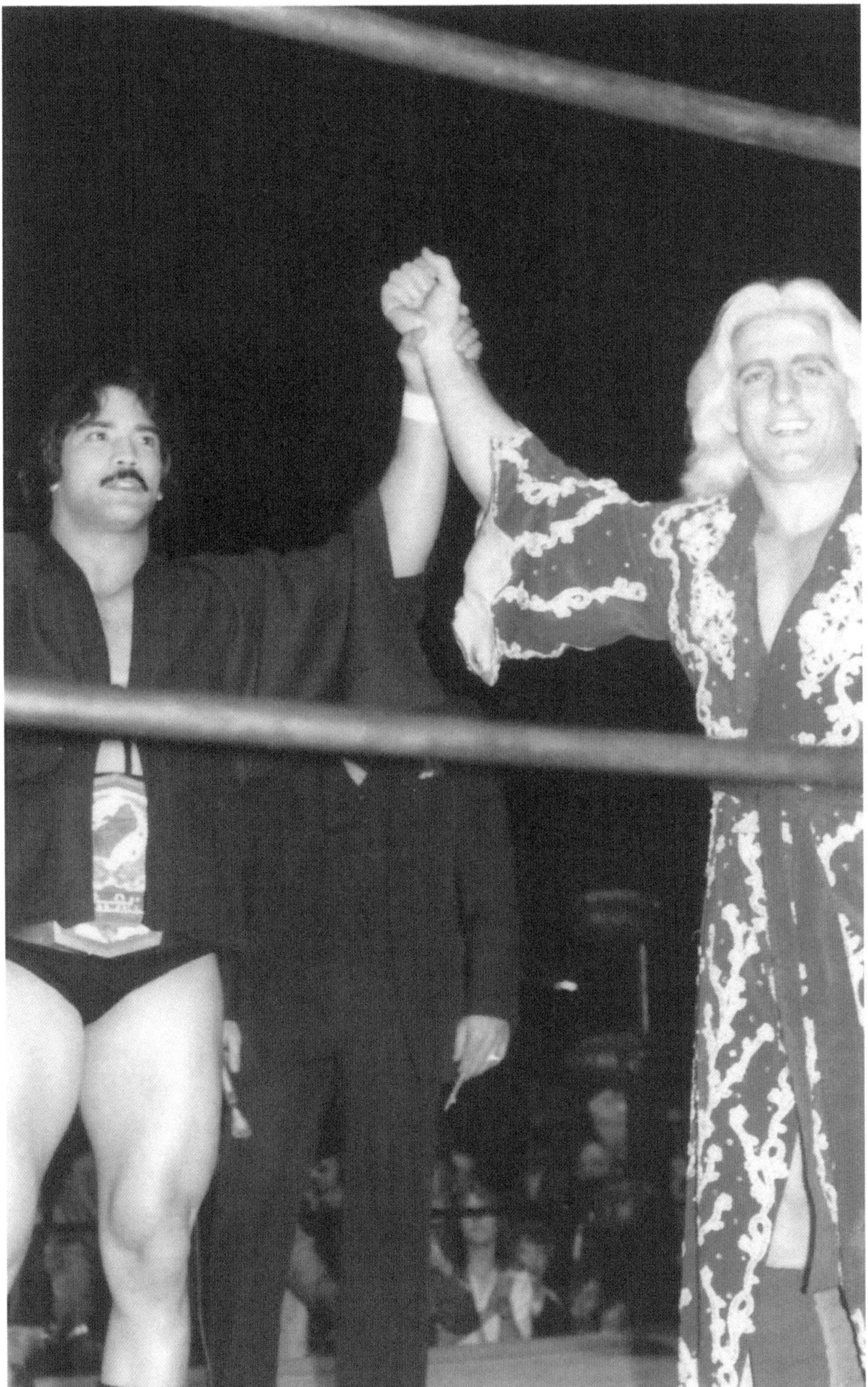

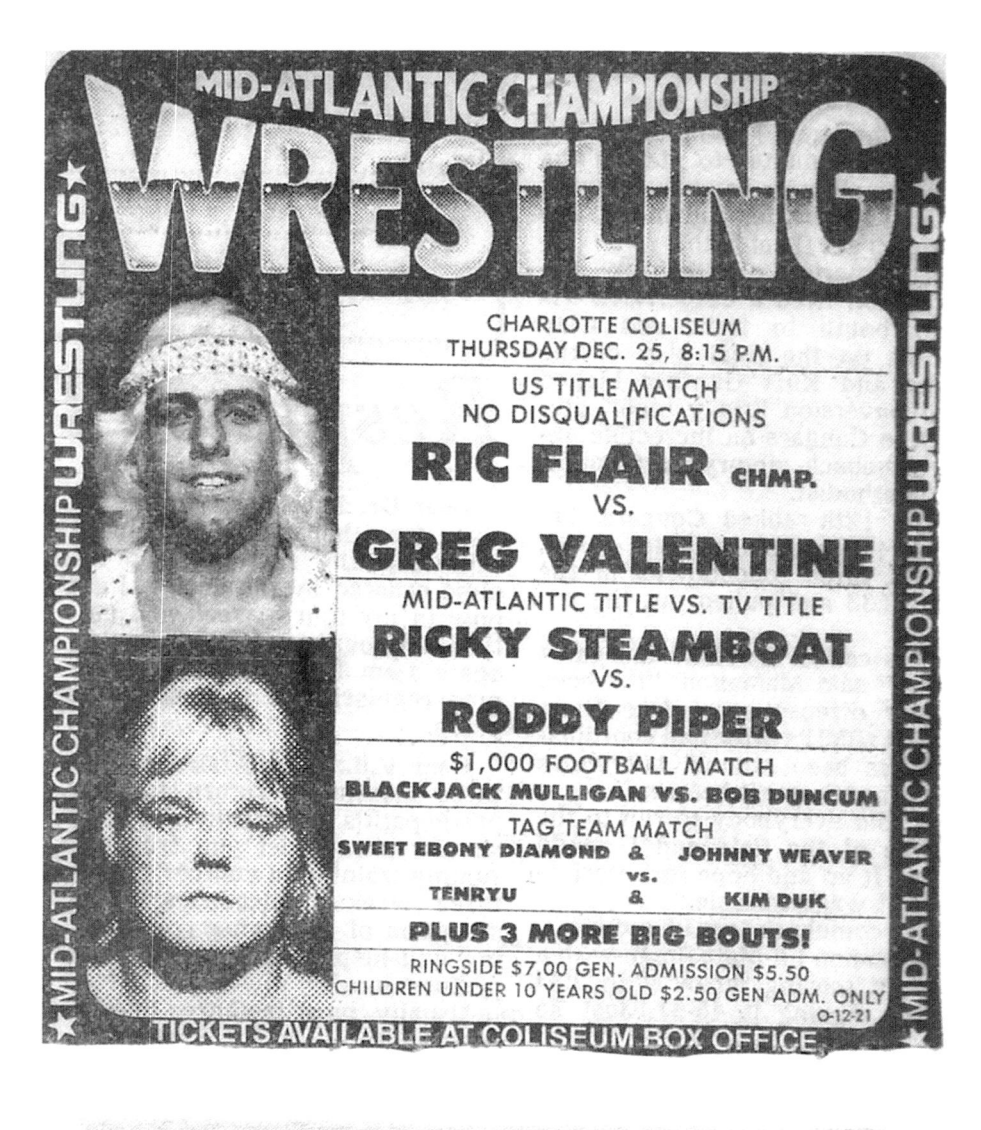

MID-ATLANTIC CHAMPIONSHIP WRESTLING

CHARLOTTE COLISEUM
THURSDAY DEC. 25, 8:15 P.M.

US TITLE MATCH
NO DISQUALIFICATIONS
RIC FLAIR CHMP.
VS.
GREG VALENTINE

MID-ATLANTIC TITLE VS. TV TITLE
RICKY STEAMBOAT
VS.
RODDY PIPER

$1,000 FOOTBALL MATCH
BLACKJACK MULLIGAN VS. BOB DUNCUM

TAG TEAM MATCH
SWEET EBONY DIAMOND & JOHNNY WEAVER
VS.
TENRYU & KIM DUK

PLUS 3 MORE BIG BOUTS!

RINGSIDE $7.00 GEN. ADMISSION $5.50
CHILDREN UNDER 10 YEARS OLD $2.50 GEN ADM. ONLY
O-12-21

TICKETS AVAILABLE AT COLISEUM BOX OFFICE

Flair Wins Pro Wrestling

Ric Flair retained his U.S. title by defeating Greg Valentine in 36 minutes in the main event of a professional wrestling card Thursday at the Coliseum.

In other matches, Ricky Steamboat defeated Roddy Piper by disqualification and Blackjack Mulligan beat Bob Duncum in the $1,000 football match. Sweet Ebony Diamond and Johnny Weaver teamed to defeat Tenryu and Kim Duk; Don Kerodle and Ron Ritchie topped Bill White and Charlie Fulton; Abe Jacobs rolled over Joe Furr, and Ricky Fererra and Frank Monte fought to a 15-minute draw.

NWA MID-ATLANTIC CHAMPIONSHIP WRESTLING

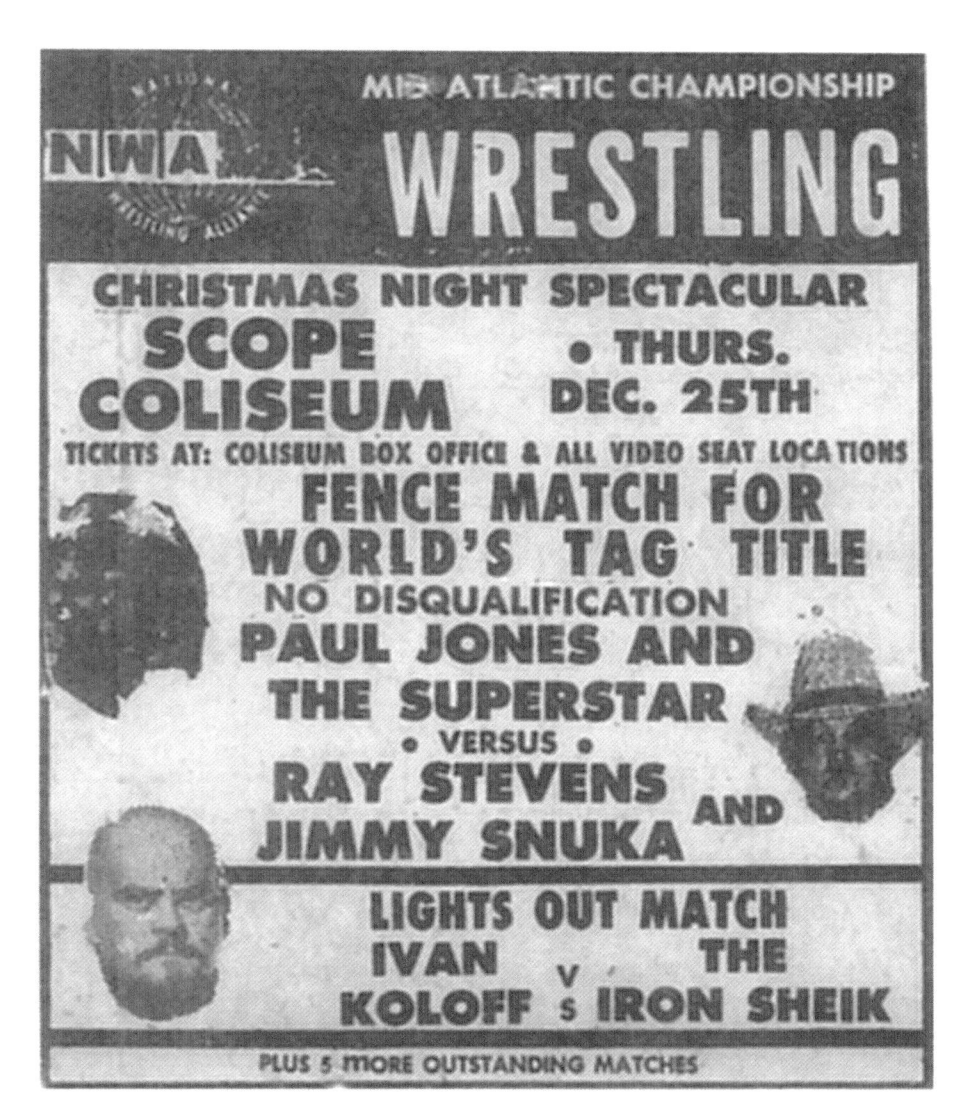

CHRISTMAS NIGHT SPECTACULAR

SCOPE COLISEUM • THURS. DEC. 25TH

TICKETS AT: COLISEUM BOX OFFICE & ALL VIDEO SEAT LOCATIONS

FENCE MATCH FOR WORLD'S TAG TITLE
NO DISQUALIFICATION

PAUL JONES AND THE SUPERSTAR
• VERSUS •
RAY STEVENS AND JIMMY SNUKA

LIGHTS OUT MATCH
IVAN KOLOFF vs THE IRON SHEIK

PLUS 5 MORE OUTSTANDING MATCHES

Jones-Superstar Win

Paul Jones and The Superstar defeated Jimmy Snuka and Ray Stevens in the feature bout of professional wrestling at scope Thursday night.

Also in tag team action, Dewey Robertson-George Wells beat Sgt. Jacques Goulet-Swede Hanson.

Also Ivan Koloff defeated the Iron Sheik, Steve Musulin downed Gene Lewis, Cy Jernigan beat Jim Nelson, Bruno Sammartino Jr. topped Ben Alexander, and Jim Nelson and Nick DeCarlo wrestled to a draw.

WIDE WORLD WRESTLING

SUNDAY DEC. 28 2:00 P.M.

DOUBLE MAIN EVENT

FEATURE MAIN EVENT T.V. TITLE MATCH

(U.S. CHAMP) **RIC FLAIR** -VS- **GREG VALENTINE**

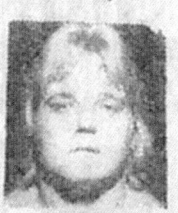

TITLE VS TITLE MAIN EVENT

(MID-ATL. CHAMP) **RICKY STEAMBOAT** -VS- T.V. CHAMP **RODDY PIPER**

GIRLS TAG MATCH

JUDY MARTIN & LILANI KAI -VS- **BETTY CLARKE & PEGGY LEE**

PLUS 2 SINGLE MATCHES

BOX OFFICE—255-5771 • RINGSIDE - $6.00
General Admission $5.00 • Children Under 10 $3.00
Box Office Open Mon.-Fri. 10:00-5:30; Sat. 11:00-4:00; Day of Match 1:00 P.M.
NO CHECKS OR CREDIT CARDS DAY OF MATCH

SEE NWA WORLD WIDE WRESTLING SATURDAY
ON WLOS-TV CHANNEL 13 1:30 PM-12:30 AM

Asheville Civic Center

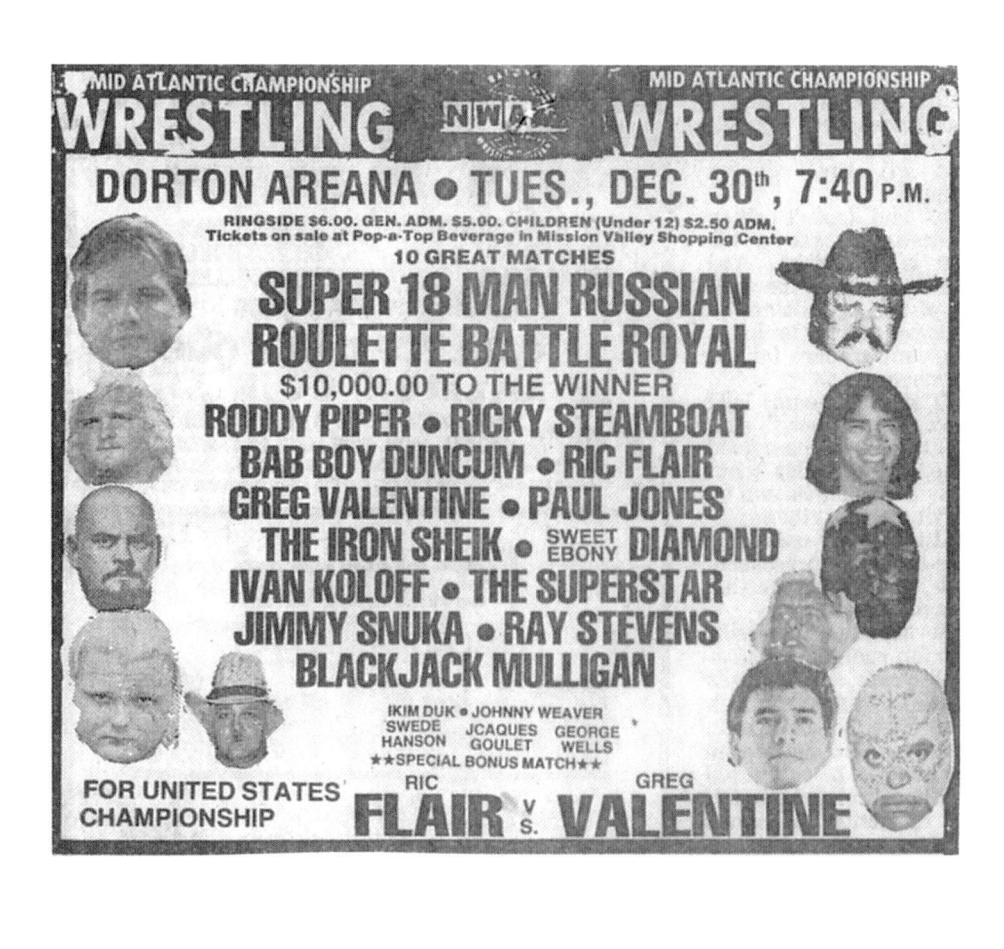

MID ATLANTIC CHAMPIONSHIP WRESTLING — NWA — **MID ATLANTIC CHAMPIONSHIP WRESTLING**

DORTON AREANA • TUES., DEC. 30th, 7:40 P.M.

RINGSIDE $6.00. GEN. ADM. $5.00. CHILDREN (Under 12) $2.50 ADM.
Tickets on sale at Pop-a-Top Beverage in Mission Valley Shopping Center

10 GREAT MATCHES

SUPER 18 MAN RUSSIAN ROULETTE BATTLE ROYAL
$10,000.00 TO THE WINNER

- RODDY PIPER • RICKY STEAMBOAT
- BAB BOY DUNCUM • RIC FLAIR
- GREG VALENTINE • PAUL JONES
- THE IRON SHEIK • SWEET EBONY DIAMOND
- IVAN KOLOFF • THE SUPERSTAR
- JIMMY SNUKA • RAY STEVENS
- BLACKJACK MULLIGAN

IKIM DUK • JOHNNY WEAVER
SWEDE HANSON • JCAQUES GOULET • GEORGE WELLS

★★SPECIAL BONUS MATCH★★

FOR UNITED STATES CHAMPIONSHIP

RIC FLAIR vs. GREG VALENTINE

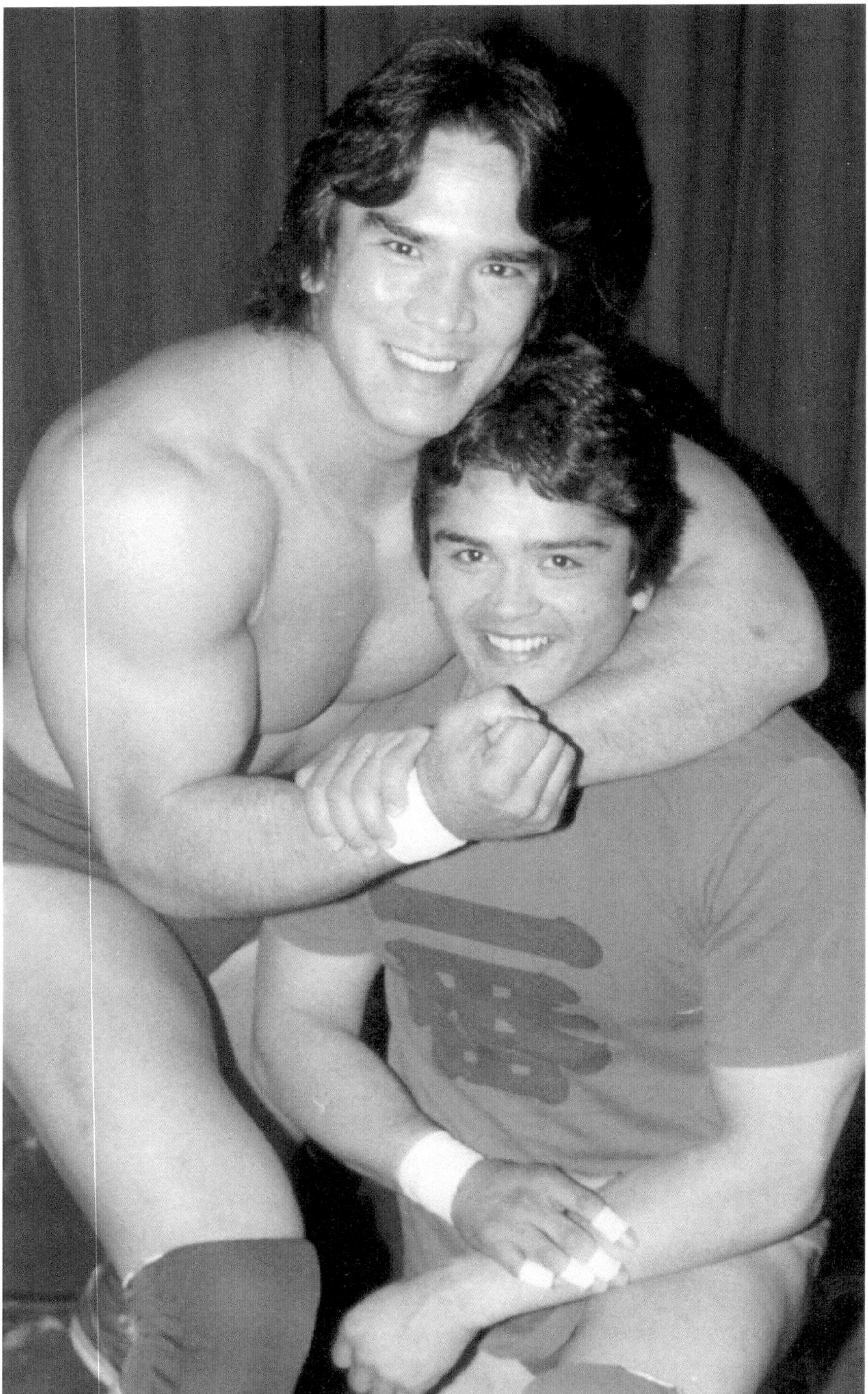

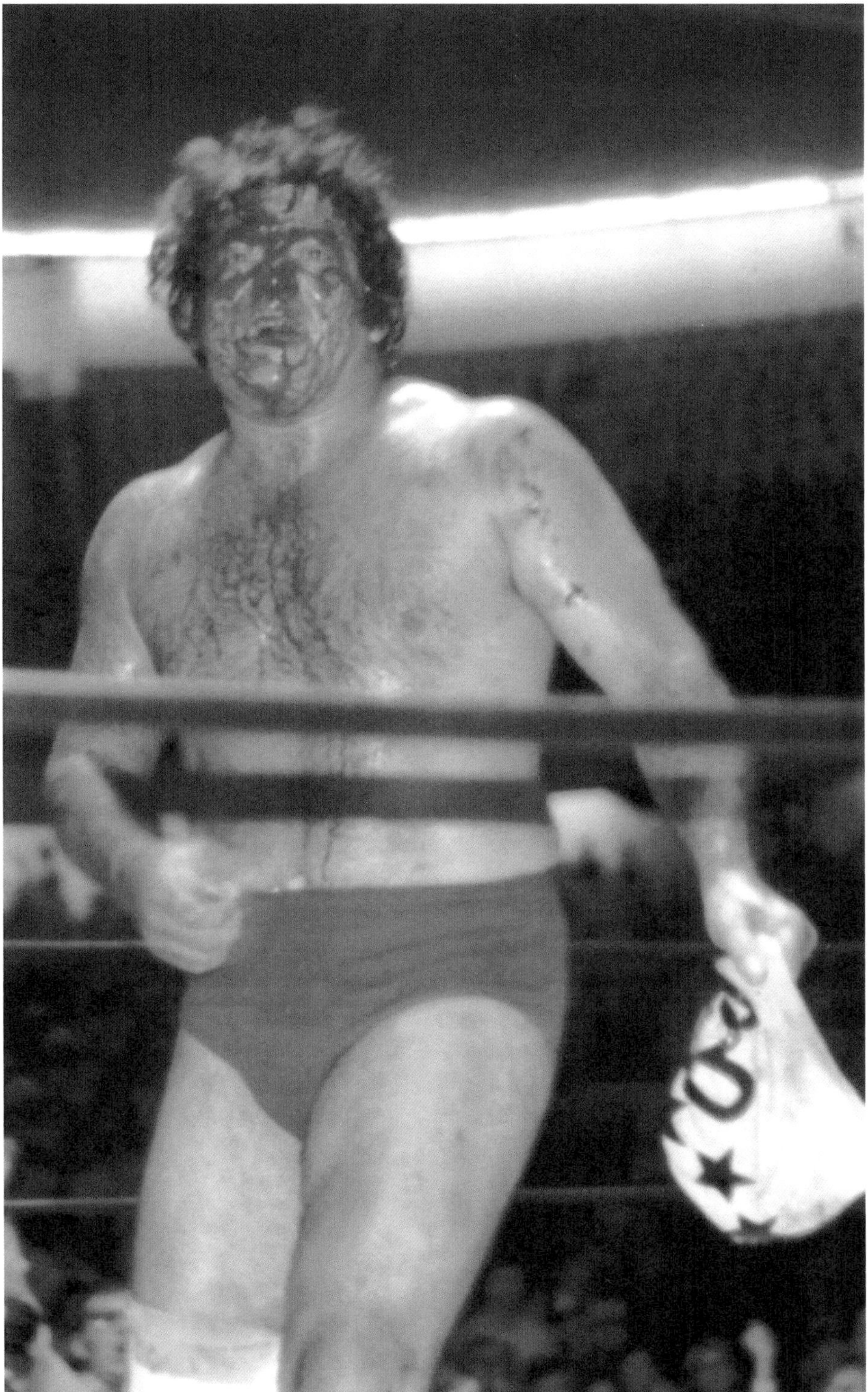